the anti-anxiety diet

the anti-anxiety diet

A Whole-Body Program to Stop
Racing Thoughts, Banish Worry
and Live Panic-Free

Ali Miller, RD, LD, CDE

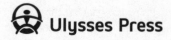 Ulysses Press

Published in the United States by:
ULYSSES PRESS
P.O. Box 3440
Berkeley, CA 94703
www.ulyssespress.com

ISBN: 978-1-61243-802-3
Library of Congress Control Number: 2018930753

Printed in Canada by Marquis Book Printing
10 9 8 7 6 5 4 3

Acquisitions editor: Bridget Thoreson
Managing editor: Claire Chun
Editor: Renee Rutledge
Proofreader: Shayna Keyles
Indexer: Sayre Van Young
Front cover design: Rebecca Lown
Cover photos: salmon © Tim UR/shutterstock.com; avocados © Valentyn Volkov/ shutterstock.com; berries © Valentina Razumova/shutterstock.com; broccoli © Serhiy Shullye/shutterstock.com

NOTE TO READERS: This book has been written and published strictly for informational and educational purposes only. It is not intended to serve as medical advice or to be any form of medical treatment. You should always consult your physician before altering or changing any aspect of your medical treatment and/or undertaking a diet regimen, including the guidelines as described in this book. Do not stop or change any prescription medications without the guidance and advice of your physician. Any use of the information in this book is made on the reader's good judgment after consulting with his or her physician and is the reader's sole responsibility. This book is not intended to diagnose or treat any medical condition and is not a substitute for a physician.

This book is independently authored and published and no sponsorship or endorsement of this book by, and no affiliation with, any trademarked brands or other products mentioned within is claimed or suggested. All trademarks that appear in ingredient lists and elsewhere in this book belong to their respective owners and are used here for informational purposes only. The author and publisher encourage readers to patronize the quality brands mentioned and pictured in this book.

To all of you readers and food-as-medicine warriors:
may you find hope and direction with a pathway toward mental
clarity, improved mood, and a mellow state of mind.
Take the time and energy to apply the recommendations and
honor your body. You are worth it!

Contents

Introduction

My Journey into Functional Medicine

Growing up as a dancer I was always very health conscious. I considered my body a machine and worked to fuel it with healthy foods. Skim milk, whole grain, high-fiber processed products, and diet soda were among my "healthy choices." In college, I transitioned from majoring in dance to nutritional sciences, with a newfound environmental consciousness, which led me to get involved with sustainable food production and the farm-to-table movement. Inspired by animal welfare networks, I became vegetarian at age 19, then vegan at age 20, substituting animal proteins for soy and meat analogues; they were cholesterol-free, after all, and sustainable, right?

During this time, my hunger for spreading "healthy eating" and changing the world with vegan advocacy was growing. I wanted to do whatever I could to immerse myself in the field of nutrition and get experience as a dietitian. While taking courses to become a registered dietitian, I worked in a hospital as a diet technician, where I was in charge of adjusting plates to be compliant with guidelines for diabetes, sodium restriction, postpartum nourishment, etc. I coordinated formulas for tube feedings and supplemental shakes with products (often recommended by physicians) that contained corn syrup solids, highly refined soybean oil, canola oil, high-fructose corn syrup, soy protein isolate, and other food-like substances with artificial colorants and flavors to boot.

I knew that this was not real food or anywhere on the path to nutrition as I imagined it, but it was a step toward understanding how the current medical system views food. In attempts to share the influence of food as medicine with the hospital and staff, I offered a class on probiotics. The class was well received, with nurses, dietitians, and doctors giving positive feedback and asking questions. I had found my calling! I needed a learning environment that would teach me how to use food as medicine rather than as a mere calorie filler.

I completed my nutrition education at a naturopathic college, Bastyr University, where my philosophies on food were greatly expanded and challenged. I learned about food on a biochemical level: how nutrients, phytocompounds, antioxidants, and enzymes influence the function of the body. I learned about anti-nutrients, or compounds in particular foods (including soy, legumes, and many vegetarian forms of protein) that block the absorption of vitamins, minerals, and nutritional elements. I also learned that the bioavailability of nutrients varies from vegetable to animal. For example, a mere 30 percent of iron is absorbed in the body from vegetarian sources as opposed to 100 percent from grass-fed beef or bison! I became fervently invested in nutritional sciences, picking up any elective courses and opportunities available to immerse myself in a deeper understanding of how food could be medicine. Yet, as the stress of my workload and courses increased, my drive increased, which led to racing thoughts, lack of sleep, and ultimately, a toll on my body.

During the last quarter of my first year at Bastyr, I did a span of four months as a raw vegan. My system did not receive this well; I was constantly bloated, fatigued, and started getting neuropathy with pain, tingling, and loss of sensation in my hands and feet. Unable to ground my floating brain, I was overwhelmed with constant racing thoughts. My circulatory system was stagnant and I was always cold and clammy, but my commitment to the cause of vegetarianism silenced the signals of my body. After the third year as a vegan and a four-month run as a raw vegan, I started experiencing shortness of breath and significant brain fog, and for the first time, I experienced a chronic onset of anxiety. Beyond persistent worry and negative thoughts, I was also starting to experience panic attacks. Tunnel vision, walls closing in on me, shortness of breath, the proverbial elephant on the chest, and exhausting insomnia all became the norm. I was seeing an acupuncturist, taking Chinese herbs, and stopped eating a raw diet to include more warming foods, but I was not improving. If anything, I was declining. The more I obsessed and searched for a cure, the sicker I became.

Finally, I went up to the naturopathic clinic and did extensive blood work. I learned that I had an autoimmune disease with elevated antinuclear antibodies (ANA) and a diagnosis of Hashimoto's thyroiditis, along with B12 deficiency and iron deficiency. It was starting to make sense: the neuropathy, the brain fog, and the shortness of breath, the vegan diet void of these nutrients! My naturopathic doctor prescribed a B12 sublingual supplement and an easily absorbable iron supplement for my deficiencies, and provided a handout of vegetarian sources of these nutrients. Even though I had been eating those foods in focused high amounts, I was still deficient!

I started to see improvement in the shortness of breath and severity of pain but felt that there was something more to it. I still didn't feel grounded or balanced. As a future practitioner who wanted to use food as medicine, I needed to start with myself, and in this case, that meant incorporating animal products into my diet in order to meet my body's increased demand for nutrients. I would need to bypass the anti-nutrients in many plant-based foods, and take full advantage of the enhanced bioavailability of animal-sourced nutrients. I had to make peace with becoming an omnivore again to fully heal. I committed to only consuming animal products that were free of antibiotics and growth hormones, and raised in a humane, small-scale environments on a traditional pasture-centered diet. I started with raw egg yolks in my green smoothies, then lightly poached eggs from pasture-raised chickens, then wild fish. Over the course of six weeks, I was consuming two biological sources of protein daily.

Reincorporating animal products into my diet played a great role in my recovery. It allowed me to lower my consumption of grains and completely eliminate processed grain and soy products, which accelerated my rebound to balanced health! This book will highlight the unique attributes of animal products and how traditional foods such as bone broth and organ pâté, as well as daily inclusion of meat, poultry, fish, and eggs, supports balancing your brain and optimizing mood stability.

Unfortunately, my healing journey was not complete. While some of my nutrient deficiencies were from inadequate intake, others were from inadequate absorption. I put myself on a quality digestive enzyme to help my body break down food and denser proteins while reducing the inflammatory properties of dairy and gluten.

Years later, I went to a Wise Traditions conference and met Dr. Natasha Campbell-McBride, author of *Gut and Psychology Syndrome* and creator of the GAPS diet. Learning about leaky gut and its role in driving inflammation throughout the body (Chapter 4), as well as driving autism, ADHD, anxiety, bipolar disorder, dyslexia, and depression, was mind-blowing!

I started to alter my diet to reduce inflammatory compounds and focus on restoring my gut lining and gut microbiome with therapeutic supplements and strategic diet support. I started to realize that it was the function of my body that was driving imbalance with anxiety and autoimmune flares, which then drove the nutrient deficiency and exacerbated symptoms.

During my last year in school, I was introduced to functional medicine in my work at the Bastyr Naturopathic Clinic. Here, I was challenged to develop patient interventions beyond a nutritional handout or natural foods approach. For example, when treating a patient with constipation, I would be encouraged to think hard about whether the individual truly needed a handout on fiber-rich foods and a reminder to drink more fluid, or whether the peristalsis (process that moves food through the intestines) was paralyzed by the stress response. I was challenged to try to understand why dysfunction was occurring with my patient rather than simply come up with a way to treat the symptom. I took an elective course, Functional Medicine for the Nutrition Practitioner, and something clicked. It was the missing piece of my educational and clinical experience: learning to get to the root of the patient's problems.

For the first time, I understood how to treat *people*, not diseases! Now focused on an individualized approach, I began treating the whole person and looking to resolve the root cause of dysfunction, rather than managing a symptom, which often yields temporary outcomes. This was the synergy that I craved, to use food as medicine to functionally address imbalance in the body. I began creating targeted treatment protocols using diet and supplement support founded on data unique to each patient and their personal expression of imbalance.

Finally, through the work of Dr. Jeff Bland and Linus Pauling, I learned about orthomolecular medicine, using nutritional supplementation to support optimized function, and the concept of nutrigenomics, the role of nutritional compounds in influencing genetic expression. I learned that high-dose nutrients could reverse disease, and that our genes are not our destiny but an opportunity! The idea that we could no longer blame our genes for disease was both enlightening and empowering, and this sealed my commitment to functional medicine. I started to understand more thoroughly the roles of stress, mental health, toxins, and hormones as the epigenome, or the lifestyle elements that influence genetic expression. This is where meditation and mindfulness as medication make sense, and the idea that stress can kill is validated.

What Is Food as Medicine?

Food as medicine is the understanding that food can contribute to disease and dysfunction or drive optimal organ function and treat or prevent disease. By avoiding inflammatory, processed, or toxic ingredients and food-like substances through a whole food diet, you can begin to experience the benefits of food as medicine. You can take it further by enhancing your diet with the addition of therapeutic ingredients that promote healthy function and lead to optimal metabolic balance. With the use of food as medicine, not only do you avoid the side effects of pharmaceutical drugs, but you may also gain a multitude of benefits.

When treating a cold, for instance, over-the-counter expectorants can break up mucus or phlegm, but they can cause nausea, nervousness, insomnia, and/or drowsiness. Bone broth, however, can break up mucus and phlegm, and beyond alleviating congestion, it will support your immune system by boosting production of white blood cells and aid in relining the gut microvilli. Bone broth also provides support for anxiety and reduced cravings. Pretty cool for a mug of broth!

How Is This Program Different?

The foods we eat play a dynamic role, both good and bad, on our brain chemistry. In fact, foods can regulate mood, emotions, and brain-signaling pathways. Some choices, such as chocolate, even have psychoactive compounds. Unfortunately, during times of anxiety, one is more likely to overindulge in sugary or processed super-flavored foods to create a dopamine spike, numb the racing mind, or redirect thought patterns from restlessness and worry to bliss.

Research has shown that emotional eating or using food as a coping mechanism can drive obesity, which in turn promotes vulnerability to more severe depression or anxiety. Physiological and hormonal changes, such as increased stress sensitivity and altered cortisol levels, are also seen with high-calorie intake or anxiety-induced binge eating, which only perpetuates the vicious cycle. Refined carbohydrates and processed foods can leach minerals, deplete B vitamins, and drive blood sugar imbalance, perpetuating mood instability, cravings, and dissatisfaction.

Just as anxiety can be the crux in preventing weight loss or healing, addressing anxiety and improving the status of your gut can greatly enhance the function of your brain and, ultimately, your entire body. When the brain is running on high-octane fuel supported by essential nutritional compounds without inflammatory distraction, the reciprocal relationship of brain chemistry and mood stability on whole body physiology is favorable.

I created *The Anti-Anxiety Diet* to be your guide to get you back in the driver's seat of the vehicle of your body. This is the manual to learn how to thrive versus simply survive! Adopting an anti-anxiety diet helps reduce inflammation, repair gut integrity, and provide necessary nutrients in abundance with enhanced absorption. As the body's nutritional status is optimized and stress signals are reduced, the systems that regulate hormones and stress chemicals are able to downshift from high-alert, chronic anxiety to reactive only in times of need. This creates a more even-keeled mood and mental processing with balanced physical responses, which then relaxes the body and gives positive feedback to the mind.

The foods you select can function as drivers of deficiency or building blocks for restoration. *The Anti-Anxiety Diet* will provide you with a plan to nourish your body while satiating cravings and supporting your brain signaling.

This program includes a focus on animal products, as they are rich in bioavailable forms of glycine, glutamine, collagen/gelatin, B12, zinc, B6, and other important compounds that you will soon learn more about! Although it is possible to follow some of the guidelines of the anti-anxiety diet as a vegetarian, you will likely need more supplemental support from protein powders, animal by-products (fish collagen/bone broth), and nutritional supplements. Also, be prepared for a heavy reliance on eggs (12 to 16 per week, minimum) because dairy is not recommended in the foundational levels of this program. If you are a vegetarian open to consuming bone broth and high amounts of eggs, then this program will still be very effective!

Rather than solely focusing on what you can't have, this diet is about prescribing an abundance of certain foods to aid in tonifying the body. Phase 1 of the anti-anxiety diet is a six-week high-fat, low-carb (HFLC) ketogenic approach that allows the body to starve off bacteria, start gut restoration if treating leaky gut, reduce food sensitivities, improve insulin signaling, and promote hormonal balance. This program offers a synergistic platform to many autoimmune, inflammatory, and dysbiosis/candida and digestive protocols. From there, you will have the option to transition to Phase 2, a low-glycemic approach that offers a more varied and sustainable diet, or you can cycle Phase 2 with your Phase 1 HFLC plan.

Additionally, pharmaceutical grade–supplements, called nutraceuticals, are necessary to optimize outcomes in functional medicine. When a system is expressing increased demand through deficiency, it often needs support beyond that from food alone. Throughout this book, I will highlight various nutritional supplements and tools to consider in your anti-anxiety diet program. See Supplement Support for the 6 Foundational Rs (page 272), which identifies a compound, dosage range, mechanism of action, and what formula I use at the Naturally Nourished clinic.

During your program, you will become reconnected with your body and have an opportunity to redefine your relationship with food. I developed this program so you can fall in love with the natural sweetness of a sun-ripened peach picked just off the branch; so you can learn to crave and feel satiated with real, nourishing whole foods, and free yourself from the ever-consuming thoughts of body image, withdrawal, and restriction! Not only will the structure of this diet successfully promote a reset of your system, it will likely support favorable body composition change while leaving you feeling energized, balanced, and grounded.

CHAPTER 1

Anxiety, the Driver of Dysfunction

In the past 10 years as a clinician, I have seen many trends and have directly served over 2,500 patients through my clinic, Naturally Nourished, addressing chronic illness, optimal wellness, and weight loss. Like many other functional medicine or naturopathic practitioners, I prefer to take the time with the individual to understand why certain diseases or disorders manifest. Practitioners often try to "outscience" nature by biohacking our way out of an imbalance. However, I discovered that as fancy as I got with cutting-edge genomics and other methods of advanced testing, if the mind and stress response are not sound, my patient will not heal.

For years I focused on my application of functional medicine with nutritional therapies, including strategic use of nutritional supplements, elimination diets, gut-restoration protocols, and adrenal support and hormonal rebalance, always pairing these approaches with implementation of an anti-inflammatory, low-glycemic diet. I saw good outcomes through each avenue, realizing every patient has a different entry point to the unfurling of their health, and if I could address that driving cause, the diet therapy and nutrient focus would yield desired results. However, if the driving cause was overlooked, the diet and strategic supplements would have temporary effects and constantly need to be adjusted or added to.

FUNCTIONAL MEDICINE AS DEFINED BY THE INSTITUTE OF FUNCTIONAL MEDICINE

The functional medicine model is an individualized, patient-centered, science-based approach that empowers patients and practitioners to work together to address the underlying causes of disease and promote optimal wellness. It relies on a detailed understanding of each patient's genetic, biochemical, and lifestyle factors and leverages that data to direct personalized treatment plans that lead to improved patient outcomes.

By addressing root cause rather than symptoms, practitioners become oriented to identifying the complexity of disease. They may find one condition has many different causes and, likewise, one cause may result in many different conditions. As a result, functional medicine treatment targets the specific manifestations of disease in each individual.

When working with a patient I take on the role of detective of their body. I seek to determine the antecedent, or driving cause, of their imbalance, essentially discovering the Achilles' heel interfering with their path of healing. In an initial session, I spend 90 minutes thoroughly getting to know my patient's story, what steps and incidents drove them to simply surviving versus thriving. All too often, stress and anxiety are overlooked or unacknowledged.

Anxiety can create an imbalance in hormones, driving infertility, polycystic ovarian syndrome (PCOS), loss of or irregular menstruation, and weight gain. It can also create an imbalance in digestion and inflammatory compounds, leading to over- or under-reactive immune function.

Time and time again, I find that my clients feel that stress and anxiety are something they just have to deal with. They are dragged by the bumper of the vehicle of their body and accept the repercussions as normal.

"Well, doesn't everyone get shakiness in their hands before a big lecture or a first date?"

"Doesn't everyone feel like they want to crawl out of their skin at times?"

"Isn't everyone struggling to get a good night's sleep and wake well-rested?"

None of these statements has to be true!

When identifying their level of stress and the way their body responds, most people note a coping mechanism, say they don't know what the physical response is, or reply that they just deal with it. Is this because we are so disconnected from our bodies? Or because we live in a society that believes stress and anxiety are normal and you just deal with them by continuing to take on more while ignoring the shouts from your body? Is there a negative association with anxiety as a sign of weakness or mental illness?

A typical stress and anxiety intake with a client includes questions such as the following:

1. How does stress physiologically influence your body?

2. Are you experiencing:

- Body temperature changes, either cold and clammy or hot and moist?

- Tension in the shoulders, neck, or jaw?

- Teeth grinding?

- Bloating or distention?

- Changes in digestion, such as cramping, gas, or belching?

3. Does food transit time feel different under stress? Do you feel more hungry or forget to eat?

4. Any changes in bowels, such as constipation or urgent, loose stools?

5. Any changes in heart rate, flutters, or tightness in the chest?

6. Any muscle or nerve tremors or spasms? Twitching in the eye? Shakiness in the hands?

7. Do you have changes in energy, such as a surge of energy or adrenaline, or do you get fatigued by stress? Is there a fluctuation?

8. Any insomnia? Do you have difficulty falling asleep or staying asleep without intermittent waking?

9. Does your mood shift into irritability and agitation, or do you get a short fuse?

10. Do you experience racing thoughts or difficulty concentrating?

Then I dig deeper, asking, "When in your silent mental space, are more of your thoughts focused on rumination of what was or anticipatory stress of what may be (the ever-loved "what ifs")?

Finally, I have all my clients select if they are "stressed and wired" or "stressed and tired" to determine if their fight-or-flight center, the hypothalamic-pituitary-adrenal axis (HPA-axis), is in overdrive or if they are in a state of adrenal fatigue. (I will discuss the HPA-axis in detail on page 103.)

Anxiety, although typically associated with the "stressed and wired" expression, when chronic, can drive "stressed and tired" manifestations. This can be both mental exhaustion as well as physiological. Anxiety, over time, can be debilitating, driving chronic fatigue and dissociative behavior, and causing one to miss out on opportunities that would potentially enhance their life.

Whether they are related to weight gain, inflammation, an autoimmune condition, or a digestive issue, anxiety and stress response play a vital role in the pathology of many conditions, and managing them is essential in recovery.

When mismanaged, anxiety throws off our neurotransmitters, which can create more alarm bells in the brain, which then stimulates more cortisol response from the adrenals. This tells the body to store more visceral body fat, which drives weight gain and insulin resistance, elevating blood sugars. The higher amount of sugar in the blood can drive elevated blood pressure and diabetes. Additionally, the stress response can have a sterilizing hit on the gut microbiome, and this, paired with elevated blood sugars, drives yeast and bacterial overgrowth, which further influences neurotransmitters, as 90 percent of our serotonin and a majority of our dopamine is produced in the gut.

Inflammation and autoimmune disease are directly related to the HPA-axis and anxiety management as well. Cortisol, produced by the adrenal glands, has anti-inflammatory mechanisms, such as reducing histamine reactivity, so an ample amount of cortisol is healthy. However, under ongoing anxiety, the adrenal glands get exhausted from overreactivity and then respond with deficiency. This is when inflammatory cascades go on high release as the cortisol dam that was holding back the inflammation breaks down. Also, when under anxiety and high stress, the body goes into hyperactivity mode, often driving autoimmune disease, when the body perceives itself as an invader and goes into auto-attack. As you can see, unmanaged anxiety can play a significant role in an array of diseases. Similarly, when mechanisms in the body are imbalanced, anxiety can be greater expressed.

Regardless of where I start with a client on a functional medicine level, I am assessing inflammation, the gut bacterial status (microbiome), micronutrient needs, adrenal stress gland status, and the expression of neurotransmitters. For a preliminary diet, I always start with either the low-glycemic diet with a healthy fat focus

(Phase 2 of the anti-anxiety diet) or a more aggressive jump into a high-fat, low-carb ketogenic diet (Phase 1 of the anti-anxiety diet).

The Anti-Anxiety Diet Foundational 6 Rs

I developed the anti-anxiety diet as a way to reset multiple processes of the body using my Foundational 6 R approach to accelerate mind-body balance and promote optimal health. The food therapy recommended in this book is focused on fueling the body with vitamins, minerals, and amino acids to aid with providing building blocks for neurotransmitters and signals in the brain that aid in managing mood, reducing cravings, and resolving anxiety. In the following chapters, we'll discuss each of the six Rs in detail.

REMOVE Inflammatory Foods: In Chapter 2, we will kick off by identifying foods that drive inflammation in the body and replace these with alternatives that are less irritating. Not only will this cool and soothe your GI tract, but your immune system will be less burdened by compounds in the bloodstream and will start to call your inflammatory army to retreat.

RESET Gut Microbiome: In Chapter 3, we will identify drivers of gut bacteria imbalance and discuss how to starve off bad bacteria overgrowth, as well as tools to promote viability of beneficial bugs to support healthy neurotransmitter production. When you are able to get those bugs working for you versus against you, you may benefit beyond the increase of feel-good neurotransmitters such as serotonin and gamma-aminobutyric acid (GABA), and experience improved regularity, less bloating, and clearer skin.

REPAIR GI Lining: Now that the primary dietary irritants are removed, we will talk about healing your gut lining to support absorption of nutrients and reduce inflammatory reactions. We will work with therapeutic foods to "seal the tank" of your GI tract, preventing leaky gut reactivity. This will be the final stage of gut restoration, ensuring we have removed irritants, reinoculated good bacteria, and finally, repaired any gut damage. See Chapter 4.

RESTORE Micronutrient Status: In Chapter 5, we will discuss synergistic eating to aid in absorption and bioavailability of nutrients. We will discuss primary nutrients that are integral to mood regularity and management of the stress response. Beyond foods that are potent in nutrients of need, this section will include nutritional supplementation recommendations to get you "above water," and then discuss a timeline in which you will be able to maintain management with primarily diet.

REBOUND Adrenals: In Chapter 6, we will discuss the symphony of the sympathetic nervous system and how the stress axis can cause over- or underreactivity in the body, ultimately influencing adrenal gland output and function. You will learn how to reduce excessive output as well as rebound fatigued adrenals to gain support of the feel-good influence without excessive excitatory response. We will dive into the role of cortisol and how it acts in both excess or deficiency, and learn about the other products of the adrenals, including the hormone precursor dehydroepiandrosterone (DHEA).

REBALANCE Neurotransmitters: Finally, in Chapter 7, we will talk about how to assess the output of the stress hormone catecholamine, and how anxiety can be managed with amino acid therapy to produce deficient neurotransmitters or those needed in higher demand. You will learn about foods that contribute to production and regulation. You will understand the broad function of neurotransmitters beyond contributing as drivers of mood stability, including management of inflammation, enhanced cognition, and piloting many autonomic nervous system functions.

CHAPTER 2

Remove Inflammatory Foods

Chronic inflammation is associated with many diseases, especially age-related diseases, including atherosclerosis, cancer, arthritis, obesity, allergies, stroke, diabetes, congestive heart failure, digestive disorders, Alzheimer's disease, mood imbalance, and more. The suffix "itis" translates to inflammation; any disease with this suffix (e.g., arthritis, diverticulitis), can benefit from anti-inflammatory mechanisms.

The natural process of aging sets the foundation for increased inflammation as the production of destructive chemicals known as cytokines increases. Many lifestyle factors also contribute to increased inflammation, such as diet, quality of sleep, psychological stress, environmental exposure to toxic chemicals (smoking, environmental pollutants, unpurified water), and dietary consumption of inflammatory foods.

In this chapter, I will teach you about what inflammation is, why it matters for your mood, and how to navigate an anti-inflammatory diet.

What Is Inflammation?

Inflammation has been coined "the silent killer" as it can often lurk in the body, causing destruction slowly, seemingly silent until the inflammatory chemicals build up so high that disease or a dynamic symptom strikes. Although inflammation is a normal and essential bodily response, when the immune system and metabolic function of the body is overwhelmed with inflammatory foods and processed ingredients, the body responds with imbalanced and excessive inflammatory reaction.

The natural immune response of inflammation occurs in reaction to a bodily insult by a foreign invader such as a virus, bacteria, or fungi, or to an injury like a cut, impact, or chemical exposure. Five cardinal signs associated with inflammation are essential in the process of healing the injury while protecting it from spreading. I was educated by their Latin names: *rubor*, *calore*, *tumor*, *dolor*, and *functio laesa*.

Rubor (redness) and *calore* (heat) occur from increased blood flow to the area of injury when the immune system delivers its natural fighters. Resident immune cells in the GALT (gut associated lymphoid tissue) are also stimulated to battle the invader. In this process, *tumor* (swelling) occurs as fluid leaks from the blood vessels into the tissue space to protect the injury or insult from spreading. *Dolor* (pain) occurs when increased fluid in the tissue causes increased pressure on the nerves. Finally, *functio laesa* (loss of function) occurs where the inflamed areas have reduced functionality to promote healing.

A healthy and balanced body is capable of shutting off the inflammatory response; however, in an unbalanced state, the inflammatory response may perpetuate, leading to chronic, asymptomatic inflammation that can wreak silent havoc or cause painful flare-ups.

So, what happens when the injury isn't something traumatic like a car accident? What if it is a food you are eating? A corn chip? A piece of whole wheat bread? A salad at a restaurant? What happens when your body responds with inflammation based on your diet, and how does that impact your mood and your mind?

Inflammation and Anxiety

Before discussing what to remove from your diet, I'd like to empower you with an understanding of the role of inflammation and the gut on the brain. Throughout this book I will reference the brain-gut axis, which is essentially the communication loop between these two areas of the body.

The past decade of psychology and neurology research has correlated the presence of inflammatory chemicals in the body with mood instability, depression, and anxiety. There is a chicken-egg relationship in that those who have anxiety, brain fog, and racing thoughts have a higher amount of inflammatory chemicals in their body. They get a surge of excitatory neurotransmitters in response to the inflammatory chemicals, further perpetuating feelings of anxiousness or panic. This creates a chronic fight-or-flight worried mode.

To add insult to injury, in response to dietary inflammation, the gut can drive swelling or bloating in the belly as well as reduce digestive function, causing bowel irregularity and limiting the production of feel-good neurotransmitters. In a healthy gut, over 90 percent of the brain's serotonin, a key anti-anxiety compound, is manufactured, but in a gut that is inflamed and damaged, production of serotonin is hindered—limiting an individual's ability to respond to stress.

Anxiety is also connected to gut inflammation via the concept of leaky gut. I will speak more on this in Chapter 4, Repair GI Lining, but here's a basic rundown.

When the gut is inflamed, the barrier lining of the gut, which is supposed to keep food particles in and absorb nutrients, doesn't stay tight. Food particles that are too large cross into the bloodstream and drive immunological response as well as inflammation.

In this scenario, the gastrointestinal (GI) tract of the individual is permeable to more food compounds during consumption, which activates an individual's immune system into overreactivity due to excess foreign invaders (antigens) in the bloodstream. The immune system responds to these particles as if there is a high pollen day, but instead of histamine alone, it produces a whole gamut of inflammatory chemicals. Also, when very large particles cross the gut lining into the bloodstream, they have the potential to also cross the blood-brain barrier and directly drive mood disturbances.

The Top 5 Inflammatory Foods

Now that you understand how inflammation is a root cause of anxiety, let's get back to that question of what happens when inflammation is in response to a food consumed rather than an injury. Could something you are eating be driving inflammation, reducing healthy neurotransmitter production, and promoting leaky gut? The answer is YES! This section will start with stripping away the top five drivers of inflammation in the diet: gluten, corn, soy, sugar, and dairy.

Remember, food is a double-edged sword; it can provide nourishment as building blocks for brain and mood health, as well as destroy brain and body function. Although I will highlight the removal of inflammatory foods, I ensure you that the anti-anxiety diet provides ample replacements to satisfy your palate and support optimal function in your body. The recipes provided in Chapter 9 will support your brain and provide compounds to balance mood while curbing cravings and satisfying your taste buds.

Food became complicated and more of a driver of disease when mass production and packaging started all the way back in the Industrial Revolution of the 18th and 19th centuries. The more people separated themselves from food production and small-scale family farms, distancing themselves further from the hunting and gathering tradition, the more convenience drove nutritional deficiency, obesity, and inflammatory conditions.

The Standard American Diet (SAD) is predominately made up of carbohydrates and all but devoid of healthy fats, nourishing proteins, and antioxidant-rich, non-starchy veggies. This diet, which is high in carbohydrates, especially those from refined carbohydrates such as flour-based foods and added sugars, causes the body to become familiar with carbohydrates as primary fuel and drives imbalanced metabolism with inflammatory reactions, such as excessive insulin and imbalanced satiety signals.

Beyond carbohydrates and excessive sugar, the SAD diet is loaded with toxic additives and chemicals that hinder our metabolic processes, which distresses the liver and kidneys and reduces production of essential mood stabilizing and anti-inflammatory compounds. This leads to chronic illnesses such as neurological disorders, hormonal imbalance, diabetes, cardiovascular disease, behavioral conditions, and cancer.

When the body is overwhelmed with an excess load on metabolic detoxification pathways and not supported with adequate nutrition to fuel them, toxins are stuffed into storage packages—fat cells! Medical research now shows that our fat cells are functioning as endocrine cells (a type of hormone) and interfering with our metabolic pathways, causing irregularly elevated blood sugar, decreasing calorie-burning activity, and promoting additional fat storage versus burn. This creates a vicious cycle of fat cells telling the body to make more fat.

Eating a diet comprised of whole, unprocessed foods is a great place to start to reduce inflammation and resolve anxiety. These five foods are the primary focus of REMOVE.

Gluten

Gluten is a protein found in various grains of wheat (spelt, kamut, triticale, etc.) as well as in barley, farro, and rye. The rise of gluten intolerance has been dramatic over the past decade, and the even more severe celiac disease is now said to affect 1 in 133 Americans according to the Centers for Disease Control and Prevention (CDC). Although wheat is not genetically modified like other pro-inflammatory crops such as corn and soy, wheat has been hybrid-ized many times to selectively increase yield, resistance, and calorie density. Wheat available in the grocery store in whole wheat or white flour (as well as their respective food products) comes from the most commonly available crop, short dwarf wheat, which is significantly higher in gluten and gliadin, the primary inflammatory compound in gluten.

Gliadin is not easily digested or broken down by enzymes in the digestive tract and can cause havoc to the body, leading to fatigue, acne, loose stools, constipation, depression, anxiety, joint pain, and more. Beyond the inflammatory response, gliadin plays a role on opioid receptors in the brain that can lead to addictive tendencies and mood disturbances. Gluteomorphin proteins, found in gliadin, have highly addictive effects and have been hypothesized as drivers of inflammation in the blood-brain barrier, contributing to anxiety, depression, and schizophrenia.

Pain, weight gain, addictive tendencies, and mood disturbances are compelling enough responses to a food for me to rule it out of a balanced diet, but there's more: Refined grains can play a nega-tive role on gut bacteria and the microvilli that line our intestines. The combination of gluten as an abrasive sticky protein (the Latin translation of gluten is "glue") and lectins found in all grains create wear and tear on the gut lining, which can contribute further to intestinal enteropathy, or leaky gut. One easy way to end this vicious cycle is to remove gluten and gluten-containing products.

On your anti-anxiety diet, you will discover if you have gluten sensitivity during the 12-week removal of all grains, and you will fill the void with more nourishing alternatives that can satisfy your sweet tooth and your need for that nice chew or crunch!

Corn

Most corn is made from genetically modified organism (GMO) crops. The two main GMO corn crops are *Bacillus thuringiensis* (Bt endotoxin) corn and Roundup Ready corn. The Bt GMO crop was designed to kill a susceptible insect; a part of the plant that contains the Bt protein must be ingested by the crop pest. Within minutes, the protein binds to the gut wall and the insect stops feeding. Within hours, the gut wall breaks down and gut bacteria invade the body cavity. The insect dies of septicemia as bacteria multiply in the blood after the colon explosion...yuck! Increased exposure to this gut wall–destroying protein can play a role in increased food sensitivities as a primary contributor toward leaky gut.

The other GMO corn crop, Roundup Ready, is able to withstand higher amounts of the herbicide glyphosate, the active ingredient in the agricultural chemical RoundUp. Research has identified glyphosate as a neurotoxin and endocrine disruptor that throws off neurotransmitters that regulate mood and stress response as well as cause nerve damage, diabetes, and hormonal imbalance. There are fears that both the Bt endotoxin or RoundUp GMO corn disrupt the gut bacteria balance, impair digestion, and direct damage to the intestinal wall, which can lead to immune activation and increase allergies and food sensitivity. Unfortunately, according to FDA.gov, 88 percent of the corn on the market is GMO, and this means a majority of the products that contain corn as an ingredient are likely to have a residue of these chemicals.

If you are able to find certified organic corn or organic blue corn and their products, keep in mind they still create inflammation in the body due to the plant's composition. Corn is high in linoleic acid, a type of polyunsaturated fat known as an omega-6. One important element in controlling inflammation is ensuring a proper ratio of omega-6 fatty acids, which are pro-inflammatory, to omega-3 fatty acids, which are anti-inflammatory. Because these fatty acids fight each other for a place within the cells, the goal is to reach a ratio as close to 1:1 as possible so inflammation levels can be regulated. Research published in the *American Journal of Clinical Nutrition* hypothesizes that hunter-gatherers were at a ratio of 4:1 or even 3:1, whereas modern society tends to trend at a 25:1 ratio.

PUT THE FRIES DOWN!

The primary source of omega-6 in the diet is fried and processed foods. Frying oils are generally vegetable, meaning corn, soy, or canola oil. These oils are all high in omega-6, and they are significantly processed from a grain to a clear odorless oil that has a high smoke point to withstand frying temperatures. Industrialized oils are extracted using solvents and bleach, then they are degummed, winterized, and deodorized, all steps involving toxic chemical ingredients and creating oxidative damage.

An anti-anxiety diet is geared toward an increased intake of omega-3 rich foods, including wild-caught fish, leafy greens, nuts/seeds, pasture-raised eggs, and grass-fed meats. The diet is devoid of processed foods that are extremely high in omega-6 fatty acids, with corn and soy being the primary contributors. By making an effort to eat whole fruits and vegetables in their natural state, you take steps toward decreasing inflammation in your body.

Soy

Soy is also predominantly GMO, with 93 percent of soybeans as a GMO crop, according to FDA.gov. A majority of the GMO soybeans produced are also RoundUp Ready, bearing similar consequences to that of corn in regard to glyphosate toxic residue. Beyond its role as a neurotoxin and endocrine disruptor, glyphosate kills plants by interfering with the production of the essential amino acids phenylalanine, tyrosine, and tryptophan. All three have influences on mood stability and anxiety, tryptophan being the most well-known as a precursor to serotonin. These amino acids cannot be made by humans; only plants and microorganisms can make them, and animals get them by eating these plants.

Common processing byproducts of soy, such as soy protein isolate and partially hydrogenated soybean oil, cause inflammation via oxidation and trans fats. Additionally soy has goitrogenic effects, which can work against the thyroid, driving reduced thyroid function or hypothyroidism.

Structurally, soy may be unfit for human consumption due to its high phytate concentration. Phytates are components of plants that can block nutrient absorption, driving nutritional deficiency. Traditional soy as consumed in Asia is fermented or aged to reduce phytate concentration. Some sources of traditionally prepared soy, including tamari (gluten-free soy sauce), tempeh, natto, and miso paste, when organic, are okay in moderation and have some unique benefits due to isoflavones and probiotic synergy from fermentation. However, most soy in processed foods is not fermented. It is raw or heated, which does not break down the phytates. This means consumption of soy foods can deplete your body of mood-stabilizing nutrients such as magnesium, zinc, and calcium.

Sugar

Sugar may be the most addictive inflammatory food that you will remove. Brain scans demonstrate that people who eat a lot of sugar and high-glycemic food show similar addictive patterns to those who take cocaine. Carbohydrates stimulate serotonin and endorphin release, which aids in a feel-good signal in our brain. The intake of simple or refined sugars accelerates this process, which leads to a rapid pick-me-up or "sugar high"; however, just as rapidly as we get a kick, we notice an almost more dynamic drop or slump in energy levels and mood. This can truly create a vicious cycle of excessive sugar intake, such as a candy bar after a high-carbohydrate lunch, then a soda as a pick-me-up following the candy bar, and so on.

Often the sugar train can traverse peaks and valleys of energy and mood, with anxiety present on either end. A sugar high can include symptoms of brain fog, fatigue, and blurred vision; often, confusion can drive anxiety and panic, along with the feeling of loss of control. On the other hand, a sugar low or blood sugar crash can include symptoms of shakiness, tension, and irritability, which can drive panic-like reactivity. Withdrawal from sugar has proven to be as destructive as blood sugar highs, with studies showing that a diet of binging on sugar followed by restriction creates a state that involves anxiety and altered brain chemical balance.

Refined sugar and excessive carbohydrate intake is also linked to obesity, hypertension, hypoglycemia, depression, headaches, fatigue, nervous tension, aching limbs, diabetes, acne, IBS, skin irritation, stiffening of arteries, advancement in cognitive decline, violent behavior, and more. Although often referred to as "empty calories," sugar is anything but neutral. Sugar quickly dissolves into the bloodstream and shocks the pancreas, which taxes the glucose-insulin response, leading to excessive insulin production. In our body's attempts to lower blood sugar levels, excess energy is stored as fat driven by inflammatory insulin. Over time, excessive sugar drives glycation, which is the coating of sugar that can build up on cells and nerves, creating plaque and creating havoc. These advanced glycation end products (AGEs) play a role in Alzheimer's, cognitive decline, neuropathy, cardiovascular disease, aging, and diabetes. In fact, the primary blood lab marker of diabetic control, HgbA1c%, looks at how glycosilated or coated red blood cells are in sugar.

Dairy

Dairy has two primary irritants: lactose and casein. Most adults who are lactose intolerant lack the enzyme lactase, and therefore can't digest milk sugar lactose. This can cause GI discomfort, bloating, and irritation, triggering inflammation. This can be easily addressed with taking lactase enzyme in a digestive enzyme formula or consuming raw milk, which has not lost its enzymes through heat processing. Difficulty digesting casein, the primary protein in dairy, can cause a lot more drama in the body. Those with low stomach acid, poor digestion, and inflammation in the gastrointestinal tract will react more adversely to casein.

Studies have linked casein consumption with opioid activity–induced mood disturbances and antioxidant depletion in those with autism and ADHD, which negatively impacts mental health. Like gluten, casein has morphine-like influence by producing casomorphines, which drive addictive tendency and mood disturbance. Finally, for those with celiac disease, casein can lead to inflammation by cross-reacting with gluten or being mistaken by the body as gluten. Also like gluten, regardless of the casomorphine property, the large particle size of casein can often cross a leaky gut and the blood-brain barrier to influence brain function.

Dairy, like soy, has some health-redeeming properties, which come down to quality of source and how the dairy is processed. Ghee or clarified butter is free of casein and lactose, as the process of slow cooking and clarifying removes these compounds. This is a great fat to use in cooking and, when sourced from grass-fed cows, can provide a variety of nutrients, including vitamins A, D, and E, and conjugated linoleic acids (CLAs), a healthy fatty acid that can help burn visceral fat and build the immune system.

Grass-fed whey is a bioavailable protein that is easy to absorb. Whey is the opposing protein to casein in dairy, so it is free of casein and will likely be free of lactose as well. A quality whey, such as the Naturally Nourished grass-fed whey, will be low-heat processed or non-denatured. This will allow it to maintain active immunoglobulins and antioxidants, such as glutathione, which actually reduce inflammation. If not sure if you tolerate dairy, try to eliminate all forms for the first 12 weeks on the anti-anxiety diet; however, you may consider bringing back casein-free options such as ghee and grass-fed whey at week 7, beginning with Phase 2 of the diet. If you choose to reintroduce dairy products, be sure to add one food per week to distinguish reactivity, if any.

Most processed foods contain gluten, corn, soy, dairy, and/or sugar, but foods and food products are not the only sources. Encapsulated medications or supplements, cosmetics, and even detergents can contain these inflammatory ingredients. Become a label reader and focus on local, non-GMO, pesticide-free whole foods. Stock your home with toxin-free natural products and remove items with inflammatory ingredients, like those found in fried, processed, mass-prepared foods. Here is a chart of some common sources of inflammatory foods to remove from your diet:

Sources and Replacements for Gluten, Corn, Soy, Sugar, and Dairy

	Sources	Hidden Sources
Gluten	Wheat, barley, rye, spelt, and their byproducts, including wheat and white flours	Malted barley, malt syrup, malt vinegar, brewer's yeast, seitan (wheat gluten), soy sauce, gravy, sauces, and thickened dressings
Corn	Popcorn, cornstarch, cornmeal, high-fructose corn syrup, corn oil or Mazola (sometimes called vegetable oil), and grits	Baking powder, maltodextrin, dextrin, dextrose, maltitol, mannitol, MSG, iodized salt (Morton's), calcium citrate, sorbitol, sucralose, Sweet'N Low, xylitol, xanthan gum
Soy	Edamame, soy sauce, tofu, tempeh, miso, soy milk, soy protein powder, textured vegetable protein, isolated soy protein, and vegetable oil	Sugar icings, processed meats, soy lecithin (may be just noted as lecithin), baked goods, vegetable broth, artificial and natural flavoring, thickening agents, cooking sprays, and protein bars and products
Sugar	Cane and GMO-beet sugar, evaporated cane juice, fructose, sucrose, glucose, corn syrup, high-fructose corn syrup, agave, maltose, and all sweets and sweetened foods	Breads, condiments, salad dressings, bars, cereals, most processed foods
Dairy	Milk, cheese, butter, cream, yogurt, cream cheese, sour cream, and milk protein. Avoid at least 6 weeks: whey and ghee.	Processed meats, artificial and natural flavoring, high protein flour, granola mixes, canned tuna, broths and stocks, medications and vitamins, cosmetics, fat replacements

One way we can limit the amount of toxins we are exposed to is by choosing local, non-GMO, pesticide-free whole foods and products. Take the first step to lowering your inflammation by eliminating these five foods for at least 12 weeks and, in the removal process, ensure your replacements are comprised of low-carb, antioxidant-rich, organic ingredients. This chart provides simple substitutions for the removed foods:

Inflammatory food	Replacement	Recipe inspiration
Gluten/carbs as pasta	Zoodles (zucchini noodles) or other spiralized veggies	Sauté with olive oil and herbs, top with protein and sauce of choice.
Gluten/carbs as pizza crust	Cauliflower crust, almond/coconut flour blend, or spaghetti squash boat	Top with your favorite herbed olive oil, grilled veggies, and meats of choice.
Soy/soy sauce	Coconut liquid aminos	Use soy sauce and coconut liquid aminos 1:1 in any stir fry or umami flavor application, or as dip for sushi.
Dairy as a beverage	Coconut milk, almond milk, or any nut milk of choice, unsweetened (look for options free of binders and fillers such as carrageenan and guar gum)	For a boost of selenium, mix 2 cups of Brazil nuts with 5 cups filtered water, vanilla, salt, and optional raw honey to sweeten.
Vegetable seed oils and industrialized oils	Virgin coconut oil, refined coconut oil*, tallow*, lard*, virgin avocado oil, refined avocado oil*, macadamia nut oil, olive oil *Can be used for high heat application over 350°F	*These fats can be used in the oven for roasting or in a marinade on a high-heat grill. Choose unrefined or extra-virgin oils to retain most nutrients at lower heat, such as a light sauté, herbed oil sauce, or salad dressing.
Cheese	Other savory snacks or toppings such as avocado, olives, or nut cheese options	Cashew Cheeze Dip (page 218)
Yogurt	Homemade coconut yogurt using a quality probiotic capsule	Quick Coconut Yogurt (page 198)

The recipes in *The Anti-Anxiety Diet* support your body, providing nourishment along with a functional approach to aid in the Remove, Reset, Repair, Restore, Rebound, and Rebalance phases of mood stability and mental health. The variety in flavor profiles and textures will support sustained outcomes, as you will find you can make an anti-anxiety diet alternative to any food craving! As you continue to explore new foods and flavors, you will also discover you don't miss prior foods that were causing "yuck" in your body while driving anxiety or lack of clarity in your mind.

Elimination Diet Approach

The elimination diet is the gold standard in assessment of food sensitivity. Digestive processes and gut bacteria can be unique for each person and results of a blood test will vary. A trial-and-error approach strategically eliminates primary groups of inflammatory foods for a period of time, followed with the introduction of one food group at a time for results-based information.

During the elimination period, including both Phase 1 and Phase 2 of the anti-anxiety diet, it is important to be mindful of hidden sources of inflammatory ingredients and carefully read all food labels. Once the foods have been removed for the three-month period, they can be reintroduced one at a time with careful attention to any symptoms experienced.

Symptoms of irritation from a food can include water retention, headache, digestive issues, bloating, reflux, fatigue, or unexplained muscle aches, as well as anxiety, insomnia, and brain fog. My recommendation would be to start the reintroduction period at week 13, but if you are not able to maintain that length of time, follow a strategic reintroduction to determine which of the removed foods is most volatile for you and your body.

Reintroduction consists of eating a single food for three days in a row followed by a buffer period of three to four days with only one new food group per week.

Day 1: Eat a small portion of the reintroduced food. This should be smaller than a typical serving size.

Day 2: Eat a slightly larger portion of the same food that resembles more of a typical serving size.

Day 3: Eat a portion that is larger than a typical serving size.

Example: Dairy

When reintroducing dairy, you may want to do one week per form of the food group as the protein structures, enzymes, and irritants differ based on processing.

Week 1: Butter three-day introduction: 1 teaspoon, 1 tablespoon, 2 tablespoons

Week 2: Yogurt three-day introduction: ¼ cup, ⅔ cup, 1 cup

Week 3: Hard aged raw cheese three-day introduction: 1 ounce, 2 ounces, 3 ounces

WHY THE MRT BLOOD TEST IS SUPERIOR AND HOW IT CAN START YOUR JOURNEY

The Mediator Release Test (MRT), also known as the MRT Inflammatory Food Panel, or MRT Blood Test, is the most accurate and comprehensive blood test available for food and food-chemical reactions. MRT can serve as your jump-start to improved well-being and systemic balance. With the results from an MRT, you will be able to identify your triggers to begin a systematic process in determining your optimal diet. If you are experiencing digestive distress or inflammatory reactions in your body that proceed beyond the first four weeks of avoiding the top five inflammatory foods in this chapter, consider running the MRT panel to get a personalized GPS map of what foods are best for your body.

If symptoms that had resolved with removal of these foods begin to present again, stop eating the food and wait until symptoms clear before introducing a new food. If no symptoms are present a new food can be reintroduced after the buffer period. Test one food per week. After testing all challenge foods, any that previously presented symptoms upon reintroduction can be retested.

Carb Control Is Key!

At my functional nutrition clinic, Naturally Nourished, one of our mantras is "bread is dead." When grain is processed into flour, including a whole wheat flour, the nutrients are stripped out, leaving it devoid of nutritional value. To reduce onset of folate deficiency, even organic non-bleached flours are synthetically re-enriched to compensate for the processing. Unfortunately, the fortification used on flour foods is synthetic and provides a synthetic folic acid versus the bioavailable form of folate, methylfolate (more on this in Chapter 5 and how methylation is key to mood stability!).

In addition, consuming flour-based foods actually depletes some nutrients from the body's storage, including magnesium, B vitamins, and antioxidants. The anti-anxiety diet is grain-free to support a low-glycemic, high-fat, low-carb approach to mood stability. Removing refined carbs from both gluten and non-gluten grains, as well as corn and sugar, aids in balancing blood sugar levels, which supports a more even-keeled mood and energy level.

Removal of Carbohydrates: Ketosis as Medicine for Anxiety

In the anti-anxiety diet, you will be focusing on keeping carbohydrates to a minimal level and launching into ketosis in the first phase of the diet program to accelerate your mood stability. The process of ketosis, or entering into a ketogenic state, occurs after restricting carbohydrates in the diet to 30 or less grams daily. As carbohydrates are reduced, the body's use of glucose (blood sugar) as fuel is depleted along with stores of glycogen in the muscle and liver. After a couple days of restriction, the body is forced to manufacture ketones as an alternative energy source. Ketones are made by fat in the body as well as fat from the diet, and they serve as a high-octane fuel source, providing a cleaner, more constant fuel as opposed to glucose, which has substantial fluctuations, often resulting in mood and energy shifts.

As glucose levels regulate at a low, steady level from absence of carbohydrates in the diet, insulin levels also fall. Insulin is a hormone that drives fat storage in response to blood-sugar spikes; it is also inflammatory in its mechanisms, and studies demonstrate unfavorable influence of elevated insulin on brain health. According to the *Journal of Diabetic Complications*, researchers have found individuals with elevated blood sugar levels are more than twice as likely to develop depressive illness. In addition to regulating glucose and insulin levels, ketone production also supports the release of other mood stabilizers and metabolic regulators, such as HGH (human growth hormone), that can aid in amino acid utilization and neuron function.

The ketogenic diet was first brought into the medical realm as a treatment option for epilepsy due to its ability to reduce overactivity of excitatory compounds in the brain. Studies have demonstrated clinical overlap in mechanisms of epilepsy and bipolar disorder. Ketones sit on brain receptors and encourage a mellow mood. They can cross the blood-brain barrier and act on neuropeptides, directly reducing anxious signaling. This impact is being studied as a tool to support treatment of neurological conditions such as multiple sclerosis and Parkinson's, as well as certain cancers and autoimmune diseases.

Ketones have a favorable influence on the brain, supporting stabilized mood and reduction of anxiety. They also aid in reducing stress response feedback to the fight-or-flight HPA-axis of the body. In summary, a ketogenic or high-fat, low-carb diet can enhance your mind and mood by regulating a consistent low glucose level, which reduces insulin response and has anti-inflammatory mechanisms while reducing excitatory neuron activity, thus mellowing out and stabilizing your body and mind.

SATISFYING YOUR SWEET TOOTH

Sometimes a girl has to have a little sweet. Although the ketogenic Phase 1 of the anti-anxiety diet will prohibit all sweeteners, if you are to cycle or transition to the low-glycemic Phase 2 or incorporate a carb cycle, you may include, on occasion, the following: dates, raw unfiltered honey, coconut sugar, dark amber maple syrup, molasses, sucanat, and organic dried fruit. These foods provide nourishment with their contribution of natural sweetness and once you "break up with sugar" through the program, your palate adjusts so a little bit will go a long way.

To achieve ketosis and a balanced state of mind, you will be limiting total carbohydrates to no more than 30 grams daily and ensuring ample protein for lean body mass maintenance or gain while primarily nourishing with whole food fats. Phase 1's six-week ketogenic protocol slashes the Standard American diet (SAD) to one-tenth the amount of carbs typically consumed. After allowing your body to convert to the use of fat versus sugar as fuel, you will have an opportunity to transition or intermittently cycle the less restrictive HFLC Phase 2, which is low-glycemic with an upper limit of 90 grams of carbs. The logistics and application of these phases is discussed in Chapter 8 starting on page 158, which includes a two-week meal plan. Feel free to skip ahead if you are ready to get to the diet program now, but the remaining chapters will continue to empower you on the "why" and provide specific functional medicine application to the "how."

Removing Inflammatory Foods

The recipes of focus in this section aid in replacement of refined carbs and provide a focus on healthy fats. The variety of flavors and textures in these recipes paired with your body and brain's anti-inflammatory effects will have you coming back for more of these dishes, no longer seeing them as a replacement for a temporary program but as a desired upgrade to your daily diet!

❖ *Caramelized Onion, Turkey, and Kale Egg Muffins, page 192*

❖ *Sweet Potato Avocado Toast, page 194*

❖ *Prosciutto Egg Cups, page 196*

❖ *Smoked Wild Salmon Scramble, page 197*

❖ *Paleo Pumpkin Protein Pancakes, page 199*

❖ *Mango Zen Fuego Nutballz, page 212*

❖ *Cashew Cheeze Dip, page 218*

❖ *Almond Flour Chicken Piccata, page 240*

❖ *Chia Cherry Thumbprint Cookies, page 250*

CHAPTER 3

Reset Gut Microbiome

Your body has over 100 trillion cells of bacteria and yeast that line the mucosal membranes of your mouth, skin, and gut. These 3 to 5 pounds of living bacteria, known as the microbiome, have the ability to work with or against your body. When the microbiome is working in your favor, your body produces ample neurotransmitters such as serotonin and GABA (an inhibitory neurotransmitter that reduces feelings of fear and anxiety), and other complex mechanisms are activated to regulate your stress and anxiety response.

This chapter focuses on resetting your gut bacteria (also known as gut microbes or microbiota) and supporting the system with pro-biotic- and prebiotic-rich foods. Excessive intake of carbohydrates, foods high in yeast, and refined sugars can drive dysbiosis with bacterial or yeast overgrowth. Maintaining a low-glycemic diet and jumpstarting your anti-anxiety program with a HFLC ketogenic diet approach will work to not only reduce your body's blood sugar, by producing ketones to use as fuel, it will also serve to starve off or weaken dysbiotic bacteria and yeast.

Why Do Bacteria Matter?

Starting as early as your birth, your bacteria exposure, the environmental influence of bacteria, and your dietary influence promote the growth of positive or negative strains of bacteria that play a significant role in mood and whole-body health. This initial thumbprint of bacteria inoculation begins with the introduction of vaginal bacteria during a vaginal delivery. Breast milk then provides immunoglobulins to aid in lining the GI tract. Supported by human milk oligosaccharides (HMOs), specific fibers in breast milk work to prevent growth of bad bacteria while feeding positive influencing strains. Beyond immunoglobulins and HMOs, breast milk provides live active cultures in the form of probiotics, bacteria strains that have a positive influence on the human body.

C-SECTIONS AND VAGINAL INOCULATION

If you have a C-section, you can request a manual vaginal inoculation. Yes, it is what it sounds like. Specifically, a vaginal inoculation is the practice of exposing a newborn to the mother's vaginal cultures (which occurs naturally during vaginal birth) by swabbing the mucous membranes of baby, including mouth, nose, eyes, and ears, with non-sterile gauze that was inserted in the mother's vaginal canal. This is something I support. When my natural waterbirth became an emergency C-section, we did what we could to reduce sterility in my baby's birthing experience and had a vaginal inoculation done.

Once in the stomach, the microbes present in the GI tract have the potential to act in a favorable, deleterious, or neutral manner depending on the ratio of good to bad bacteria. If the beneficial bacteria dominate, then the body is in a state of symbiosis. When in a state of symbiosis, the gut bacteria are able to reduce inflammation in the body, regulate immune and digestive function, enhance nutrient absorption, and produce serotonin and other natural mood stabilizers.

On the contrary, when in the state of dysbiosis, "bad," or pathogenic, strains of bacteria can take over, leading to gas, bloating, constipation, diarrhea, inflammation, immune dysfunction, and imbalanced neurotransmitter production. Often, dysbiosis drives excessive epinephrine and excitatory neurotransmitter response, which fuels expression of a pathogen. In other words, our bodies' stress signaling perpetuates the growth and spread of pathogens, which only drives more anxiety expression. As a result, serotonin is exhausted and under produced. Yeast overgrowth, another culprit of dysbiosis that is often seen as an excessive presence of *Candida albicans*, can be identified through belching, distention or bloating, excessive sugar cravings, anxiety, and brain fog.

For optimal health we should strive for our GI tract to be in a state of symbiosis, rather than dysbiosis.

What Fuels Dysbiosis?

Many factors of your day-to-day function greatly influence your gut bacteria balance. Your stress levels, drug interactions, and dietary intake can either provoke or prevent dysbiosis.

The digestive process begins as soon as food enters the mouth, where enzymes and bacteria in the saliva play a role in turning food bites into a slurry. Then, as the food passes through the gastric pouch, ideally being denatured by hydrocholoric acid and additional enzyme exposure, microbes in the small and large intestines complete the digestion process. The metabolic end products in the presence of probiotics (beneficial microbes) are short chain fatty acids (SCFA), including butyrate and organic acids (lactic and acetic acids). SCFA tend to lower the pH of the intestinal contents, creating conditions less desirable for harmful bacteria and cancer while providing a fuel source for healthy cells. They are also able to regulate the environment so helpful bacteria can thrive, influence the memory and learning process, balance the sympathetic nervous system, and support neurotransmitter release while promoting serotonin secretions. In this sense, the end products of bacterial balance have a final say on mental health.

When the body is under stress, we produce less saliva, which means our bodies provide less bacteria battling and digestive enzyme support. Stress can also hinder your digestive processes by slowing down food breakdown. This drives a stagnant fermentation state in the gut where bad bacteria, when overgrown, can have a heyday eating the foods you just consumed. Dysbiosis paired with stress or unregulated anxiety can be a big driver of the "food baby," where some individuals experience dynamic bloating of greater than 2 inches post meal consumption. Essentially, the bad bacteria or yeast strains are attempting to brew beer or bake bread in your digestive system!

In addition, when your body is under high stress or a state of anxiety, the sympathetic nervous system (which controls fight-or-flight responses) will likely reduce the amount of good bacteria and increase susceptibility to pathogens, further perpetuating a dysbiotic environment. Hence stress management and anxiety go hand in hand with optimizing your microbiome. Research also demonstrates that adding probiotics to the gut can alleviate schizophrenia, mania, and anxiety.

Managing stress in the time of anxiety may seem like an uphill battle. The areas where you potentially have the most control over your microbiome are your medications and diet, both of which have a significant influence on driving dysbiosis. Antibiotics kill most bacteria in the gut, yet the undesirable bacteria tend to be resistant or resilient, quickly reappearing and leading to dysbiosis. These unfriendly microorganisms, such as pathogens, yeasts, fungi, and parasites, can upset the balance by taking over the tract if probiotics are not there to defend it. Antacids, including both PPIs (proton pump inhibitors) such as Protonix and Nexium, and over-the-counter chews or drinks such as Tums or Pepto-Bismol, may soothe the burn of acid reflux temporarily; however, over time, this basic elevated pH of the stomach sets up an environment that supports bacterial and yeast overgrowth, only fueling the fire! Beyond drugs, medical intervention such as radiation and surgery can be sterilizing to the gut bacteria, reducing probiotic function and allowing bad bacteria overgrowth.

Two of the most damaging substances to intestinal flora balance are chlorine and sodium fluoride, both present in most city water. Drinking filtered water is important in avoiding these sterilizing compounds. Drinking alcoholic beverages, taking birth control pills, and many other NSAID pain-relieving medications can also cause damage to intestinal lining and flora. In addition, poor eating habits, including a diet high in refined sugar and excessive carbohydrates, drive and fuel continued dysbiosis and bacterial imbalance. On the contrary, diets that are low-glycemic and balanced with ample fiber can support a healthy gut ecology, driving symbiosis.

Drivers of Dysbiosis

Birth and early infant nourishment: A sterile C-section and formula-fed babies will have less favorable bacterial state.

Stress: Suppresses the production of probiotics and reduces stomach acidity.

Antibiotic use: Acts as a "bomb" to good bacteria; bad bacteria or opportunistic yeast typically rebound more quickly and aggressively than good bacteria.

Steroid use: Inhibits the immune system's ability to respond with inflammation so the yeast or bacteria can spread; often, thrush is seen with oral inhalers.

Use of PPIs or antacids: Reduces stomach acidity, which increases environment for pathogenic bacteria and yeast.

Excessive alcohol use: Weakens the immune system, alters the stomach pH, and can kill off probiotics.

Oral contraceptives: Alters gut bacteria; estrogen in excess (often seen with synthetic form in birth control) can promote yeast growth.

A diet high in sugar and refined carbohydrates: Fuels yeast growth and activity.

Bacteria and Mood Connection

Now that you understand the impact of stress, medications, and diet on your microbiome, it is important to emphasize the role of the microbiome on your mental health. The gut is also known as the enteric nervous system (ENS), which controls heart rate, digestion, respiratory rate, and sexual arousal, and serves as the primary driver of fight-or-flight response. The ENS has over 500 neurons, only secondary to the brain; this is why the gut is often deemed the second brain of the body. It can work in connection with or independent of the central nervous system in response to rest-and-digest mode or fight-or-flight mode. The gut serves as the manufacturing plant for over 30 neurotransmitters, most of which act in the same way as those neurotransmitters in the brain. In fact, over 90 percent of the body's serotonin is manufactured and stored within the gut as well as about 50 percent of the body's dopamine.

The vagus nerve is the largest nerve of the autonomic nervous system. It goes from the brain stem to colon and works in both parasympathetic (relaxed) and sympathetic (stressed) response. This highway of information carries signals from the microbiome, which can either instigate an anti-inflammatory and anti-anxiety response or drive dysfunction in the HPA-axis.

Neurotransmitters and Probiotics

Neurotransmitter	Function of neurotransmitter	Probiotic producers
GABA	Feel-good inhibitory compound, natural anti-anxiety effects	*Lactobacillus* and *Bifidobacterium*
Serotonin	Most popular known contributor to a feeling of well-being and happiness, plays a role in blood pressure regulation and digestion while reducing anxiety and stress response	*Lactobacillus* and *Bifidobacterium*
Norepinephrine	Increases arousal and alertness, promotes vigilance; in excess, can drive racing thoughts and difficulty concentrating; increases restlessness and anxiety	*Escherichia, Bacillus,* and *Saccharomyces*
Dopamine	Excitatory compound playing a significant role in reward mechanisms; in deficiency, can drive restless leg and even neurological conditions such as Parkinson's; in excess, can drive mania and schizophrenia	*Bacillus* and *Serratia*
Acetylcholine	Aids in REM cycle and memory; in stress response, stimulates norepinephrine; plays a role with calcium channels in activating muscle response as well as vasodilation, or widening, of blood vessels, increasing blood flow	*Lactobacillus*

In this sense, optimizing your microbiome supports not only digestive and immune health, but also promotes optimal neurotransmitter production and mood stability. Social stress and anxiety drives excessive output of stress-responding neurotransmitters, including dopamine, norepinephrine, and epinephrine, to be released, which influences the growth of imbalanced gut bacteria, further emphasizing the two-way street of brain-gut connection.

As you work to reset your microbiome to a more favorable symbiotic state, the probiotics in your gut will enhance neurotransmitter production to aid as inhibitory compounds that promote relaxation and reduced anxiety. Increased production of serotonin and GABA will aid neurochemically, resulting in less anxiety or stress response, and thus, less output of stress-responding neurotransmitters. You will also have fewer stress chemical compounds as a result of lower levels of dysbiotic bacteria.

View the table on page 43 to learn about specific neurotransmitters, their functions, and which probiotic strains support their production. As you will see, *Lactobacillus* and *Bifidobacterium* are the primary strains of focus for the two major anti-anxiety neurotransmitters, GABA and serotonin.

Beyond neurotransmitters, the microbiome influences the brain-derived neurotrophic factor (BDNF), a specific protein that works on growth, maintenance, and stability of neurons. A study published by the *Journal of Gastroenterology* demonstrates the influence of good bacteria on the brain. Researchers examined the influence of antibiotics and gut sterility on BDNF, specifically focusing on the hippocampus and amygdala. When levels of BDNF drop in the hippocampus, depression and anxiety are seen at higher rates. Thus, some anti-anxiety medications are targeted at increasing BDNF in this brain region. However, in the fear center of the brain, the amygdala, low levels are associated with less anxiety as to not upregulate fear response. An increase of BDNF in the hippocampus and a reduction of it in the amygdala aids in more exploratory behavior and reduced anxiety expression.

BEYOND BLOATING...FINDING MYSELF!

Laurie was seeking a solution for her chronic bloating and constipation and came to the Naturally Nourished clinic with a desire to get off her daily Miralax and flatten her abdomen. In our initial consultation, we determined she was a likely candidate for dysbiosis and set up to do a 3-day stool test. Upon review of panel we identified a pathogenic bacteria, *Proteus mirabilis*, often associated with UTIs and trended in research studies with anxiety and panic. Laurie was working as a busy attorney, so she often wrote off her panic attacks as just a part of the job. I worked with Laurie using my a 6-week cleanse to address dysbiosis and candida. At our 4-week check-in, Laurie shared something phenomenal: not only was she experiencing bowel regularity and less bloating, but she was thinking clearer, sleeping better, and experiencing fewer palpitations. Following our 6-week cleanse, we worked on rebuilding her gut microbiome with the Targeted Strength probiotic, providing 60 billion CFU in a 50:50 blend of lacto and bifido strains. She didn't just tolerate the probiotic; she found herself more social, laughing more, and ultimately feeling like herself again. Not only is she experiencing less bloating with improved bowel regularity, she is panic-free, even-keeled, and living in a balanced, joyful state of mind.

Getting Your Microbiome to Work For You

You know the significant role that gut bacteria have on brain chemistry and understand that the gut is like a second brain due to the amount of nerves and neurological production in the GI tract. Now, you can empower yourself by managing mood with regulation of your microbiome. In this sense, probiotics can be seen as "nature's Prozac." A symbiotic gut drives a happy, mellow mind.

Probiotics exhibit direct effects in the GI tract and indirect effects in other parts of the body and brain. Effects on joints, skin, and the brain are due to the impact that probiotics have on immunity via changes in inflammatory mediators making the overall body less reactive. As probiotics in the digestive tract aid in breaking down foods, absorption and digestibility of nutrients increases, leading to increased production of proteins, vitamins, and other functional compounds in the body. Symptoms and conditions that can be treated with probiotics include diarrhea, gastroenteritis, irritable bowel syndrome, inflammatory bowel disease (IBD), Crohn's disease and ulcerative colitis, cancer, depressed immune function, food allergies, low weight or malnourishment, depression and anxiety, obesity, and liver disease.

All probiotics can be well-received and proliferate if welcomed by prebiotics, non-digestible fibers that selectively stimulate the growth and activity of beneficial bugs. When probiotics and prebiotics are mixed together, they encourage a symbiotic, synergistic relationship that is beneficial to the host. However, if the gut is in a state of dysbiosis, prebiotics can fuel growth of bad bacteria, instead. Also, in dysbiosis there often isn't room for the probiotic to grow, and there can be intolerance or a battle-like environment.

Using the anti-anxiety diet, you will starve off potential bad bacteria during your ketogenic state. You will have the opportunity to reset your bacterial balance in the low-glycemic phase by bringing prebiotic fibers into synergy with an abundance of probiotic cultures. Beyond mellowing out your mood and supporting a healthy production of feel-good brain chemicals, this phase of microbiome reset may aid in brain fog, difficulty concentrating, bloating and distension, and stubborn metabolism.

Plowing the GI Tract with a Bacterial and Yeast Cleanse

The best way to understand the microbiome is to envision a garden bed. There is only so much room for things to grow. You will see the beneficial vegetation you intended to grow, wild flowers, and weeds. In some cases of dysbiosis, the garden bed is filled with so many weeds or even overgrown with wildflowers that there is no room for intended vegetation (probiotics) to thrive. As there is an upper capacity in your microbiome, when in a state of dysbiosis, you may not be able to resolve the situation with a probiotic food or supplement. Probiotics may help on some level but in order to reset the microbiome, one must plow the fields of the garden bed to allow space for good bacteria to thrive and then fertilize and support healthy growth for symbiotic effects.

Low in carbohydrates and refined sugars, the anti-anxiety diet is supportive of a bacterial and yeast cleanse to starve off bacteria. During this time it is recommended to consider a cleanse with antimicrobial and antifungal supplemental support to remove potential overgrowth of bad dysbiotic strains and make room for beneficial probiotics to set up camp and proliferate. Taking supplements to support a bacterial and yeast cleanse would be especially recommended if you have experienced intolerance to a probiotic supplement or food or experience significant bloating, bowel irregularity, dermatological flares, or have taken multiple rounds of antibiotics. Take the Gut Bacteria Balance Quiz below to determine if your gut is in a state of dysbiosis. Learn more about advanced approaches in the Appendix supplements and labs sections.

Gut Bacteria Balance Quiz

Respond to the following questions with Never, Sometimes, or Often. Give yourself a score of 2 for each Often response, 1 for

Sometimes, and 0 for Never. This quiz will be used as a tool to determine if yeast, small intestinal bacterial overgrowth (SIBO), and gut bacteria imbalance or dysbiosis is a root cause of your anxiety, requiring additional support such as advanced testing or nutritional supplementation.

The recommendations on the following pages correspond to formulas carried in my clinic. In Supplement Support for the Foundational 6 Rs (page 272), you will find information on dosage, active ingredients, and mechanism of action so you can determine if these formulas are a good fit, or find comparable ones that have similar composition.

1. Have you taken antibiotics in the past three years? Give yourself a score of 4 for frequent use of more than twice per year and/or long-term use of tetracycline, Bactrim, or another antibiotic for over a month.

❏ Never   ❏ Sometimes   ❏ Often

2. Have you taken prednisone, corticosteroids, or steroid inhalers over the past three years?

❏ Never   ❏ Sometimes   ❏ Often

3 a. Women: Do you get yeast infections, UTIs, and/or vaginosis, or have you been with a partner that has these conditions or a man that has had penile thrush?

❏ Never   ❏ Sometimes   ❏ Often

3 b. Men: Have you been with a partner that suffers from yeast infections, UTIs, and/or vaginosis, or have you had penile thrush?

❏ Never   ❏ Sometimes   ❏ Often

4. Do you experience athlete's foot, ear wax, or other chronic fungal infections of the skin or nails?

❏ Never   ❏ Sometimes   ❏ Often

5. Do you regularly consume alcoholic beverages or experience alcohol intolerance?

❏ Never   ❏ Sometimes   ❏ Often

6. Do you experience significant bread and sugar cravings?

❏ Never   ❏ Sometimes   ❏ Often

7. Have you struggled with blood sugar irregularities such as shaking, irritability, crashing in energy, or headaches?

❏ Never   ❏ Sometimes   ❏ Often

8. Do you experience bloating and distension in the abdomen?

❏ Never   ❏ Sometimes   ❏ Often

9. Do you wake with a flat abdomen but as the day goes on, get more bloated and notice brain fog following meals?

❏ Never   ❏ Sometimes   ❏ Often

10. Do you have irregular bowel movements, such as constipation or diarrhea?

❏ Never   ❏ Sometimes   ❏ Often

11. Does your stool have a fruity odor, flaky or sticky texture, or mucus?

❏ Never   ❏ Sometimes   ❏ Often

12. Do you have bad breath, a white-coated tongue, or dry mouth?

❏ Never   ❏ Sometimes   ❏ Often

13. Do you experience aches in the soft tissue of your fascia or muscles?

❏ Never   ❏ Sometimes   ❏ Often

14. Do you experience brain fog or difficulty concentrating in general?

❏ Never   ❏ Sometimes   ❏ Often

Total Scoring:

Less than 10

It looks like your gut is not imbalanced and the addition of probiotic-rich foods with prebiotic fibers will be enough to set up your gut to produce serotonin, GABA, and other feel-good mood stabilizers! Consider a 50:50 blend of bifido and lacto bacteria strains, such as Restore Baseline Probiotic, to optimize probiotic function for digestive health and beyond.

Less than 15

You are likely experiencing some level of dysbiosis, which can be based on yeast or pathogenic bacteria overgrowth. Phase 1 dietary protocol with carbohydrate restriction will help starve off bad bacteria or yeast. Enjoy a cultured food four times per week. The addition of these probiotic-rich foods with prebiotic fibers support your gut to produce serotonin, GABA, and other feel-good mood stabilizers! In addition, it is recommended to take at least 15 billion CFU of a 50:50 blend of bifido and lacto bacteria strains, such as Restore Baseline Probiotic, to optimize probiotic function for digestive health and beyond. If the addition of this probiotic supplement or probiotic- and prebiotic-rich foods exacerbates symptoms, it is likely that dysbiosis is severe enough to proceed with a bacterial cleanse.

Greater than 15

This score points to definite dysbiosis, which can be based on yeast or pathogenic bacteria. Follow the Phase 1 dietary protocol with carbohydrate restriction, and withhold probiotics and prebiotics while proceeding with the six-week gut reset protocol detailed in this chapter. During the six-week cleanse you will starve off and weaken the overgrowth, and also attack the bacteria and yeast with the natural antimicrobial, antifungal, and detoxifying compounds. Following the gut reset protocol, you will add probiotic-rich foods with prebiotic fibers in your diet to support the rebuild in your gut to produce serotonin, GABA, and other feel-good mood stabilizers! Due to the severity of dysbiosis, following your gut reset protocol, it is recommended to take at least 50 billion CFU of a 50:50 blend of bifido and lacto bacteria strains, such as Targeted Strength Probiotic paired with *S. Boulardii*–rich Spectrum Probiotic to combat regrowth of bacteria and yeast while optimizing probiotic function for digestive health and beyond. If post-cleanse, following four weeks of the probiotic support, you are still experiencing symptoms of dysbiosis, you may consider advanced functional testing of stool (see Advanced Functional Labs on page 287 for details).

If you score with a high value and suspect you are a candidate for dysbiosis, I would encourage removing yeast and vinegar-based foods for six weeks as a supplement to your anti-anxiety diet. Also, restrict probiotic foods for the first three weeks, reintroducing them at weeks four to six.

The removal of all long-chain carbs, such as grains and beans, during the anti-anxiety diet supports resetting the microbiome, as bad bacteria can ferment these fibers, perpetuating dysbiosis. Your first phase of the program will work to starve off bacteria to support a successful dysbiosis reset and cleanse, if necessary.

Supplements to Support Your Microbiome Reset

When looking to remove the overgrowth of unwanted pathogenic yeast or bacteria, first remove foods from the diet that might be feeding them. High-carbohydrate foods, especially those with refined sugar and added yeast, are known to feed bad bacteria and yeast overgrowth in the small intestine and should be removed if dysbiosis is suspected.

The strategic use of natural plant compounds, nutrients, and probi-otics is a helpful tool to help kill off pathogenic bacteria or yeast and promote optimal digestion and neurotransmitter production. This is preferred over the use of antibiotics, which can have a sterilizing effect, killing off the good bacteria and reducing our powerhouse of production.

A benefit to using natural compounds such as berberine root from Oregon Grape is that they can have antiviral, antibacterial, and antifungal support while also working to promote bile flow, balance blood sugar levels, and fight against cancer. Food as medicine offers a synergy and unintentional beneficial influence versus the deleterious side effects of drugs. Consumption of bitters, such as dandelion and lemon, can promote the production of bile flow, stimulating liver and gallbladder function while further supporting bacterial balance.

Supplements to Remove Yeast or Bacterial Overgrowth

These supplements will support a balanced microbiome and a bacterial, fungal, or yeast cleanse. See Supplement Support for the 6 Foundational Rs on page 272 for specific dosages and details.

• Berberine supplement (page 275) such as Berberine Boost

• Aromatic, antimicrobial, and antifungal herbs (page 276) such as CandiActivator

• Bacteriophage/probiotic combination formula (page 277), such as GI Cleanup

• Phase 2 liver detox supportive formula (page 277), such as Ultimate Detox

Supplements to Support Your Rebuild of Healthy Gut Bacteria

After a bacterial cleanse, it is important to rebuild your army of beneficial bacteria. Prebiotics from the Phytofiber in combination with different targeted strains of probiotic will work to prevent relapse and support a healthy gut microbiome!

- Restore Baseline Probiotic, page 278
- Broad-Spectrum Probiotic/Rebuild Baseline Probiotic, page 278
- Prebiotic fiber blend/PhytoFiber, page 279

Lifestyle Support for Your Cleanse

If you do go into a cleanse, you may experience a Herxheimer reaction, where your symptoms get worse before they get better. As you are plowing the garden bed, those weeds may kick up pollen or bad seeds, and the bacteria or yeast fight back. I like to recommend locking down and moving forward with the cleanse during these symptoms, as this is a sign of the excess activity that needs to get removed. You can support symptom management and reduction with anti-inflammatory and detox-promoting foods and activities. Focus on high-antioxidant, low-carb foods such as green tea, rooibos, turmeric, leafy greens, avocado, cacao, and seeds such as hemp, chia, pumpkin, and sunflower. These foods will support healthy cells in a time of cleanse and reduce inflammation.

Supporting the excretion pathways of the liver should be another primary focus. Sulfur-rich cruciferous vegetables such as broccoli, cauliflower, cabbage, kale, Brussels sprouts, and bok choy have indole-3-carbinoles that increase detox activity in excretion pathways, aiding in gathering the dust from die-off and reducing symptoms.

If anxiety gets severe during a cleanse, consider using GABA or other inhibitory compounds to aid in managing anxiety reactivity. If anxiety prevails after 5 days, bring in a 5–15 billion CFU, 50:50 *Lactobaccilus* and *Bifidobacterium* probiotic blend (even if anxiety occurs earlier than week 4, depending on circumstance).

Beyond diet, moving your body will support lymphatic tissue function, which in turn supports detox and removal of bacteria, yeast, and their debris, as well as reduces the inflammation in the body. Additionally, massage and Epsom salt baths are two of my favorite recommendations to soothe and support removal.

Common symptoms of pathogen die-off include:

- Loose stools or diarrhea
- Nausea
- Flu-like symptoms
- Body aches, muscle aches, and joint pain
- Fatigue
- Brain fog and headaches
- Increased insomnia or anxiety

Dietary and Lifestyle Support Action List

- Keep probiotic supplements and foods out for first three weeks! (See note above for exceptions per severe anxiety reactivity.)
- At week 4, start to bring in small amounts of probiotic foods.
- Aim for >80g of protein in biological form, per day. Use 2 tablespoons of coconut oil daily (see sidebar on page 56).
- Consume ½ to 1 cup of cooked cruciferous vegetables daily.

- Drink turmeric lemonade (find a recipe at www.alimillerRD.com; omit the honey).

- Aim for 6 to 8 ounces of (chicken, beef, turkey, or pork) bone broth daily.

- Reduce vinegar intake, keeping to a maximum of 1 tablespoon/day for weeks 1 to 6 of active cleanse.

- Keep carbs at <60g/day, with no refined sugar or yeast foods, following Phase 1 of the anti-anxiety diet.

- Practice gentle movement therapy! Walk, incorporating hills, and try yoga, Pilates, or bar resistance.

- Stretch using a foam roller.

- Shower using hydrotherapy HOT to COLD, plus body brushing.

- Indulge in a sauna or Epsom salt bath.

- Consider a massage at least once a month, or twice during the cleanse.

- Incorporate oil pulling three to four times a week (page 56), with 1 tablespoon of coconut oil.

- Use coconut oil topically.

The Power of Fermented Foods

As noted, the human gut is said to contain nearly 5 pounds of live active culture. Eating lacto-fermented foods provides the body with beneficial bacteria that aid in fighting off bad bacteria in the intestine. The healthy, friendly bacteria in our gut not only aid in digestion, it is also responsible for synthesizing various nutrients, such as vitamin K2, vitamin B12, and biotin. If you tolerate probiotic-rich foods and don't have dysbiosis, incorporate these foods for significant anti-anxiety effects. If you do not tolerate them, keep them out of the diet until you are halfway into your cleanse.

Perhaps the highest influential shift in your microbiome will occur when adding in fermented vegetables that increase *Lactobacillus* and *Bifidobacterium*, which, with colonization in the gut, increase GABA production and expression. GABA is the major chill pill of the brain, having inhibitory influence on anxiety activity. Beyond balancing mood and mellowing out the mind, GABA can have anti-inflammatory effects on the gut itself. This reduces the response of inflammatory chemicals as well as stress chemical compounds, such as epinephrine, which in excess can drive panic, worry, irritability, and distress.

PREVENT TRANSLOCATION OF BACTERIA AND YEAST

As you work to cleanse your gut and weaken the bad bacteria strains, often they will translocate to other areas of the microbiome that are less targeted. This is exemplified when women get yeast infections following antibiotic use. With a *Candida* (yeast) and bacteria cleanse, bacteria may shift to other areas outside of the gut, causing changes to skin with rashes, itching, hives, phlegm or thrush on the mouth or tongue, excess wax in the ears, or styes and mucus shifts in the eyes. To prevent this unpleasant experience and support true removal of the bad bacteria and yeast, consider using coconut oil for oil pulling and topical use. Oil pulling is the process of essentially swishing coconut oil in your mouth for about 5 to 10 minutes and then spitting it out. This aids in circulation of blood and delivers antimicrobial and antifungal compounds to your periodontal tissue and mouth. Also, consider gargling with a mouthwash containing wild harvested herbs with antimicrobial effects.

Benefits of Consuming Probiotic and Lacto-Fermented Foods

- Enhances digestibility and absorption of nutrients
- Activates immune system, supporting the body's defense system
- Improves bowel regularity
- Enhances production of serotonin and GABA for brain balance
- Improves metabolism
- Reduces risk for cancer by reducing free radicals and increasing natural killer cell activity

Probiotic Challenge

Try this to see if you are a good candidate for a candida and bacterial cleanse. Oftentimes with candida or bacterial overgrowth, probiotic foods and supplements will not be tolerated well due to competitive inhibition. This challenge is an easy and cost-effective way to evaluate the need to dig deeper with a cleanse!

Restore Baseline Probiotic offers a 50:50 blend of lacto and bifido probiotic strains to support the bowel without fermentable fiber that can throw off gut bacteria. This makes it a great probiotic to use in a test of tolerance.

Here's how to do it:

Supplies: Sewing tape, a notebook, and a bottle of Restore Baseline Probiotic.

Step 1: Take your waist circumference measurement at your belly button for three days in a row from rising to bedtime and record as a baseline.

Step 2: Start the probiotic at 1 capsule at bed for three days. Continue to measure waist circumference at rising and at bedtime.

Step 3: Increase by 1 capsule every three days for ten days until you reach four per night (not counting initial reads without the probiotic).

Step 4: Try to continue at 4 per night for 3 days. Note changes in waist circumference as well as any changes in GI, such as cramping, bowel movements, belching, or gas during the challenge.

If you experience increased bloat or increased GI symptoms, this indicates dysbiosis and requires a cleanse; in this case discontinue probiotics.

If you experience a flatter abdomen or no change and reduced GI symptoms, this is a pass and sign of symbiosis. Continue taking 1 probiotic at bedtime; if well-tolerated, take the full dosage of 4 per night. If you notice when you reduce back to only 1 capsule as your baseline that your symptoms decline from where they were at 4, you may consider a targeted strength probiotic that provides 60 billion CFU versus 15 billion.

FOOD AS MEDICINE

Reset and Cleanse Your Microbiome

These recipes have ingredients with antimicrobial, antifungal, and antiviral activity and provide antioxidants and detox support.

❖ *Coconut No-Oatmeal, page 202*

❖ *Curry Roasted Cauliflower, page 214*

❖ *Bacteria-Battling Chimichurri, page 248*

❖ *Lime in the Coconut Fat Bomb, page 254*

Support Symbiosis and Healthy Gut Flora

These recipes contain probiotic-rich ingredients and prebiotic fibers to aid in fertilizing a balanced gut biome. Beyond direct favorable effects of promoting production of GABA and serotonin, these foods will defend against bad bacteria to aid in maintaining continued sustainable neurotransmitter production. Prebiotics and probiotic-rich foods fight against pathogens and dysbiosis with strength in numbers and keep your targeted *lactobaccilus* and bifido strains in your probiotic supplement alive and viable.

❖ *Quick Coconut Yogurt, page 198*

❖ *Creamy Green Chile Chicken Soup, page 225*

❖ *Coconut Chia Seed Pudding, page 255*

CHAPTER 4

Repair GI Lining

The gut refers to both the small and large intestines. With this anti-anxiety Foundational R, you will target these organs and their role in inflammation, bacterial imbalance, and malabsorption of nutrients, which drive nutritional deficiency.

This chapter takes you into the structural influence of the primary barrier regulating what enters your bloodstream and how your body responds to the compound that enters. If needed, you will learn how to repair your gut lining for whole-body health. If the gut is in an optimal state of health, the lining will be intact, able to prevent large particles or irritants from entering the bloodstream while providing space for good bacteria to thrive and enhancing nutrient absorption. But when the gut is in a leaky state with damage to the delicate internal lining (in medical terms, intestinal enteropathy) you are at risk for increased food and chemical sensitivity because the damaged barrier allows large compounds into the bloodstream, creating an overactive inflammatory response on an immunological level. Also, if the gut lining is not sound, the gut bacteria have less space to proliferate and grow, which means you will have less defense mechanisms against bad bacteria and less space to absorb nutrients.

Gut Anatomy 101

The intestines' primary function is the absorption of nutrients and water. The small intestines, which are 20 feet or so of a narrow, winding mass, directly connect to the stomach, the colon, and large intestines, all the way to the anus. Beyond absorption, the intestines play a great role in housing gut bacteria, which in turn support neurotransmitter production, and the large intestine especially plays a great role in detoxification and electrolyte stability.

The tissue of the submucosa (the external part of organ) is resilient, whereas the internal layers of the mucosal lining (the internal part of the intestines) are quite delicate. The thin mucosal lining has a significant role in your immune health. It houses the GALT, which has the largest storage of immune cells, such as T cells (made in the thymus), and B cells (made in bone marrow). These specialized white blood cells play a role in tagging and attacking foreign invaders, such as harmful viral and bacterial influencers, while providing an adaptive immune response to things inside and outside the cells. One role of B cells is determining what is friend or foe. If the B cell tags a food or chemical as harmful (reactive), the immune system has inflammatory reactions. The thickness and integrity of the gut lining where the GALT resides is strongly correlated to how reactive the immune cells will be to foods and chemicals. If the gut lining is damaged, there will be more antigen reactivity, as seen with food sensitivity and inflammatory conditions.

The most internal lining of the intestines, called the epithelial lining, has finger-like projections called villi and microvilli, which are delicate projections that enhance surface area for optimal absorption of nutrients as they work to scoot food particles along what is called the brush border. This border includes an area where nutrients are exposed to bacteria and digestive enzymes, further enhancing breakdown of food particles for absorption while regulating pH and defending against invaders.

What Is Leaky Gut?

Leaky gut, or intestinal permeability, is the condition in which larger-than-desired particles, including metabolic byproducts of food and gut microbes, enter the bloodstream. This overburdening of compounds in the bloodstream triggers a chain of events where the body drives an immune response and attacks otherwise neutral molecules, thinking that they are "invaders."

In attack mode, inflammatory chemical mediators are released from immune cells to battle these compounds. However, many of the compounds that cross the gut-blood barrier in the case of leaky gut are otherwise harmless food compounds that don't necessitate an attack. In this state the body goes into overreactive mode as a hypervigilant immune response, which drives chronic inflammation and excessive immune reactivity. Studies show that these attacks play a role in the development of autoimmune diseases.

The main culprits of this leaking are gut-damaging chemicals and medications, inflammatory foods, infections, bad bacteria, and toxins. As discussed in Chapter 2, gluten is the number one cause of leaky gut, with abrasive activity of gliadin, a pro-inflammatory compound. Another concern with gliadin is its production of zonulin proteins in gut cells, which unlock tight junctions in the gut lining. In this sense, gluten can cause both inflammatory irritation and, in the role of gatekeeper, drive the opening for more destruction by letting larger particles cross the gut-blood barrier. Here are some symptoms that are associated with leaky gut:

- **Brain:** Brain fog, depression, ADHD, anxiety
- **Skin:** Acne, psoriasis, eczema, rosacea, hives, dermatitis
- **Thyroid:** Hashimoto's, hypothyroidism, hyperthyroidism
- **Colon:** Constipation, diarrhea, colitis, Crohn's, IBS

- **Ear, nose, throat:** Phlegm, allergies, difficulty swallowing, frequent colds, mucus

- **Structural system:** Fibromyalgia, arthritis, joint pain, headaches

- **Adrenals:** Chronic fatigue syndrome, histamine reactivity, panic attacks

- **Autoimmune:** Multiple sclerosis (MS), neuropathy, Parkinson's, lupus, chronic inflammatory demyelinating polyneuropathy (CIPD)

Chemicals and Medications that Drive Leaky Gut

Prevention is always the most powerful tool in optimized health! Below are the common irritants and drivers of leaky gut. After reading, take the Anti-Anxiety Diet Leaky Gut Quiz (page 68) to understand the state your gut lining may be in, which will determine the level of intervention and supplementation warranted.

Chlorine. Chlorine in drinking water can be damaging to the gut by sterilizing gut flora. Other commonly consumed chemicals include food additives or preservatives that act as stabilizers, fillers, or emulsifiers. These chemical additives are found throughout processed or even natural products such as almond milk. Food chemicals such as carrageenan, cellulose gum, and polysorbate 80 destroy mucosal membranes and can allow bad bacteria to pass the gut lining, plowing through with damaging effects.

Non-steroidal anti-inflammatory drugs (NSAIDs) and antibiotics. These two top drivers of leaky gut are very irritating to the GI tract, causing a separation of gut lining junctions. They can even cause hemorrhaging or bleeding to the intestinal lining, especially if combined with alcohol use. NSAIDs include over-the-counter drugs such as Advil, Aleve, Ibuprofen, and their higher dose counterparts Meloxicam, Celebrex, and Naproxen Sodium, to name a few.

It is important to emphasize the influence of these seemingly harmless drugs, as many people take daily doses of NSAIDs to cope with muscle and joint aches and pains that may be resolved with reduction of inflammatory foods in the diet and support to repair leaky gut. However, instead of reducing the driving causes, they take a drug that provides short-term relief while providing a more long-term hit to the gut lining, which perpetuates the body's inflammatory response.

Antibiotics. Antibiotics have a less direct but very important role in leaky gut. These drugs sterilize the gut microbiome, including the protective probiotic colonies that seal the gut lining junctions and aid in the further breakdown of foods. When the gut microbiome is weakened through the use of antibiotics, the epithelial gut lining function is compromised. The use of antibiotics also drives imbalance of the microbiome (see Chapter 3).

Unfortunately, like many drugs, we are just starting to see the long-term effects of use. In fact, the first antibiotic, penicillin, did not hit mainstream healthcare until 1939, and since the 1950s it has been increasingly prescribed for both necessary conditions like blood, bone, and organ infection as well as unnecessary conditions like common ear infections, sore throat, and bronchitis, which may have viral influence in which antibiotics serve no beneficial purpose.

Cancer treatments. Cancer treatment, including both the toxic exposure of chemotherapy as well as the sterilizing effects of radiation, can also drive leaky gut. Chemotherapy, in its focus to attack abnormal cells and malignancy, can also hit the epithelial lining of the gut, reducing digestive enzyme production and bloating as well as increasing permeability in the intestines. Radiation has similar outcomes but with more of a mechanical damage from exposure.

Both chemotherapy and radiation reduce probiotic activity, as well, which can lead to less protective activity on the lining.

PPIs. Another more commonly prescribed drug category of concern that is now available over the counter is proton pump inhibitors (PPIs), from Nexium and Protonix to the generic omeprazole and pantoprazole. These drugs work to reduce the production of stomach acid. Many people take them for heartburn, reflux, or indigestion; however, often the cause of these conditions is the exact opposite—too little stomach acidity. In fact, stomach acid is supposed to be quite acidic, with a pH of 1 to 2.

Bacterial imbalance, stress, and other drugs can neutralize the stomach acid, causing more bloating and impeding optimal digestive function. When stomach acid gets too low, foods are not properly broken down, which only exacerbates the issue. When these drugs are taken as a response to bloating or acidity in the esophagus often they will resolve the acidity by neutralizing it, but the individual will be prone to vitamin and mineral deficiency as the hydrochloric acid (HCl) levels in the stomach need to be optimized to activate certain enzymes to break down and absorb nutrients. In fact, one of the drivers of B12 deficiency anemia and bone demineralization is associated with use of PPIs. In addition, when B12 levels drop, anxiety peaks, as B12 has calming effects to stabilize mood.

Foods that Drive Leaky Gut

We make over 300 food-related decisions per day. We can choose to consume foods that soothe and heal or that damage and inflame. Food can influence leaky gut by causing structural damage, bacterial imbalance, and the inflammatory process. Foods contributing to leaky gut contain lectins and phytates (primarily in wheat, grains, and legumes), refined processed sugar, excessive carbohydrate, and omega-6 fatty acids from industrialized oils (corn, soy, cottonseed, safflower, to name a few). Familiarize yourself with the foods to remove covered in Chapter 2, Remove Inflammatory Foods.

Infections and Pathogens that Drive Leaky Gut

The presence of pathogenic (bad) bacteria in the gut can cause an imbalance in gastrointestinal lining function. This has been shown to be a primary cause of mortality in poverty-stricken countries where malnourishment is widespread. In fact, research done on the villi of the gut when a pathogen is induced in both healthy and malnourished rats determined that the malnourished state accelerates damage of the gut lining in the presence of a pathogen and that there is greater risk of translocation, which is when the pathogen crosses the gut lining and enters other areas of the body.

Bacteria and infections in the body influence gut integrity on an immunological level. Specific immune T helper cells (Th17, Th22) play a role in maintaining the epithelial lining of the gut via production of interleukin-22 (IL-22), which is optimized in a healthy, balanced gut. When the immune system is distressed it will reduce its production of IL-22, which drives leaky gut. In IL-22 deficient mice, research has shown higher mortality when exposed to *Clostridium difficile (C. diff),* a known pathogen, as the low levels of IL-22 allow the *C. diff* to cross the gut barrier, hitting other vital organs and driving dysfunction on a whole-body level.

Toxins and Leaky Gut

Industrialized chemicals in our food, water, air, and households can contribute to gut damage via direct chemical insult as well as sterility of gut biome. The US consumes more GMO crops than the rest of the world, and we allow many chemical substances in our food system that are banned in other developed nations. Additives, stabilizers, flavor enhancers, and other ingredients are found ubiquitously within the Standard American Diet.

Agriculture for both consumed crops and industrial crops like cotton, as well as confined animal feeding operations (CAFO) for conventional meat production with use of growth hormone, antibiotics, and mismanaged feces, contribute to chemical toxicity in our water systems. The bisphenol A (BPA) in plastics for food and beverage containers adds insult to injury as a contributor to toxicity and hormone imbalance in the body, driving immune and gut distress.

Volatile chemicals from petrofuels, toxic metals from the mining industry (mercury, lead, asbestos, arsenic, cadmium), and dangerous inhalants in flame retardants and adhesives found in most upholstery and furniture (mattresses, curtains, car seats, to name a few) can all find their way into our air and water systems. Even an individual with an organic and clean diet can be exposed to toxic overload due to the dirty industrialized world we live in. It is estimated that each year, 6 billion pounds of toxic chemicals are released into our environment. Things like arsenic, toxic metals, pesticides, flame retardants, and rocket fuel have all been found in significant levels in most Americans! In fact, according to the Fourth National Report on Human Exposure to Environmental Chemicals, the CDC has found traces of 212 chemicals in typical urinary output, and over 200 different industrial chemicals have been found in the umbilical cords of babies. These toxins can accumulate in the body and negatively impact your overall health.

Your body has the natural ability to rid itself of toxins and waste; however, most of our systems are overwhelmed with far more toxins than the body can get rid of. Excess toxins and waste in the body can lead to symptoms such as:

• Anxiety

• Depression and irritability

- Chronic fatigue

- Skin conditions

- Weight gain

- Joint pain

- Headaches and muscle aches

- Allergies

- Gastrointestinal distress

Stress and Leaky Gut

Stress indirectly causes changes in the microbiome. Research has discovered that lipopolysaccharide (LPS), which is released in the presence of pathogenic bacteria and infection, can drive leaky gut by reducing function of tight junctions of the gut. Emotional and social stress further affect the gut because LPS is released in higher amounts in depressed or anxious individuals. The release of inflammatory chemicals as a response to the leaky gut further drives the anxiety and stress response and perpetuates the cycle. When the parasympathetic fight-or-flight system is turned on from a stress response, it has a significant influence on the intestinal immune system on a bacterial, inflammatory, and gut lining integrity level.

Anti-Anxiety Leaky Gut Quiz

Respond to the following questions with Never, Sometimes, or Often. Give yourself a score of 2 for each Often response, 1 for Sometimes, and 0 for Never. (Where appropriate, use 2 for Yes, 0 for No.)

This quiz will be used as a tool to determine if leaky gut and inflammatory foods are a root cause of your anxiety, requiring additional support such as advanced testing or nutritional supplementation.

The recommendations on the following pages correspond to formulas carried in my clinic. In Supplement Support for the 6 Foundational Rs on page 272, you will find information on dosage, active ingredients, and mechanism of action so you can determine if these formulas are a good fit or find comparable ones that have similar composition.

1. Have you been diagnosed with an autoimmune condition (e.g., Hashimoto's, rheumatoid arthritis, fibromyalgia, MS)?

❏ Never   ❏ Sometimes   ❏ Often

2. Do you suffer from acne?

❏ Never   ❏ Sometimes   ❏ Often

3. Do you suffer from or have a history of other dermatological concerns (e.g., eczema, hives, psoriasis, rosacea)?

❏ Never   ❏ Sometimes   ❏ Often

4. Do you experience joint or neuromuscular pain?

❏ Never   ❏ Sometimes   ❏ Often

5. Do you experience bloating?

❏ Never   ❏ Sometimes   ❏ Often

6. Do you have irregular bowel movements, such as constipation or diarrhea?

❏ Never   ❏ Sometimes   ❏ Often

7. Do you experience heartburn, reflux, rawness in the stomach, and/or are you on a PPI for heartburn or reflux?

❏ Never   ❏ Sometimes   ❏ Often

8. Are there foods or additives that you are sensitive to with a digestive, dermatological, or neurological reaction? (If you experience more than three known reactions, give yourself a score of 4.)

❏ Never   ❏ Sometimes   ❏ Often

9. Do you experience difficulty concentrating or focusing (i.e., brain fog)?

☐ Never   ☐ Sometimes   ☐ Often

10. Do you find yourself fatigued or mentally drained after meals?

☐ Never   ☐ Sometimes   ☐ Often

11. Have you been diagnosed with gastritis or IBD such as Crohn's, ulcerative colitis, or diverticulitis?

☐ Never   ☐ Sometimes   ☐ Often

12. Do you have micronutrient deficiency symptoms such as muscle twitches, hair loss, brittle breaking nails, anemia, weakness, shortness of breath, and/or poor immune function?

☐ Never   ☐ Sometimes   ☐ Often

13. Do you experience ear, nose, and/or throat irritation such as phlegm, mucus, and/or runny nose?

☐ Never   ☐ Sometimes   ☐ Often

Total Score: _____

Less than 10
Keep gluten out of your diet for at least 12 weeks to further support your gut lining, then limit consumption to two to three times per week, if at all. Consider taking Naturally Nourished Digestaid Enzyme with DPPIV to break down gliadin, when mindfully consuming. Strategically reintroduce gluten after three months using the guidelines in Chapter 2 to reintroduce eliminations. Consume 4 to 6 ounces of bone broth four times per week to continue to support your healthy gut.

Less than 15
Keep gluten out of your diet for six months minimum and consume 4 to 6 ounces of bone broth five to seven times per week to start to repair and soothe your gut. Consider taking 2 to 3 grams of L-glutamine in combination with aloe and DGL, such as the Naturally Nourished GI lining powder, at bedtime to accelerate

gut repair and reduce food sensitivity. Take Digestaid Enzyme with DPPIV when dining out to break down gliadin and casein from potential cross contamination. Follow a strategic reintroduction after three months of removing the other four inflammatory foods (while keeping gluten out strictly for six months). Use the guidelines in Chapter 2 to reintroduce eliminations to determine reactivity and if you need to dig deeper on irritants to your gut and body with the MRT blood test.

Greater than 15

In addition to following the supplement recommendations for a score of less than 15, keep gluten out of your diet for 12 months minimum, and the other four inflammatory foods for three months. Use the guidelines in Chapter 2 to reintroduce eliminations after a 1-year period. As this is considered serious risk for leaky gut, it is recommended to run the MRT blood test to learn more about individualized food sensitivity and inflammatory food reactions beyond those eliminated in Chapter 2. Learn more about the Mediator Release Test (MRT) in the Appendix on page 288.

Gut-Blood Barrier and Immune Reactivity

When addressing the root causes of anxiety, gut integrity is a top area of focus. There is strong evidence of depression and anxiety being driven by activation of inflammatory response of the immune system, including release of cytokines and LPS, both of which are released in excess in a state of leaky gut. Secretory IgA (immunoglobulin A) is produced in the immune system as a barrier for mucosal membranes. Chronic stress and anxiety can drive imbalance of excess or deficiency. Secretory IgA drops when the immune system is pooped out and an individual is in the "stressed and tired" adrenal insufficiency mode. Elevated secretory IgA is seen when the body is under acute stress from attacking pathogenic bacteria, yeast, or viral influence in the gut. In both cases of too high or too low secretory IgA, leaky gut can be seen, with undesired particles crossing the gut-blood barrier and driving anxiety and mood instability.

Blood-Brain Barrier and Histamines

Histamine is an inflammatory compound made by the immune system in response to allergies in the environment or to gut bacteria action. Histamines can be found actively in certain foods. The role of histamine is to remove the invader from the body rapidly via sneezing, watering eyes, coughing, and other known seasonal allergy responses; however, when histamine builds up in the gut, rapid removal can be more difficult, leading to bloating, GI pain, and bowel irregularity.

Histamine buildup in the blood drives vasodilation, which drives the heart rate to speed up as the body tries to push blood through the canal with less tension. The reaction in the body can first feel like a slump or crash followed by panic and anxiety as tachycardia, or rapid heart rate, hits. Flushing or redness in the skin can further drive anxiety and unease, especially if hives or red marks appear in public.

From this explanation you may think I am going to provide you with a low-histamine food list and recommend reduced histamine intake. However, research also supports that histamine food compounds can have calming, sedative effects when they cross the blood-brain barrier. Histamine neurons project from the hypothalamus (the start of the fight-or-flight axis) in significant levels, affecting sleep and circadian rhythm, appetite regulation, cravings, and stress and anxiety. If there is not enough histamine activity in the brain, these physiological functions are disturbed.

So, too little histamine can drive mental health imbalance, as it is unable to cross the blood-brain barrier to influence regulatory function. With anything, there is a tipping point and balance. An individual who has significant bacterial dysbiosis and high amounts of histamine in the gut may benefit from a low-histamine diet while in bacteria reset. Similarly, someone with chronic fatigue syndrome and low cortisol will have increased histamine expression so, especially during allergy season, this individual would likely benefit from a low-histamine diet as well. Histamine levels can also build up in the body based on genetic metabolic influence, which we will touch on more in the next chapter with methylation and nutrient repletion.

To be clear, a low-histamine diet can help the body cope with symptoms of anxiety while addressing an underlying mechanism of imbalance, such as gut dysbiosis or adrenal fatigue, but it is not a solution for sustainable outcomes on its own. If you are dealing with anxiety and imbalance, you may consider a short-term low-histamine diet to aid with your body's rebound. The highest source of histamine in diet is not in the amino acid L-histadine itself, it is in the aging of food or a production of bacteria in foods. Fermented and cultured foods are at the top of the list, including probiotics. If an individual has a poor reaction to a probiotic supplement, it may be both a combination of dysbiosis and excessive histamine buildup. Consider reducing or removing these foods for six to eight weeks minimum during your anti-anxiety diet if your symptoms get worse during the program. As you heal your leaky gut, replete your nutrient deficiency, and rebound your adrenal glands, your histamine reactivity should reduce and be nonreactive.

Histamine Levels of Certain Foods

Very high histamine levels	Cultured foods such as aged cheese, alcohol, cured meat, kefir, kimchi, sauerkraut, vinegar, and yogurt
High histamine levels	Fish and seafood, especially if smoked or preserved
Moderate histamine levels	Avocado, canned vegetables, eggplant, spinach, tomato

Source: *The Journal of Clinical Nutrition*

Foods that have the amino acid L-histadine should not be limited, as they will help create balance in the body. This includes fresh, protein-rich foods. The less aged a food is, the better. Very sensitive individuals should avoid leftovers.

Supplements to Support Gut Lining and Reduce Inflammation

During this portion of the protocol we work with restoration of anti-inflammatory compounds, such as omega-3, and botanicals, such as curcuminoids, to reduce inflammation in the gut, which will ultimately aid in repair. You can't rebuild a house that is currently on fire! After the removal of inflammatory foods, as detailed in Chapter 2, the addition of anti-inflammatory compounds will soothe and cool the gut.

Omega-3 fatty acids, proteolytic enzymes, and specific plant compounds, including curcuminoids from turmeric and bromelain from tropical plants, have been shown to reduce inflammation in the intestines. The dietary approach removes the lighter fluid while the supplemental support can trap and put out the flames. The Appendix's Supplement Support for the 6 Foundational Rs section includes dosage, details, and unique attributes to the formulas I use in clinic to aid in reducing inflammation in the gut and throughout the body.

Glutamine and Mucilaginous Herbs

Glutamine is an amino acid that supports healthy gut cell function, aiding with both lining and repairing the GI tract and healing ulcerations or damaged areas of the leaky gut. To further support gut restoration in my clinic, I recommend a GI lining powder that includes L-glutamine, deglyclyrrhizinated licorice (DGL), and aloe, to therapeutically rebuild the GI lining. This is a great tool to more directly address leaky gut, coat and soothe the intestines, and reduce food reactivity.

Beyond the GI tract, L-glutamine can be used to tame sugar cravings and has been used in rehabilitation clinics for substance and alcohol abuse. I often recommend clients take 3 to 5 grams of L-glutamine under the tongue to curb sugar cravings.

Food as Medicine to Support Leaky Gut

Bone Broth for Gut Repair

Preparing a bone broth is an ideal way to repair the gut lining, prevent future food sensitivities or allergies, and promote tolerance. The glutamine in bone broth acts as both a nutrient source and a building block for enterocytes, the cells along the gut lining. The gelatin not only prevents muscle wasting and promotes healthy digestion; it also lines the GI tract, reducing breakdown of the gut lining. Gelatin also contains collagen, which can aid in healthy connective tissue in the hair, skin, nails, and joints.

Bone broth also supports relaxation and can actually be a driver for GABA production—the same neurotransmitter that, along with serotonin, reduces anxiety and stress response. Another anti-anxiety compound to note in bone broth is glycine, which aids in neuromuscular relaxation, sleep, and neurological regulation. Sipping on bone broth in the evening can help you find your mellow and support your gut in the healing process while building healthy connective tissue. Bone broth and gelatin gummies add a therapeutic "gut lift" and mood boost!

Suggested use: Aim to have 6 to 8 ounces of bone broth at least four times weekly. You can sip on your broth in a mug or use it as a cooking liquid or the base of a soup. Check out Grass-Fed Beef Knuckle Bone Broth on page 221.

Gelatin Gummies for Gut Repair

Gelatin is comprised of glycine and proline, two amino acids that are generally limited in the American diet as they are found abundantly in organs, bones, and fibrous animal tissues not commonly consumed. These amino acids promote collagen formation and contribute to healthy skin, as well as hair, nail, and joint strength. Their main claim to fame is the ability to line the gut and reduce inflammation caused by food allergies or inflammatory bowel disease. Gelatin has mucilaginous (aka "oopy-goopy") compounds that reline the gut, essentially servings as a face-lift for the GI tract! Beyond these benefits, there is some compelling research that it may reduce cellulite and boost weight loss!

Suggested use: Try to make a gelatin recipe or two monthly to support optimal gut lining and connective tissue health. This is a great summer option when bone broth becomes less appealing, and it is also a great delivery for kids. Your anti-anxiety diet recipes include a gelatin noted on the opposite page, as well as the Turmeric Orange Gummies (page 260).

Repair GI Lining

These recipes feature glutamine, collagen, and gelatin with additional therapeutic elements to synergize flavor and function. Learn how to make bone broth with beef bones, whip up your chicken stock into a creamy zesty soup, and play with making a gelatin pudding and an indulgent, dairy-free hot chocolate.

CHAPTER 5

Restore Micronutrient Status

Micronutrients, which include vitamins, minerals, amino acids, and antioxidants, are involved in every biological process in the body and thus have a great influence on overall health, from neuromuscular function, hormonal balance, metabolism, and energy to sleep, relaxation, and mood stability. Many symptoms of disease are correlated with micronutrient deficiencies due either to a medication's influence on micronutrient absorption or the mechanism of the disease demanding more of a nutrient. When considering repletion of micronutrients, it is important to understand the underlying cause of deficiency to promote sustained repletion and to prevent future deficiencies. The three main categories that can potentially lead to micronutrient deficiencies are increased demand, inability to absorb or use, and inadequate intake.

Increased Demand

Increased demand for a nutrient could be due to lifestyle, lifecycle, or a life stage. Both physiological and psychological demands can drive deficiency patterns. General aging, trauma, and healing from injury, pregnancy, breastfeeding, and even exercise can also influence physical demands of nutrients.

There is an increased need for nutrients following physical activity to aid in tissue recovery and repair. Also, increased oxidative stress from respiration or aerobic training can deplete antioxidant status.

Beyond running a marathon or carrying a child, there are psychological demands on nutrients. At times of mental stress or anxiety, more B vitamins are needed to act as cofactors for neurotransmitter production. Excess amounts of vitamin C are needed to support the adrenal glands in their production of cortisol. Another marker of stress demand on the body is glutamine depletion. As discussed in Chapter 4, glutamine is a fuel source for the gut cells, and anxiety can drive leaky gut, thus burning through glutamine at higher demand.

Inability to Absorb

The inability to absorb nutrients could be directly related to the efficiency of the digestive tract, including digestive enzymes, stomach acidity, bile, and the state of the gut lining. Bowel irregularity can be a marker of absorption issues, especially as seen with loose stools and clients with undigested particles of food or fat in the stool. A patient without a gallbladder is prone toward fatty acid and fat-soluble vitamin deficiency, often requiring a digestive enzyme with ox bile, hydrochloric acid (HCl), and lipase to help compensate. Alternatively, low stomach acid due to stress or use of acid-reducing medications can drive, as this acidity from HCl is actually needed to absorb nutrients such as amino acids, B12, calcium, and iron.

Medications play a significant role in nutrient deficiency trends. Cholesterol-lowering medications block the body's production of coenzyme Q10 (CoQ10), an antioxidant and enzyme demonstrated in studies to have natural antidepressant effects by supporting mitochondrial function. Blood pressure medications can reduce levels of minerals, especially those that have diuretic effects or are combined with an additional diuretic medication. Metformin, used to treat diabetes and elevations of blood sugar level, has been shown to deplete B12 levels.

The concern with these drug-induced nutrient deficiencies are that often the nutrients that drop due to prescription use are those very nutrients which are required on higher demand for regulation in the body, thus driving medication dependency and, ultimately, undesired side effects from further depletion. For example, some of the minerals that become depleted with blood pressure medications are the very nutrients that aid in vascular relaxation and blood pressure regulation effects.

On an anxiety specific approach, selective serotonin reuptake inhibitor (SSRI) drugs are no exception to this connection of prescription drugs driving deficiency and creating further need for medication. Beyond the central nervous system, serotonin receptors are found in the gut, blood vessels, and connective tissues, including smooth muscle and bone. SSRIs have been shown to have unfavorable effects on serotonin receptors for bone health, which is demonstrated with use of these drugs and increased risk of osteopenia and bone fracture. The use of common SSRIs, such as Zoloft, Prozac, and Xanax, to name a few, drive reduced calcium levels in the blood, which can drive acute anxiety and panic attacks! These drugs also can deplete levels of CoQ10, magnesium, and B-vitamins, which can result in chronic fatigue, arrhythmias, muscle tension, insomnia, and depression. Beyond the deficiency of medications on a blood level, many antidepressants and anti-anxiety drugs require higher amounts of B vitamins for optimal functionality. So, both the influence of driving depletion by interference with absorption as well as increased demand can be seen with use of anxiety medications.

Inability to Use

The inability for your body to use a nutrient is often due to genetic predisposition or mutation that would limit the conversion of nutrients from foods or supplements into the active form to be available functionally on a cellular level. Genetic single nucleotide polymorphisms (SNPs), or mutations at the genetic level, for example, include the body's inability to use, build, bind, excrete, and transfer compounds. The most known and relevant to anxiety is the genetic SNP MTHFR (methyl-tetrahydrofolate reductase). Over 40 percent of the population has methylation issues due to the MTHFR gene, which influences the body's ability to build neurotransmitters, excrete toxins, generate activated folate (vitamin B9) and convert other compounds via a methyl compound.

For someone with the genetic SNP MTHFR, taking nutrients in the inactive form, such as folic acid, might actually lead to fatigue or toxicity. Their body needs help with converting the supplement, so they would instead need to take an active form with the methyl compound, such as 5-methyltetrahydrofolate, to drive the methylation process.

In general, it is ideal for everyone to take nutritional supplements that are in the active and absorbable form regardless of genetics, as this ensures optimal utilization without having to delve into expensive genetic assessments. I will dig a bit deeper into MTHFR and this gene's role in anxiety in the B-vitamin section of this chapter.

Inadequate Intake

Nutritional deficiency is common in picky eaters, those whose diets are composed of processed foods and refined carbohydrates, or those who have little to no variety in their diet, even if it is from the "healthy" food selection (e.g., oatmeal every day for break-fast). Inadequate intake might also occur in those with a restricted diet for medical or personal reasons, such as a vegan diet low in B vitamins and bioavailable minerals. Without biological proteins consumed from meat and fish, an individual would be more likely to be deficient in B12, zinc, iron, and glycine, as vegetarian sources are limited and their forms are less bioavailable.

Next, I will walk you through trends of nutrient deficiency correlated with racing thoughts, difficulty concentrating, heart palpitations, insomnia, and generalized anxiety. Beyond your focus of meeting recommended intake, take some time to reflect back on these drivers of deficiency to address the root cause!

Genetic Drivers toward Anxiety and Nutrient Deficiency

As noted, genetic SNP MTHFR affects about 40 percent of the population and is now proposed as a major mechanism in anxiety and depression. Remember, the MTHFR gene influences your body to produce neurotransmitters, including serotonin and stress-responding norepinephrine, epinephrine, and dopamine. With over a third of the population experiencing anxiety, this correlation of genetic influence is of great interest in regard to regulation and reduction of anxiety disorder.

The science of epigenetics explores the environmental drivers, and nutrigenomics studies the influence of nutrients on genetic expression. What this means is that a genetic SNP may be present, but it does not drive destiny; it drives the tendency of how your body will respond if not provided the nutrients to compensate. In the case of MTHFR and epigenetics, environmental drivers such as mental stress, lack of sleep, exposure to toxins, and a dysbiotic state in the gut can contribute toward more accelerated MTFHR burnout, thus driving more deficiency trends with methylation nutrients, including folate, B12, and SAM-e (s-adenosyl-methionine).

Modifying stress demand and reactivity, focusing on sleep hygiene, eating a clean non-processed diet, and resetting your microbiome can all aid in reducing the effects of the MTHFR genetic SNP by reducing the demands on the process of methylation. Using nutrigenomics to fight against anxiety would include focused supplementation with methylated folate and B-12 (5-methyltetrahydrofolate and methylcobalamin) as well as providing mood-stabilizing support from SAM-e.

Now, like many things in life, too much of a good thing can drive dysfunction as well. Meet COMT, catechol-O-methyltransferase, a gene that influences the metabolism of stress-responding chemicals, supports a calm mood, and reduces estrogen dominance. An individual with COMT SNP can over-methylate due to stress driving the cycle or from excess methyl donors from over-supplementation. This buildup of stress chemicals can drive anxiety as well as brain fog, difficulty concentrating, irritability, and increased risk for estrogen-related cancers.

This is where SAM-e comes in to support the process of MTHFR as well as the COMT pathway by donating a methyl group (basically a building block) to release the buildup of stress-responding chemicals and estrogen while supporting a focused, relaxed mood. Reducing excess estrogen can reduce anxiety, worry, and panic while preventing cardiovascular, thyroid, autoimmune and cancer risks, as well as PMS, fibroids, and endometriosis in women. Methylation both regulates the amount of estrogen in the body and influences which receptors are targeted. Supporting your body's methylation pathways with essential nutrients promotes expression of beta estrogen receptors, which are known to have anxiety-reducing effects. Those that have hindered methylation will see more expression on the alpha estrogen receptors, which have an anxiogenic effect.

COMT works in hand with monoamine oxidase (MAO), another genetic SNP with similar properties, focusing on breakdown of neurotransmitters. You may be familiar with the name, as some medications for depression are MAO inhibitors working to keep higher levels of neurotransmitters in the brain. In an anxiety-induced individual, these medications can provoke the stress response in a similar way to how the genetic SNP for MAO would, by slowing removal of stress chemicals. SAM-e with its ability to reduce buildup, has a nice, calming, anti-anxiety effect on MAO and COMT pathways.

Genetic predispositions can drive higher susceptibility to anxiety, the influence of the epigenome via nutrigenomics can address genetic areas of concern through enhanced expression. The diet, supplement, and lifestyle changes recommended in this book can free you from a life of worry and anxiety regardless of your genetics by compensating for areas of enhanced need.

Ways to Address a MTHFR and COMT genetic SNP

1. Reduce stress levels and practice relaxation.

2. Reduce exposure to toxins in cosmetics, household, diet, and environment.

3. Avoid use of synthetic estrogen in birth control pills and prescription hormone replacement therapy.

4. Avoid processed enriched foods or supplements using folic acid (the only acceptable forms of folate are: natural folate, 5-methyltetrahydrofolate, 5-MTHF, and L-methylfolate). Watch out for many health products that have non-methylated B vitamins, such as folic acid and cyanocobalamin.

5. Aim for at least 7 hours of sleep per night.

6. Eat a diet rich in foliage or leafy greens such as kale, spinach, collards, and broccoli, and consider pasture-raised organs such as chicken and beef liver for bioavailable B-vitamins.

7. Take an activated B-complex to provide a moderate amount of methyl-donors, such as 5-MTHF and B6 in the form of pyridoxal 5′ phosphate (P5P).

8. If the addition of a quality B-complex drives anxiety and insomnia, consider SAM-e at 400 to 800 milligrams to support COMT and reduce over-methylation or methyl-build up.

When Eating Healthy Isn't Enough and Drugs Don't Work

Pairing all of the complexities of inability to absorb with fluctuating demands based on aging, exercise, hormonal and emotional distress, and state of dysfunction in the body, you may start to see that it's nearly impossible to provide for the body's need to heal and create balanced brain chemistry with mood stability. This is where micronutrients in a supplement form are a very powerful tool in helping you reclaim your mental health.

Research points to poor diet quality, intake of refined processed sugars, inflammation, and gut damage as primary factors of micronutrient deficiency, all of which have a strong risk association with depression and anxiety. The anti-anxiety diet program is developed to reset the foundational environment of your gut to optimize absorption of nutrients as well as the actions of neurotransmitter production.

During this therapeutic approach, it will be necessary to supplement the diet to achieve brain balance and mood stability with less panic and anxiety. In order to truly see outcomes from food as medicine in the anti-anxiety approach, it is essential to pair a therapeutic diet with strategic nutrients in concentrated form to ensure functional deficiency is repleted while improving the function of the system. Studies have found orthomolecular dosing, or dosing at mega nutrient levels beyond the dietary reference intake (DRI), to be both effective and safe interventions for anxiety and mental health.

In order to get clinical outcomes with supplementation, you will not likely get results from a product purchased at your grocery store; this will likely be a synthetic form of nutrients, manufactured at low quality, and not tested for potency and contaminants. Use the quizzes in this book to determine if you need to start supporting a leaky gut to enhance absorption, microbiome to enhance production of neurotransmitters and reduce stress to system, or adrenals to balance neurotransmitters and rebound chronic fatigue. The nutrients to follow are highlighted for their varied functions to support anti-anxiety outcomes and may be used to strategically address a specific need.

When choosing supplements, select from lines that are third-party assessed for potency, optimal absorption, purity, and contaminants to ensure you are using effective nutritional medicine. Learn more about what I use in my clinic the Appendix's Supplement Support for the 6 Foundational Rs section.

Antidepressants, anti-anxiety, and antipsychotic drugs may be effective in the short term but become ineffective or drive greater mood instability and symptoms over time. In fact, a 2014 systematic review, "Outcome of Mood Disorders Before Psychopharmocology," found "no support to the belief that pharmacological treatments have resulted in an improvement in the long-term outcome of patients with mood disorders."

Yet the use of medications as primary intervention for anxiety prevails and continues to increase in both adults and children, with a 65 percent rise over the last 15 years. At the same time, there are higher incidents of anxiety than ever. Using food as medicine paired with strategic quality nutritional supplement support, you can rebalance your brain chemistry and achieve mood stability while eliminating side effects and achieving synergistic response in your body, such as increased energy, brain clarity, weight loss, improved digestion, reduced joint pain, and overall disease risk.

Antioxidants as Anti-Anxiety Support

Oxidative damage occurs in the presence of toxins, free radicals, light, heat, and oxygen exposure. Oxidative stress in the brain drives neurological dysfunction, including depression, anxiety, panic, and acute anxiety distress. These symptoms accelerate in the state of antioxidant deficiency. Imagine lemon or lime juice on an avocado. When you mix the vitamin C (ascorbic acid) as an antioxidant with the avocado, the oxidative damage, or browning, is reduced. This is a direct mechanism of an antioxidant preventing oxidative stress or damage, and the same mechanism can protect your brain from neurological imbalance and mood instability.

To add insult to injury, research demonstrates chronic emotional stress as a driver of reactive oxygen species (ROS), which drives more oxidative damage in the brain. Beyond management of stress and reduction of exposure to toxins, a diet rich in antioxidants can be a great way to support protection against free radicals and reduce ROS activity.

Top antioxidant-providing nutrients include glutathione, cysteine, CoQ10, selenium, vitamin E, vitamin A, and vitamin C. Sulfur-containing vegetables such as broccoli, cauliflower, cabbage, and

Brussels sprouts provide a rich source of cysteine and glutathione to aid in both detoxification and antioxidant support. Glutathione is really the "granddaddy" antioxidant in the hierarchy of free radical scavengers. Beyond sulfur-containing compounds, vegetables, herbs, and fruits provide flavonoids, plant-based compounds that exert a positive health effect in neurodegenerative and anxiety disorders.

VITAMIN C AND CORTISOL CONNECTION

The most concentrated storage site of vitamin C is in the adrenal glands, which is likely due to the fact that vitamin C demands can increase tenfold in times of stress! The adrenals use vitamin C in the regulation of cortisol production and release. Vitamin C is used in the production of adrenal hormones, namely cortisol, the primary stress responder, and ample levels of vitamin C encourage the gland's optimal function. When vitamin C levels become deficient, rather than reduced cortisol production from the adrenals, they go into "freak out" mode and surge more cortisol release. Optimizing vitamin C through a diet rich in berries, bell peppers, and citrus is a priority when addressing adrenal imbalance. In the case of adrenal fatigue, vitamin C is required in amounts of 2 to 5 grams/day to rebound the function and production in the gland. As if managing cortisol wasn't enough, research demonstrates vitamin C supplementation as a way to reduce blood pressure, enhance antioxidant status, and reduce anxiety in both acute and chronic settings.

Boosting Antioxidant Status with Whole Foods

Adding fresh herbs and generous portions of spices into your food is a great way to boost antioxidant status! By eating real foods in their most whole form, you get more abundant polyphenols, which include the varied plant antioxidant forms of anthocyanins, isoflavones, and flavonoids.

Rutin, for example, is an antioxidant classified as a citrus flavonoid, and is found in the white pith and rind of citrus. When consuming lemon, lime, grapefruit, or orange juice, you get very little rutin; however, if you consume the whole fruit, the white furry fiber will enhance the citrus fruits' disease-fighting properties due to the presence of rutin. Rutin may also aid with mood stability and reduced anxiety through activation of cannabinoid mediated antidepressant activity on certain receptors in the brain.

A diet that is focused around whole foods in a spectrum of colors, providing plant antioxidants, will not only reduce free radicals and thus reduce inflammation to the brain, but will also provide drivers for optimal neurological function and mood stability.

Best Sources of Antioxidants

Berries	Blackberries, blueberries, cranberries, elderberries, goji berries, raspberries
Cacao	Cacao butter, cacao nibs, cacao powder
Roots	Ashwagandha, ginger, maca, turmeric
Herbs	Basil, cilantro, cinnamon, cumin, oregano, parsley, rosemary
Teas and coffee	Black tea, coffee, espresso, green tea, matcha, oolong, rooibos, white tea

Mood-Stabilizing Minerals

Minerals play a dynamic role on mood stability, from enzyme activation to muscle relaxation and neurotransmitter regulation. Mineral deficiency can drive dynamic mood shifts and anxiety to the level of psychosis and panic. I will highlight five minerals for food-as-medicine support for anxiety below, but first I want to discuss reasons for mineral deficiency.

I stress the recurring "chicken and egg" theme throughout this book because it is important to understand that some minerals, such as selenium and magnesium, are depleted with stress demand. As they are depleted, this further drives the anxiety and stress response. Both selenium and magnesium activate the production of thyroid hormone to support balanced energy and metabolism in times of stress.

Beyond stress-driving depletion, all minerals are at risk for deficiency with a processed diet, lack of soil diversity in farming, excessive use of fiber supplements, and/or use of medications that block nutrient absorption or drive excretion. Sugar and refined foods drive mineral depletion, as the body burns through 54 molecules of magnesium to process one molecule of sugar! As your blood sugar spikes from high carbohydrate intake, insulin responds in a surge, which uses up your zinc and chromium. Although there are many factors in mineral depletion, your transition to reduced carbohydrate intake with the anti-anxiety diet will play a foundational role in preventing deficiency and supporting rebound for sustainable mood and metabolism.

Magnesium

Magnesium is involved in over 300 enzyme pathways and has a role in both neuromuscular stress response as well as neurotransmitter and HPA-axis function. Research supports that magnesium deficiency can drive increased anxiety reactivity and stimulation of cortisol, which further drives anxiety and distress response. Diabetes, hypertension, heart disease, and inflammation are all linked to magnesium deficiency, and over 68 percent of Americans are estimated to be deficient. Magnesium has been deemed the "original chill pill" as it directly works to suppress cortisol and adrenal output via reduced release of ACTH (adrenocorticotropic hormone) from the pituitary. Also, magnesium has the unique ability to cross the blood-brain barrier, serving as gatekeeper to block the entrance of stress hormones into the brain.

Magnesium is found in dark chocolate, nuts, seeds, leafy greens, avocados, and beets.

Due to the prevalence of deficiency and significant relaxation response with low risk for toxicity, I recommend supplementation of magnesium in the form of magnesium glycinate (see Supplement Support for the 6 Foundational Rs on page 272 for recommendations). This becomes especially important when adapting to a high-fat, low-carbohydrate diet as electrolytes are often thrown off with hydration shifts in a ketogenic state.

Chromium

Chromium is known for aiding blood sugar regulation due to its role in carbohydrate metabolism. It supports the body's ability to take up and use insulin. In recent findings, researchers discovered insulin sensitivity may also support the ability of tryptophan to cross the blood-brain barrier. Tryptophan is the amino acid building block to serotonin. We will get deeper into all things neurotransmitter in Chapter 7, Rebalance your Neurotransmitters.

A rat study used chromium supplementation with exposure to chronic unpredictable mild stress (CUMS) and discovered chromium's ability to aid in delivery of tryptophan as well as reduce concentration of corticosteroid stress hormones. In this sense chromium may have the ability to modulate stress response by enhancing the delivery of feel-good mood stabilizers while reducing the influence of anxiety-driving stress hormones.

Chromium is found in broccoli, cinnamon, nuts and seeds, green beans, prunes, pasture-raised meats, and wild seafood (especially shellfish).

Selenium

Selenium is a mineral with antioxidant properties, most known for its ability to promote healthy thyroid function. It aids with glutathione generation, serving to scavenge free radicals and reduce oxidative stress in the body and brain. Selenium status has been inversely related to frequency and severity of anxiety, depression, and chronic fatigue. A study examined a five-week period of increased intake of selenium by diet and supplementation and determined an elevation in mood and, most remarkably, a reduction in anxiety.

Selenium is found in Brazil nuts, cashews, sunflower seeds, tuna, oysters, sardines, snapper, shrimp, liver, garlic, and dark meat cuts of chicken.

Zinc

Zinc plays a role in hormone regulation, both in reducing excess estrogen and enhancing testosterone expression, and it is widely acknowledged for its immune-supporting properties. But, in the anxiety world, zinc is a hero due to its effects on neurotransmitters and its ability to counteract copper.

Zinc, like magnesium, plays a role in over 300 enzymes in the body, and its use is widespread. It is depleted with stress and anxiety due to demand. The role of zinc in the connection of anxiety and brain chemistry is twofold. Zinc aids in optimized stomach acid, which in turn supports the breakdown of amino acid glutamine, which can then convert into the excitatory glutamate, which can further be metabolized under optimal conversions to the mellow-out compound GABA. Zinc competes with copper, which has been shown to drive excitatory stress hormone output seen in the primal survival part of the brain that is often overstimulated during times of panic.

A study by the *Journal of Nutrition and Metabolic Insights* found that individuals with chronic anxiety had elevated levels of copper paired with very low zinc in their plasma and demonstrated improvement of symptoms with the addition of zinc supplementation. If your body has excessive stores of copper due to improper multivitamin supplement, tap water treated with copper and leaching from copper pipes, estrogen dominance, sluggish liver, and/or adrenal fatigue, the copper buildup in your body will block use of zinc, which can further perpetuate panic and anxiety response.

Zinc is found in oysters, liver (from pasture-raised sources), grass-fed beef and lamb, egg yolk, fish, pork, turkey, pumpkin seeds, sesame seeds, dark chocolate, and nuts.

PYROLURIA: A TOXIC DRIVER OF ANXIETY?

Pyroluria is a chemical imbalance due to a genetic error in red blood cell formation. Hemoglobin is a protein that holds iron in the red blood cell, and individuals that have pyroluria experience a buildup of hemoglobin builders called kryptopyrrole (KP), which is passed in the urine in normal amounts in healthy individuals. Individuals with pyroluria have an excess of KP, which has toxic effects and binds vitamin B6 and zinc, driving deficiency of these key mood-stabilizing nutrients. Those that suffer from pyroluria cannot effectively produce serotonin, as B6 is an important cofactor in production. Pyroluria can be assessed by excessive presence of KP in urine and can often be treated and managed by optimizing B6 and zinc along with monitoring red blood cell function and buildup.

Calcium

This final mineral has a reputation for its role in bone health as a building block for bone-supporting repair, growth, and preventing injury. The use of SSRI antidepressant and anti-anxiety drugs is associated with calcium deficiency and negative impact on bone health. Serotonin receptors are located throughout the body, including in the bone cells. Calcium with SSRIs disrupts feedback mechanisms of serotonin which, on the bone level, regulates calcium resorption.

Beyond bone mass, the skeletal muscular system is influenced by calcium via biochemical pathways called the calcium channel, in which calcium is used to tighten and release muscles for development and function. Calcium channel blockers are drugs that are typically prescribed for blood pressure regulation, as they keep calcium from entering the heart and vessels, preventing tension in arteries and reduced blood pressure. Because the reduction of vascular and muscular tension can lead to generalized relaxation, calcium channel blockers are being studied as drug options for anxiety.

Although it sounds like blocking calcium activity may be a solution for relaxation, calcium is required as a mineral to regulate neurological function, and deficiency has been tied to mania, panic, confusion, and chronic anxiety. Calcium, like glutamate, has excitatory impact on a neurological level, and the neuron impact is regulated by magnesium. In simple terms, magnesium is the relaxer while calcium is the activator. For this reason, if taking a calcium supplement as recommended by your doctor for bone health, it is extremely important to balance out the calcium with magnesium to ensure optimal relationship of these minerals and aid in the utilization of calcium by the bones. Also, if using a calcium supplement, I only recommend the MCHC form of calcium, which is more available for bone cells and less prone toward excessive blood calcium deposits and calcification.

Calcium is found in grass-fed dairy products (whey and ghee are within the anti-anxiety diet), canned salmon and sardines with bones, tahini, almonds, and leafy greens.

Mood-Stabilizing Vitamins

B-Vitamins (B6, B9, B12)

From thiamin to vitamin B1 through B12 and beyond, B vitamins have long been acknowledged for their role in energy metabolism and mood stability. Like the minerals mentioned above, B vitamins are driven to deficiency under anxiety, often due to a chronic stress response. B vitamins play a role in stabilizing DNA, synthesizing neurochemicals, regulating signaling, driving methylation process, and serving as precursors or cofactors to build or activate necessary compounds for whole-body balance. Although all B vitamins are involved in managing mood and reducing anxiety, the most prominent are B6, B9, and B12 due to their roles in methylation.

Pyridoxine (B6)

Pyridoxine is potent cofactor used to activate amino acids into neurotransmitters, including dopamine, serotonin, GABA, and melatonin. Even mild levels of deficiency have been tied to suboptimal levels of serotonin and GABA, the two most potent anti-anxiety players. Supporting the body with ample B6 aids in rebounding levels of serotonin and GABA while reducing homocysteine, a vascular marker of inflammation. B6 in ample amounts can reduce homocysteine by combining with serine to produce glutathione, a favorable antioxidant. Using folate and serine as a building block, B6 drives production of glycine associated with inhibitory activity along with GABA, further driving relaxation and improved sleep quality. Ample levels of B6 activate neurotransmitters that aid in mental stability and support antioxidant levels while reducing inflammation.

Pyridoxine is found in chicken, tuna, salmon, beef, shrimp, nuts/seeds, bananas, pork, carrots, and spinach.

When selecting a supplement of B6, ensure you use the "active" B6 known as P5P (pyridoxyl-5-phosphate) to ensure absorption and utilization. Use caution to avoid high-dose intake and be sure to watch the add-up from various formulas as often stress or adrenal support supplements will provide dosages of 20 to 30 milligrams per capsule. Doses higher than 500 milligrams may cause nerve injury and damage.

Folate (B9)

Folate, made famous for its role in preventing neural tube defect and supporting healthy fetal development, has a role in DNA synthesis and repair as well as red blood cell formation. Folate deficiencies were seen to increase when refined white flour was introduced to the Standard American Diet. This drove governmental requirements of synthetic folate in processed foods in an attempt to prevent neural tube defects; however, the type of folate used in enriched products (and most over-the-counter vitamins, for that matter) are synthetic folic acid, which has very little bioavailability. Folate produces an array of compounds for whole-body health, including myelin to protect nerves, coenzyme Q10 to stabilize energy, carnitine to support fat utilization, and SAM-e to reduce anxiety and pain.

Folate is found in organ meat, leafy greens, sunflower seeds, asparagus, and avocado.

Avoid enriched foods and low-quality supplements that have synthetic added B-vitamins in non-methylated forms, as this can further drive imbalance. Select folate in the nature made form, folinic acid, or activated methyl-forms, such as 5-methyltetrahydrofolate, 5-MTHF, or L-methylfolate.

Vitamin B12

B12 has the most significant research backing its in reducing anxiety and supporting healthy neurological function. It has a vital role in the production of myelin, the protective coating of our nerves. When myelin is damaged, individuals can experience numbness, neuropathy, and delay or improper nerve impulse for mental health. Beyond nerves, B12 deficiency has been tied to anemia, specifically causing pernicious anemia. The influence of B12 on the nervous system directly, as well as the limited ability of blood cells to carry nutrients of focus, are two delivery impacts of B12 deficiency, which drives the perfect conditions for anxiety and often panic.

Hypochlorhydria, or low stomach acid, as well as stress and the increased use of antacids and PPI medications for heartburn, drive increased risk for B12 deficiency. Stimulating optimal digestive juices with Bragg Raw Apple Cider Vinegar may accelerate rebound from deficiency, aiding in your body's ability to better break down and absorb nutrients. Also, if taking an antacid or PPI drug, consider working with a functional medicine practitioner to wean off the drug and address the digestive concerns from the root cause versus silencing the symptoms and causing other areas of distress. A blood sugar stabilizing drug, metformin, has been shown to deplete B12 stores in 30 percent of patients using the drug. A diet that is low in animal products can also drive B12 deficiency. The anti-anxiety diet plan will provide stimulation to optimal digestive juices while reducing your need for blood sugar–stabilizing drugs in the low-carb, high-fat protocol. Also, the diet is rich in whole food sources of B12 to rebound and boost your body's neurological function.

B12 is found in organ meat, salmon, shellfish, octopus, beef, lobster, egg yolk, turkey, and grass-fed dairy products (whey is within the anti-anxiety diet).

Consider using 1 tablespoon of Bragg Raw Apple Cider Vinegar with 1 ounce of water as a "shooter" in the a.m. to stimulate stomach acid and enhance the digestive environment.

ORGANS AS SUPERFOODS

Liver, which is often regarded as an old-school superfood, is making a resurgence in traditional food communities, and rightly so! Organs in general are nutritional powerhouses with compact delivery of nutrient density. Liver is incredibly rich in vitamins, minerals, quality protein, and fat. Pasture-raised or grass-fed young glands are particularly rich in nutrients that support optimal brain function, including the essential fatty acids EPA and DHA as well as fat-soluble vitamins A, D, E, and K.

Organs are concentrated source of B vitamins, B12 in particular, which is essential for neurological function and is helpful in preventing and treating anxiety. Consumption of organs provides a balance of minerals such as copper, selenium, and iron; however, it is important to note that most are significant in copper while moderate in zinc. So, if consumed in excess, it may throw off anti-anxiety mineral balance. In most senses, the benefits outweigh the risk and the bioavailable nutrients in organs are quickly and easily absorbed into your body! A serving of 2 ounces twice per month is ample to provide a B vitamin boost while promoting whole-body balance.

Check out alimillerRD.com for Frozen Liver Pills and Simple Organ Pate recipes.

Vitamin D

Access to the sun and time outside is not often considered in the scope of optimizing nourishment, but in the case of vitamin D, sun bathing for 15 minutes per day and providing direct exposure of lighter areas of the skin (such as the forearms) to the sun may be the best path to optimizing levels of this necessary nutrient and regulating circadian rhythms. Vitamin D deficiency is one of the primary proposed drivers of seasonal affective disorder (SAD), including depression and mood irregularities in times of winter with shorter days and colder conditions leading to less sun exposure. Vitamin D is the only nutrient that has hormonal structure, and its expression is directly connected to fight-or-flight response as the pituitary gland, has vitamin D receptors that play a role in utilization and absorption, which may be the reason why vitamin D levels are also connected to thyroid and metabolism.

Vitamin D also has an influence on sexual hormone balance. Too much an cause excessive estrogen, and too little can result in estrogen deficiency. Vitamin D is in high demand during stress because it stimulates releases of mellow-out neurotransmitters and supports immune and inflammatory processes, which are typically thrown off in stressful events.

When vitamin D levels drop, production of serotonin and dopamine decline as well. Beyond mood stability, vitamin D has mechanisms on immune health and inflammation with low levels highly correlated to chronic illness, including cancer and autoimmune disease.

Benefits of vitamin D are enhanced in the presence of vitamin K. Also, excessive vitamin D levels from supplementation with deficient levels of vitamin K can drive calcification of soft tissues or calcium stones, creating risk of kidney stones. For this reason, a diet rich in vitamin K1 with leafy greens and vitamin K2 from bacterial fermentation in probiotic foods is important for balancing vitamin D. When considering supplementation, look for a product that pairs vitamin D3 with K1 and K2 in a blend that is 10:1 in IU:mcg; for example, 5000 IU vitamin D3 to 500mcg K1 K2 blend. See the Appendix's Supplement Support for the 6 Foundational Rs section for more information.

Vitamin D is found in liver and organs, fatty fishes, mushrooms, cheeses, and egg yolks, especially from pasture-raised products.

Restore Your Micronutrient Status

The recipes in this chapter provide rich forms of antioxidants, mood-stabilizing minerals, and bioavailable B vitamins to support nutrient repletion and the methylation process.

To support micronutrients:

❖ *Mellow Mama Dressing, page 219*

❖ *Herb-Crusted Pork Tenderloin, page 239*

❖ *Slow Cooker Carnitas, page 242*

❖ *Carnitas Burrito Bowl, page 244*

❖ *Spaghetti Squash Bolognese, page 246*

❖ *Simple Salt and Pepper Scallops, page 249*

❖ *Grain-Free Low-Carb Peanut Butter Cookies, page 256*

❖ *Matcha Coconut Gummies, page 261*

To support methylation:

❖ *Butternut and Brussels Breakfast Hash, page 190*

❖ *Electrolyte-Boosting Avocado with a Spoon, page 209*

❖ *Greek Deviled Eggs, page 210*

❖ *Whole Roasted Cauliflower, page 213*

❖ *Asian Braised Bok Choy, page 216*

❖ *Warming Chicken Thighs with Braised Greens, page 231*

CHAPTER 6

Rebound Your Adrenal Glands

Following the Remove, Reset, and Repair phases of the anti-anxiety diet, you are likely in an enhanced state of micronutrient repletion with the ability to absorb nutrients in a less inflammatory state. Additionally, you are now empowered with lists of foods to focus on to replete deficiency.

This chapter moves beyond the gut-brain axis and will focus on the adrenal gland. These walnut-sized glands that sit above your kidneys work to regulate your body's stress response. Although an independent gland, the adrenals are connected to the gut, as dysbiosis increases the adrenal demand in the production of stress neurotransmitters. In this chapter, you will learn more about the function of your adrenals in driving your fight-or-flight response via the influence of steroid hormones and neurotransmitters. An imbalance of adrenal output can drive heart palpitations, worry, distress, racing thoughts, insomnia, and ultimately, chronic anxiety.

HPA-Axis

The adrenals have both regulatory and reactive functions, which are driven by the hypothalamic-pituitary-adrenal (HPA) axis. The HPA-axis is comprised of three primary glands (hypothalamus, pituitary, and adrenals) that regulate the fight-or-flight (sympathetic) mechanisms of the body, as opposed to the rest-and-digest (para-sympathetic) mechanisms. When under chronic stress, any one of these glands can demonstrate dysfunction leading to hindered metabolism, chronic fatigue, immune system distress, and mood disturbances.

The fight-or-flight state stimulates the release of stress hormones and puts the body's metabolism and regulatory functions on hold as it focuses on survival. It often leads to cravings, increased fat storage, and difficulty with weight loss, as well as excessive antic-ipatory stress response and irritability or anxiety. Conversely, the rest-and-digest mode reduces the anxiety response, driving relax-ation of the muscles, nerves, and blood vessels while providing a surge of digestive enzymes that aid in the body's ability to metabo-lize, absorb nutrients, and effectively burn fuel.

A balanced parasympathetic response in the HPA-axis supports healthy hormone levels, relaxation, and optimized digestion to experience a grounding, balanced mental state. This is significant, as the state of the HPA-axis can greatly influence the body's abil-ity to metabolize and can imply that even a perfect diet can be unsuccessful if the mind is overworked and the body is not able to reset. The stress hormones released by an unbalanced sympathetic response can directly hinder digestive enzymes, sterilize the micro-biome, and drive leaky gut.

The adrenal glands themselves are the primary fight-or-flight responders. They provide steroids, neurotransmitters, and hormone-building blocks to respond to stressors. They also provide blood pressure and sodium regulation. The adrenal cortex, a part of the adrenal glands, regulates cortisol, the body's primary stress-responding steroid hormone, which has both reactive and regulatory function. The adrenal medulla regulates dopamine, norepinephrine, and epinephrine.

The hypothalamus gland, located in the brain, plays a primary role in homeostasis, or keeping the body at its baseline. It plays a role in thirst regulation throughout the day and satiety at meal times, telling the body when it has consumed enough fuel and is satisfied. Beyond intake regulation, this gland produces thyroid-releasing hormone and plays a key role in body temperature, which influences how thermogenic or warm the body is, ultimately impacting caloric burn at basal metabolic rate. The hypothalamus also plays a role in circadian rhythms, which regulate sleep cycles, fatigue, and energy cascades. It also analyzes information such as light exposure, stress, environmental factors, and perceived risk. In relationship to the HPA-axis, the hypothalamus responds to stress and anxiety by making corticotropin-releasing factor (CRF), which drives the pituitary to stimulate the adrenals to release cortisol and stress neurotransmitters, thus driving continued anxiety response.

Also located in the brain, the pituitary gland has a great influence on the thyroid, a major metabolic organ; the ovaries or testes as sexual hormone regulators; and the adrenal glands, the primary stress-responding agents. The pituitary releases many hormones that regulate fluid, sexual function, growth, mood instability/anxiety, pain management, and caloric burn. The pituitary produces thyroid stimulating hormone (TSH), which functions as a direct stimulant to the thyroid gland to produce thyroxine (T4) and becomes activated as triiodothyronine (T3) hormone. In a state of hypothyroidism or underactive thyroid, the TSH increases, stimulating the thyroid to increase output. Conversely, when the thyroid is overworked in a state of hyperthyroidism, TSH production in the pituitary will drop to reduce output from the thyroid. Imbalance within the thyroid gland can be an independent driver of anxiety.

When the pituitary is responding in the state of anxiety or chronic stress, it focuses all its energy on driving adrenal gland output. In an androgenic state, which is when the adrenal glands are over-used, the body suppresses thyroid and sexual hormone expression to prioritize survival function; in this sense, the parasympathetic relaxed system includes rest and digest, as well as metabolize and reproduce! Because of this, some practitioners refer to this axis as the HPA-TOG (hypothalamus-pituitary-adrenal-thyroid-ovary-gonad) axis. In women, when the HPA-axis is in overdrive, they can see irregular cycles, PCOS, infertility, and hirsutism (female facial hair growth), which is often seen with excessive testosterone or DHEA. Even though testosterone in an androgenic state is expressed in women under stress, in men testosterone is counter-regulated by cortisol, which can actually drive erectile dysfunction and low testosterone levels. In this sense, the root of hormonal imbalance often lies in anxiety or excessive stress response.

The adrenals are the primary drivers of anxiety, irritability, and panic on the HPA-axis. They release steroids such as cortisol, and stress chemicals norepinephrine and epinephrine (adrenaline). Under stress, more cortisol is released, which increases blood sugar pro-duction and release while reducing the body's ability to use fat as fuel. The adrenals also produce DHEA, a hormone-building precur-sor for estrogen and testosterone that aids in stress resilience and naturally declines with age. DHEA is also used as a precursor or building block in ketone production, which is achieved in a very low carbohydrate diet. (More on ketosis and its anti-anxiety effects in Chapters 2 and 8.)

Symptoms	Hypothalamus signal	Pituitary signal	Adrenal signal
Unbalanced fluid retention	Vasotensin	Antidiuretic hormone	Aldosterone Cortisol depletes potassium and magnesium, further increasing blood pressure
Appetite control	Leptin	Oxytocin	Dopamine Cortisol drives blood sugar spikes, influencing hunger and fat storage increase
Weight gain	TRH	TSH, growth hormone	Cortisol, which drives rT3, mimicking T3 and breaking active thyroid hormone function; also interferes with muscle function, driving fat storage
Infertility/ Hormone imbalance	GnRH	FSH, LH, Prolactin	DHEA, testosterone, estradiol, and cortisol, which steals from progesterone production
Anxiety	CRH	ATCH	Epinephrine, norepinephrine, cortisol in excess

Each gland of the HPA-axis releases hormones and neurotransmitters that not only have direct effects on the body, but also signal the next gland in the HPA-axis. This chart shows HPA-axis responses in relationship to specific symptoms.

One of the benefits of Phase 1 of the anti-anxiety diet is that ketone production can be a great regulator of excessive DHEA, thus supporting fertility in an individual with PCOS, who would likely express elevated DHEA values. However, chronic adrenal stimulation and demand over time can tax the glands, leading to reduced output of cortisol and DHEA, as seen in adrenal fatigue. In this state, the adrenals may be too fatigued to produce ketones, in which case DHEA supplementation would be recommended.

If an individual is in advanced adrenal fatigue, a strict Phase 1 ketogenic approach is not recommended to ensure that the gland is not overtaxed or DHEA depleted. Optimizing levels of DHEA aids in stress resilience and tolerance as well as sexual hormone balance. During adrenal rebound, the Phase 1 diet can be cycled with Phase 2 diet, or one may choose to stay within the freedom of low-glycemic Phase 2 only. This level can be assessed both in the blood and the saliva and is discussed further in Advanced Functional Labs on page 287.

Progesterone and Anxiety

Progesterone deficiency can play a significant role in anxiety, racing thoughts, worry, and insomnia. When the HPA-axis is off, progesterone levels often dip because the pituitary in the brain is primarily focused on stimulating the adrenals and the thyroid, so regulating reproductive hormone balance drops. Beyond its function in fertility and menstruation, progesterone has a relationship with GABA expression, and some studies demonstrate its direct anxiety-reducing effects. If you are in a time of hormonal transition such as irregular cycles, amenorrhea (loss of your period), postpartum, perimenopause, menopause, or dealing with infertility, it is recommended to measure your progesterone levels through a salivary assessment and work with a functional medicine practitioner. Learn more in the Advanced Functional Labs on page 287.

Signs of low progesterone include:

• Anxiety

• Belly fat

- Brain fog
- Breast tenderness
- Fluid retention
- Hot flashes
- Infertility
- Insomnia
- Irregular cycles or PMS
- Low libido
- Poor circulation
- Racing thoughts

BIRTH CONTROL: A ROOT CAUSE OF ANXIETY?

It is important to remember birth control has a hormonal influence on the body and can cause your body's hormones to be out of balance. Transdermal bioidentical hormone in the form of yam-derived progesterone cream may be an appropriate intervention to aid in hormone balance and anxiety relief. Maca, a Peruvian root with adaptogenic properties, may also be used at a dosage of 1 gram per day to support the pituitary gland in regulation of progesterone stimulation from ovaries. If your anxiety shifts dynamically with your cycle or you have an abnormal cycle, it is strongly advised to complete a functional hormone test to get more information.

Cortisol and Anxiety

Stimuli from anxiety can drive increased production of stress-responding compounds like cortisol. Over time, the system can become overworked, leading to inadequate response. An excessive response is seen as hyperadrenalism, and the inadequate or "pooped out" response is seen as hypoadrenalism, more commonly known as adrenal fatigue.

Cortisol can have a significant effect on anxiety and mood. Research shows high stress exposure in youth or chronic stress as an adult can have long-term influences on the hippocampus, a major area of the brain that regulates mood and anxiety, via the excessive release of CRH (otherwise known as CRF). This CRH and hippocampus connection is yet another vicious cycle of feedback in the body where stress response can drive more tendency toward anxiety due to physiological, stress-induced chemical release. Even when the cortisol levels are down or when the body is in a state of adrenal fatigue, the relationship between CRH and the hippocampus can cause the body to experience anxiety. The cortisol released during stressful events can lead to vascular restriction, increased blood pressure, irregular surges of energy and feelings of physical tension, and irregular blood sugar surges that increase fat storage. This HPA-axis is supposed to be down-regulated by the release of cortisol, which should reduce the release of CRH from the hypothalamus. However, this negative feedback loop often gets interrupted during high stress situations (during which the body perceives its survival to be at stake), which interferes with continued release of CRH, ACTH, and what is left of cortisol along with other adrenal stimulants. The adrenals might surge until they burn out, causing imbalance within the digestive, sexual, immune, and inflammatory systems.

Cortisol has two primary modes of operation: **regulatory**, which promotes the coordination of circadian events such as the sleep/

wake cycle, food intake, and inflammatory processes, and **reactive**, which provides the ability to react to, cope with, adapt to, and recover from stressful events and triggering episodes.

CHOLESTEROL AS MEDICINE?

Cholesterol is a building block of all steroid hormones, including sexual hormones, cortisol, and vitamin D. It plays an integral role in regulating inflammation as it is in the cell wall, protecting cell contents from exposure and damage as well as supporting cellular communication. Corticosteroids, namely cortisol, are manufactured from LDL cholesterol, a rich source of dietary cholesterol and high fat to provide ample building blocks for gland recovery and optimized output. The anti-anxiety diet supports intake of saturated fat from pasture-raised animal products to support the body's hormones and cellular integrity. As you remove processed foods and refined carbohydrates and start to focus on the dietary distribution of fat as your driving macronutrient, you will be providing your body with the best fuel to rebound adrenal gland function. If you are diagnosed with adrenal fatigue and your DHEA is suboptimal, you may consider staying on the low glycemic Phase 2 while supporting glands with strategic supplements and introducing nourishing fats.

In the Regulatory mode, cortisol peaks in the morning, allowing a natural awakening response that provides a balanced sense of energy where one would report waking well-rested. A healthy cortisol response will gently cascade throughout the day, allowing for a deep, uninterrupted sleep in the evening. If the body is not taxed or overworked by physical or emotional stress, which drives the reactive mode, the individual will maintain optimal energy, sleep, mood stability, metabolism, and immune function. Cortisol in balance also has anti-inflammatory effects as well as the ability to inhibit excessive histamine response. When cortisol levels are low, as seen in adrenal fatigue, often an individual will have increased allergies, food sensitivities, and inflammation.

In the Reactive mode, cortisol does not have a predictable cascade or optimal flow. The peaks of cortisol are in response to emotional or physical stressors at a time of stimulation, driving anxiety reactivity during the event or at a delay with intermittent peaks, such as the middle of the night, driving insomnia. Emotional or mental stress can be from an argument, worrying about a parent or a child, financial woes, professional struggles, or generalized anxiety disorder. Physical stressors can come from recovering from an accident or injury, carrying a child, and even exercise, especially HIIT (high intensity interval) exercise, which can be perceived by the adrenals as "running from a cheetah," so the body goes into cortisol surge through fight-or-flight response. In this fight-or-flight response, the blood pressure rises, the breath becomes shallow, blood sugar spills out from the liver into the bloodstream, and digestive processes shut down. In fact, as you may recall from Chapter 3, in fight-or-flight the body only makes a quarter of the necessary digestive compounds, leading to bloating, indigestion, weight gain, inflammation, and increased susceptibility to food sensitivities!

"Stressed and Wired" or "Stressed and Tired"?

Many of us thrive on adrenaline in fight-or-flight mode based on lifestyle, external demands, or the way we react to stressors. Although welcomed at moments of need, unmanaged excessive demand of adrenaline can drive imbalanced expression, which results in anxiety, panic attack, worry, racing thoughts, and difficulty resetting after times of stress demand. This can be seen as an example of "stressed and wired," an over-reactive HPA-axis.

"Stressed and tired" occurs later on, once the adrenals have become fatigued. In this under-reactive HPA-axis, the adrenals don't have surges of cortisol or catecholamines to release. It is very possible to express both an overactive HPA-axis and underactive HPA-axis, and bounce back and forth from "stressed and wired" to "stressed and tired," but generally, people go hyper or overreactive first and then follow with hypo or underreactive when the gland gets fatigued from overuse.

HPA-AXIS UNDER STRESS AND ANXIETY

In an anxiety-induced individual, the glands in the HPA-axis are in overdrive. Certain functions are reduced, including production of oxytocin, and others are increased, such as production of the stress hormone cortisol.

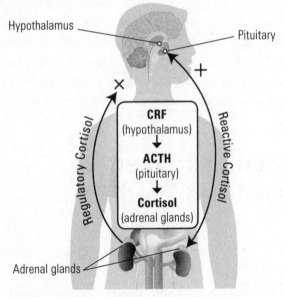

+ Reactive functions increased by anxiety and stress.
× Regulatory functions reduced by anxiety and stress.

HPA-Axis Impact on Your Immune System

The immune system is often impacted when the body's regulatory function is skewed for an extended period. When the adrenals are in overdrive, the immune system is over-stressed, the adrenals are hyper-reactive, and the body goes into auto-attack mode. One might be more prone to autoimmune flare-ups, including rheumatoid arthritis, Crohn's, ulcerative colitis, lupus, multiple sclerosis, and other autoimmune diseases. Conversely, when the adrenals are fatigued and hypo-reactive, the body produces less cortisol, DHEA, and catecholamine. The immune system is insufficient at this time and may allow pathogens, yeast, cancers, and other invaders to proliferate, without having the ability to upregulate the anti-inflammatory and immunological army. Additionally, in this fatigue state, the body is more prone to histamine reactions and inflammation, because cortisol has a natural anti-histamine, anti-inflammatory impact. Stress from both mental and physical stimuli will greatly determine how your immune system responds to the many threats it encounters and ultimately impact your body's resilience.

Cortisol Levels

Excess Cortisol (Stressed and Wired)	Insufficient Cortisol or Adrenal Fatigue (Stressed and Tired)
Apple body or excess abdominal fat	Low energy
Immune resistance, less susceptibility to cold/virus, and potential autoimmune reactivity (hyper-immune response)	Increased histamine response (more susceptible to seasonal or food allergies/sensitivities) and bloating
Insomnia	Brain fog and difficulty concentrating
Irritability, tension	Flat affect/depression
Anxiety	Anxiety

Are you over- or under-reactive in your HPA-axis? Use the Adrenal Fatigue and HPA-Axis Imbalance Quiz to assess your body's state of reactivity and need.

Adrenal Fatigue and HPA-Axis Imbalance Quiz

Respond to the following questions with Never, Sometimes, or Often. Give yourself a score of 2 for each Often response, 1 for Sometimes, and 0 for Never. This quiz will be used as a tool to determine if adrenal fatigue and HPA-axis imbalance are your root causes of anxiety, requiring additional support such as advanced testing or nutritional supplementation.

The recommendations on the following pages correspond to formulas carried in my clinic. In the Appendix's Supplement Support for the 6 Foundational Rs section, you will find information on dosage, active ingredients, and mechanism of action so you can determine if these formulas are a good fit, or find comparable ones that have similar composition.

1. Do you feel chronically fatigued, even after a good night's sleep?

❏ Never   ❏ Sometimes   ❏ Often

2. Do you experience insomnia or sleep issues?

❏ Never   ❏ Sometimes   ❏ Often

3. Are you apathetic or indifferent, even in areas of your passion or interests, and/or do you feel wildly impassioned and uncontrollably motivated with difficulty winding down?

❏ Never   ❏ Sometimes   ❏ Often

4. Do you suffer from seasonal allergies or rely on antihistamines (natural or over the counter)?

❏ Never   ❏ Sometimes   ❏ Often

5. Do you have poor circulation, cold extremities, or difficulty regulating body temperature?

❑ Never   ❑ Sometimes   ❑ Often

6. Do you crave salt or experience constant thirst?

❑ Never   ❑ Sometimes   ❑ Often

7. Does your mind feel thin or overworked, and/or do you experience racing thoughts?

❑ Never   ❑ Sometimes   ❑ Often

8. Is it difficult to complete tasks and multitask, and/or do you often finding yourself distracted?

❑ Never   ❑ Sometimes   ❑ Often

9. Do you experience pain throughout your body?

❑ Never   ❑ Sometimes   ❑ Often

10. Do you get heart palpitations or tightness in your chest?

❑ Never   ❑ Sometimes   ❑ Often

11. Do you feel impulsive, irritable, and reactive or snappy?

❑ Never   ❑ Sometimes   ❑ Often

12. Do you rely on exercise as the one time you feel good or energized?

❑ Never   ❑ Sometimes   ❑ Often

13. Do you have a low libido/sex drive?

❑ Never   ❑ Sometimes   ❑ Often

14. Do you experience dizziness and have issues with low or high blood pressure?

❑ Never   ❑ Sometimes   ❑ Often

Total Score: _____

Less than 10

It looks like your adrenals are functioning optimally and your stress axis is in check! You may benefit from the use of adaptogenic herbs during times of stress and fatigue to support your body's resilience. Consider using AdaptogenBoost to optimize your HPA-axis during times of stress demand.

Less than 15

It looks like your adrenals could use some TLC and your stress axis may be in overdrive. To preserve your adrenal function, use adaptogenic herbs daily in the form of a capsule or warm herbal decoction with tea to support your body's stress response. Consider using AdaptogenBoost to optimize your HPA-axis and aid in stress-induced fatigue on a daily basis. Increase salt intake if venturing into the Phase 1 ketogenic diet, as your adrenals will need some support in electrolyte stability with reduced carbohydrates during transition. Limit caffeine to one coffee or espresso daily. Matcha is recommended as an alternate or can be consumed additionally to provide L-theanine to modulate caffeine effects. Beyond adaptogens to support adrenal rebound, a quality bioavailable B-complex with active B6, such as Naturally Nourished B-Complex, is recommended to aid in neurotransmitter production. Consider GABA in chewable form, such as GABA Calm, to serve as a tool at times of need, acute anxiety, tightness, or "white-knuckle effect" from stress.

Greater than 15

It looks like you are suffering from adrenal fatigue and your stress axis is imbalanced. Due to the state of adrenal fatigue, it is recommended to wait at least four weeks into the foundational anti-anxiety diet with adrenal supplemental support prior to venturing into Phase 1 ketosis with carbohydrate restriction. If considering ketosis after the first month of this program, be sure to increase salt intake, as your adrenals will need some support in electrolyte stability with reduced carbohydrates during transition. In addition to following the supplement recommendations for those with a score of less than 10 and less than 15, it is recommended to completely eliminate coffee and espresso, with matcha as the only form of caffeine. Due to the elevated scoring and serious potential of adrenal fatigue, consider additional supplemental support, such as Calm and Clear, which can be brought initially while waiting on additional testing for strategic adrenal and neurotransmitter support. Adaptogen Boost, Calm and Clear, and GABA can be taken preliminarily without advanced testing to modulate anxiety and stress effects; however, some more intensive formulas, such as glandulars in Adrenal Support, should be used only if needed per advanced testing to confirm low levels of both DHEA and cortisol.

Slowing the Anxiety Drive

Beyond cortisol and DHEA, the adrenals play a role in neurotransmitter expression. Chapter 7 will delve deeper into how neurotransmitters work; however, when focusing on rebounding the adrenals, I want to dig into catecholamines, the neurotransmitters made in the medulla of the adrenals.

Catecholamines are stress-responding neurotransmitters, including epinephrine, norepinephrine, and dopamine, that are stimulated by cortisol and ACTH release. These excitatory neurotransmitters in excess drive anxiety and over time, often following prolonged stress response, dopamine becomes depleted, driving issues with motor skills, with extreme cases being seen in Parkinson's disease. As norepinephrine declines, an individual may experience memory issues, brain fog, and reduced cognitive function; however, in excess, norepinephrine can drive heart palpitations, sweats, racing thoughts, panic, and anxiety response. Similar effects are seen with epinephrine.

With neurotransmitters, both excess and deficiency can have significant effects on mental and physiological imbalance. The influence of catecholamines can be countered by higher levels of inhibitory neurotransmitters GABA and serotonin, which can serve as landing gear to mellow out stress response.

Supplements for Adrenal Fatigue and Stress Resilience

The adrenal glands take much of the hit of stress on your body and can become insufficient if overworked. The glands generally start in overdrive mode, which can attribute more of the "stressed and wired" influence on the body seen with insomnia, panic, palpitations, and excessive stress response. Both burnout and excessive output can create cortisol and HPA-axis imbalance. Some supplement formulas may be appropriate for both approaches, and the food recommendations that follow are the foundation to support both rebound and recovery in the adrenal gland.

Adaptogens to Support Stress Demands

Adaptogens are a group of traditional herbs that help us to be more resilient to stress, improving our ability to handle stress demands without getting overwhelmed or fatigued. These herbs are very tonifying to the body and optimize mitochondrial and thyroid activity. Rather than targeting one pathway, adaptogens are multifocal, hitting many physiological influences in the body. They support immune function, focus, sustained energy, and the ability to take on stress-stimulating activity without going into overdrive or burnout. By definition, in order for an herb to be classified as an adaptogen, it must be non-toxic to the recipient and must yield support for homeostasis via the HPA-axis glands, driving balance throughout the body and regulating cortisol.

Adaptogenic herbs, when sourced from a company that tests for mold, contamination, potency and purity, and organically grown or wild sourced where possible, provide active influence on supporting balanced mind and memory while improving cognitive function and reducing anxiety. Use adaptogens as a tool to prevent HPA-axis imbalance or to manage it with additional formulas as needed. Pair them with lifestyle support discussed in Chapter 8 for optimal outcomes. These herbs can be consumed in tea, tincture, or pill form and should be a first line of defense for stress, aiding in your ability to adapt to whatever life throws at you with ease.

Adaptogen formulas include ashwagandha, panax ginseng, rhodiola, cordyceps, eleuthero, schisandra, maca, tulsi (holy basil), astragalus, and licorice root.

Nervines to Help You Find Your Mellow

Nervines are a group of traditional herbs that support healthy nervous system response, reducing excitatory activity and protecting nerve function. They can have a physiological influence on the central nervous system, with nerve and muscle relaxation, as seen with skullcap, or nourishing influences. Oat tops protect nerves from damage and aid in caffeine withdrawal. Mentally, the effects of nervines can range from mild anti-anxiety influence, as seen with oat tops and chamomile; to moderate effects of lemon balm and passion flower, which reduce tension and restlessness; to the level of sedative effects seen with valerian and poppy.

Nervine formulas include oat tops (*Avena sativa*), chamomile, catnip, passion flower, lemon balm, lavender, hops, skullcap, valerian, poppy.

Recommended Supplements

I use the following formulas in clinic to aid in rebounding from adrenal fatigue and balancing the HPA-axis.

Adaptogen blend/Adaptogen Boost: See page 284

Adrenal glandular: When an individual has suboptimal cortisol along with low adrenal output overall, a glandular compound is often warranted. A glandular is an animal gland that is desiccated but retains its bioactive properties. Adrenal glandular is typically derived from cows. It is important to look for a product that is third-party assessed for purity as well as toxicity.

Nervine and adaptogen blend with L-theanine/Calm and Clear: See page 283

High-dose vitamin C: Promotes healthy adrenal output and reduces stress impact to the body. The adrenals are the highest concentrated storage of vitamin C in the body and they use it in production and management of cortisol. Start with 2–3 grams per day as a base dosage and look for a form that is buffered to aid in absorption and reduce GI distress. Dosages upwards of 5–10 grams may be warranted in individuals experiencing immune distress and low platelet count.

Sleep Support: A blend of tonifying nervines with sedative nervines and melatonin, this Naturally Nourished formula is a safe, effective alternative to sleeping medications. It supports relaxation and reduced tension while promoting a restful night of sleep and generalized state of calm.

Note: If dealing with low serotonin levels, melatonin may be needed for a period of time as your production increases, as serotonin is manufactured from melatonin.

Rebound Your Adrenal Glands

Nutritional support for adrenals and HPA -axis in the anti-anxiety diet program includes rich sources of B vitamins to rebound the gland, including animal proteins, leafy greens, and avocado; and magnesium for relaxation of muscles, improved sleep, and cortisol metabolism. The recipes in this chapter also feature vitamin C to boost immune system and fight brain cell damage from prolonged cortisol hormone exposure. You will also get to experience consumption of adaptogens in the steamer and nutball caramels, helping you rock through your day feeling resilient.

❖ *Anti-Inflammatory Electrolyte Elixir, page 204*

❖ *Stress-Stabilizing Steamer, page 205*

❖ *Citrus Burst Smoothie, page 208*

❖ *Roasted Colored Peppers, page 220*

❖ *Walnut Maca Caramels, page 258*

❖ *Turmeric Orange Gummies, page 260*

❖ *Matcha Coconut Gummies, page 261*

CHAPTER 7

Rebalance Your Neurotransmitters

I want to close my 6 Foundational Rs of anti-anxiety with the most direct system for mood stability and anti-anxiety effects, the neurotransmitters. Remember, when the gut is inflamed and the HPA-axis is imbalanced, this often causes imbalance or depletion of neurotransmitters, leading to anxiety, agitation, panic, and chronic distress.

Traditional approaches to regulate mood and reduce anxiety focus on the imbalance of neurotransmitters. In fact, the pharmaceutical industry brings in over 15 billion dollars per year in antidepressant and anti-anxiety drugs targeting neurotransmitter function. Topping the list of these drugs are reuptake inhibiting drugs that perpetuate selective neurotransmitter signals. Selective serotonin reuptake inhibitor (SSRI) medications, along with a newer class of drugs that target the adrenal neurotransmitter norepinephrine, selective serotonin norepinephrine reuptake inhibitor (SNRI), are used on millions of people. However, 30–50 percent of this population suffers from drug side effects. Unfortunately, these drugs do not increase the stores of the neurotransmitters; they simply recycle the already low neurotransmitters, which can often lead to even lower production, driving more symptoms and mood instability.

Rather, a person can use food as medicine, as well as targeted nutrient supplemental support, to balance or replete neurotransmitters.

What Are Neurotransmitters?

In simplistic terms, neurotransmitters are chemical messengers that carry signals from one neuron to another. The autonomic nervous system (ANS) is comprised of both the fight-or-flight sympathetic and rest-and-digest parasympathetic systems discussed in the last chapter. It runs through the spine, driving most unconscious activity such as heart rate, respiratory rate, digestion, pupil dilation, and many reflexes. In the craniosacral areas of the spine, the parasympathetic nerves are expressed, and between these regions, in the thoracic lumbar area, the sympathetic stress response is expressed. The ANS communicates through a complex networking system of ports and threads from these spinal regions to peripheral glands of focus and directly to the GI tract. Fibrous nerves carry messages of neurotransmitters to and from the central nervous system, targeting any of the 30 billion neurons in your brain.

Neurons form connections with other neurons known as synapses, and messages cross the synapse from one neuron to another via chemical communication of neurotransmitters. Beyond neurons in your brain, a neurotransmitter can signal and communicate with neurons in the gut and can even communicate with non-neuron cells such as muscle and gland cells.

There are over 100 unique neurotransmitters, which play an integral role in daily function, cognitive processing, and perception. Protein compounds, called amino acids, are the building blocks for creating neurotransmitters, which are combined in the presence of specific enzymes and cofactor nutrients.

The direct neurotransmitters of focus for anxiety are the inhibitory signals serotonin and GABA, which help the mind mellow out and reset following anxiety stimulation. The drivers of distress are the excitatory neurotransmitters, including acetylcholine, epinephrine, norepinephrine, dopamine, and glutamate, which stimulate stress activity and anxiety response.

Anxiety can be seen due to an excess of excitatory neurotransmitters or a deficiency of inhibitory neurotransmitters, or relative dominance and imbalance seen within the symphony of your brain's expression. If one neurotransmitter plays louder than it should or is overexpressed, or if there are many neurotransmitters playing out of turn, this can throw off the harmony of the brain, causing panic, worry, racing thoughts, or crippling panic. A state of chronic anxiety can drive constant imbalanced neurotransmitters as the anxiety reaction continues to drive demand and further depletion. When there aren't appropriate conditions to manufacture neurotransmitters due to microbiome imbalance or lacking the building blocks due to deficiency of nutrients, it is difficult to get out of anxiety as a vicious cycle.

What Influences the Expression of Neurotransmitters?

Neurotransmitters are influenced by production pathways and precursors, or amino-acid building blocks, available. The level of need of a particular neurotransmitter is relative to the demand on which it is needed based on environment and perception of the individual. For instance, an individual who works 10+ hours a day and gets poor sleep is likely running on adrenaline, so they may be burning through or making an excess of epinephrine, and their brain may be trying to balance this surge by spilling out more inhibitory compounds serotonin and GABA. Over time, based on demand and limitations of the building materials, precursor amino acids, and cofactors, imbalance will be seen in symptoms of anxiety, insomnia, difficulty concentrating, brain fog, and more!

Providing building blocks of deficient neurotransmitters is one step in focused support of rebalance; however, activating that production is also essential. Most amino acids or building blocks are able to cross the blood-brain barrier, aiding in production of neurotransmitters. When focused on therapeutic effects, it is important to take supplemental forms of amino acids separately from protein-containing meals. This will help the body absorb neurotransmitter-building amino acids without competition from the amino acids found in foods.

A diet rich in bioavailable protein provides foundational support for ample building blocks or precursors. Although strategic use of amino acids in supplement form should be separated from protein-containing meals to get targeted effects, it is important to note that overall, a low-protein diet very well may drive deficiency of building blocks in general. If an individual is not consuming ample protein, their body will spare the limited amino acids for the varied functions of the body, including metabolic, immune-related, and structural function.

Starting with a low-protein diet limits intake of amino acids, which drives higher susceptibility to depression and anxiety. Selecting wild-caught fish or grass-fed, pasture-raised meats will provide a higher quality source of nutrients without the taxation of pro-inflammatory compounds found in conventional sources. A diet rich in the amino acids tryptophan, tyrosine, and glycine will increase GABA production and have a calming effect. This can be achieved with a diet of amino acids found in clean sources of pasture-raised poultry and pork, grass-fed beef, as well as bone broth, gelatin, and pork skins.

CALCULATE YOUR BODY'S PROTEIN NEEDS

1. Take your body weight in pounds and divide it by 2.2 to convert pounds into kilograms

Weight in pounds _____ / 2.2 = _____ kg

2. Calculate your protein needs at lower range

lower value x weight in kg = _____

3. Calculate your protein needs at higher range (see g of protein per kg body weight below)
higher value x weight in kg = _____

4. Plug in numbers for your ideal protein range:
_____ – _____ g/day

Recommended Daily Protein Intake Based on Body Weight

If you are within 10 pounds of an ideal weight (see note below)	Consume 1 to 1.4 g protein per kg of body weight
If you are overweight by 50 pounds or less	Consume 0.8 to 1.2 g protein per kg of body weigh
If you are overweight by greater than 50 pounds	Consume 0.8 to 1.0 g protein per kg of body weight
Lower levels are suggested for overweight individuals based on the assumption of restriction of calories, focusing on feeding ideal body weight to aid in results of weight loss.	

Ideal weight is defined as:

106 pounds at 5 feet + 6 pounds per inch for men

100 pounds at 5 feet + 5 pounds per inch for women

If you are under 5 feet tall, subtract 3 pounds per inch.

Please note: I do not use body weight as a primary judge of health. I consider body composition and percent body fat as a stronger indicator of disease risk and optimal health as well as consider various biomarkers that can be seen in people at heavier weights. I am using this "ideal weight" concept to ensure ample protein provided scaled to body size without overconsumption or promotion of a high-protein diet.

As with everything in the body, it is important to focus on ample amounts to prevent depletion and support your needs, but maxing out is not the goal, as more does not translate to better! In fact, a diet that is too high in protein can drive cortisol output, which will drive anxiety and stress response. There seems to be a sweet spot of optimal protein range that works best when accompanied with a diet rich in phytocompounds, antioxidants, and minerals, as seen in your anti-anxiety diet program.

When looking at macronutrient caloric distribution of carbs, protein, and fat, the anti-anxiety diet should be predominantly fat (>50 percent), followed by protein (15 to 30 percent) and moderate carbs (5 to 20 percent). The first phase of your anti-anxiety diet uses the ketogenic approach to teach your body to become fat adapted, coating and protecting your brain and nervous system. This phase should be 70 to 85 percent fat, 15 to 20 percent protein, and 5 to 10 percent carbs. Learn more about the anti-anxiety diet guidelines in the following chapter.

Regulating the physiological demands of stress can help to rebalance your neurotransmitters as well. As noted, if you are burning the candle at both ends, your body will be in a constant state of burn, and you will likely experience more symptoms of imbalance. As I always say to my clients, you can't out-supplement lifestyle! You have to find a balance at both ends of the equation where you undo deficiency trends and prevent the burnout.

With this being said, many of us are under chronic stress from environmental or emotional drivers that we are not able to modify, such as divorce, death of a loved one, a child struggling, situations at work, etc. In this case, working on perspective and those things you can control may be the most powerful tool, supported by adaptogens and specific nutrients of focus.

Employing deep-breathing techniques such as the 4-7-8 breathing of Dr. Andrew Weil is one way to truly harness the wild stallion in your brain, sending relaxation signals down the vagus nerve from the body to the brain and back. See Chapter 8 in lifestyle support for an explanation on how to follow 4-7-8 breathing. Beyond breath, focusing on sleep hygiene or routine to set up the mind and body for a restful night's sleep can be a powerful way to reduce anxiety. Research supports that seven to nine hours a night can reset stress hormones and reduce anxiety!

Then, of course, to get you "out of the water" and optimize brain function, the use of amino acids can be beneficial. Studies demonstrate when putting people at an increased state of physiological stress, supplementation with the amino acid tyrosine can aid in mood stability and reduced panic or anxiety.

Beyond deficiency of the building blocks and demands of the neurotransmitters, the receptors that neurotransmitters target may be equally important. Excess stimulants, both in medications such as Adderall and in foods such as caffeine, have been shown to strip the receptors, making them less receptive to neurotransmitters, thus expressing low levels even in abundance of the compound itself.

How to optimize your neurotransmitter levels:

- Eat adequate protein.
- Support utilization and absorption of protein with a digestive enzyme.

- Get seven to nine hours of sleep at night.

- Practice deep breathing and 4-7-8 breathing.

- Adjust environment to reduce stress and learn to say "no."

- Practice perspective and gratitude.

- Consider amino acid supplementation.

You can find more on the lifestyle application of the anti-anxiety diet program in Chapter 8.

Get to Know Your Neurotransmitters

Let's meet the primary players in your brain's symphony of cognition and mood regulation. We will start with the inhibitory, or mellow-out, neurotransmitters, followed by a carrier messenger, and then finish with the excitatory drivers of stress response. As discussed, anxiety can be due to a complex chemical equation of imbalance of these compounds: either deficiency of the inhibitory or an excess of the excitatory!

Serotonin

Probably the most famous neurotransmitter of the group, serotonin is an inhibitory compound that aids in relaxation, anxiety, depression, memory, socialization, sexual function, sleep, blood pressure stability, pain, appetite, and digestive regularity. Serotonin receptors, although concentrated in the forebrain, are found throughout the body, including the intestines, heart, blood vessels, uterus, and ovaries. Beyond its direct effects, serotonin has the ability to modulate the release of other neurotransmitters as well as hormones that regulate sexual function and stress response. There are many types of serotonin receptors but the most well-known are 5-HT1, which is the primary inhibitory receptor, and 5-HT2, which is primarily excitatory and the focused hit for many psychedelic drugs, driving hallucinations in excessive stimulation. Drug therapies have been developed to work on both receptors, either to suppress or enhance activity for reduction in anxiety and mood stability.

Regardless of medication use and supplementation support, consuming a diet rich in tryptophan food sources can aid in production and utilization of serotonin. There are no known food sources of 5-HTP (a precursor to serotonin), but tryptophan is found in poultry, beef, fish, dairy, seeds, dates, chocolate, and spirulina, to name a few. If not on an anti-anxiety medication, supplementing with 5-HTP at 50 to 200 milligrams in a synergy formula, including B6 as a cofactor, could be of benefit. However, long-term use of 5-HTP can, over time, dampen mood by depleting your dopamine and other excitatory compounds. To prevent depression, I suggest minimizing supplementation with 5-HTP to no more than three to six months of daily use unless monitored and advised by a practitioner.

Low blood levels of tryptophan have been correlated to anxiety and depression. Inflammation in the body drives depletion of tryptophan, so removing the pro-inflammatory foods discussed in Chapter 2 can be equally as important as the abundance focus in supporting all 6 Rs of this program!

As you may also recall, serotonin is primarily manufactured in the gut by the probiotic strain, *Lactobacillus*. In fact, it is estimated that greater than 90 percent of the serotonin of the body resides and is produced in the gut! Supporting your body with a serving of probiotics daily can enhance your body's production of serotonin, aiding in a stable, healthy mood. Consider 5-HTP or tryptophan as supplemental support for short-term targeting of serotonin to give a "leg up" and rebound, and a quality probiotic formula with a focus on *Lactobacillus* and *Bifidobacterium* strains as a foundational supplement with broad support for your system. Beyond serotonin production, these healthy gut bacteria strains are correlated with GABA.

Signs of low serotonin:

- Aches throughout the body (muscular, fascia related)
- Anticipatory distress
- Anxiety
- Constipation
- Depression
- Flat affect (emotionally low, difficult to excite)
- Lack of pleasure
- Loose stools
- Poor sleep
- Ruminating thoughts

GABA

Rapid anxiety relief can be seen with release and use of GABA, the main inhibitory neurotransmitter in the central nervous system targeting the brain's conscious and behavioral center. GABA works both as relaxer and anxiolytic, a reducer of anxiety, with rapid effects that can influence the brain and body for hours. GABA is also sought for its ability to reduce seizure activity with epilepsy, rigidity, and neuromuscular spasms. It is used as a neuroprotectant in Parkinson's and multiple sclerosis, and has even been sought out for use in PMS and migraines to reduce pain and stabilize mood. As discussed previously, active neurotransmitters are not able to cross the blood-brain barrier; however, in the case of GABA, there seems to be a workaround via the gut and peripheral tissues.

Similar to serotonin, the majority of GABA is produced in the enteric nervous system of the gut, and signals are carried back and forth from brain to gut via the vagus nerve. *Lactobacillus* and *Bifidobacterium* strains seem to have the greatest effect on GABA production, specifically a strain called *Lactobacillus rhamnosus*. Studies confirm both consumption of these probiotics as well as forms of PharmaGABA, a fermented form of GABA molecule, reduce anxiety and support relaxation via reduction of cortisol, reported symptom reduction, and reduced blood pressure.

GABA supplementation seems to be a rapid-acting tool with limited side effects. I explain GABA in its chewable form to have the ability to reduce the "white knuckle effect" of stress. It tends to take the physiological tension, impulsivity, and irritability of anxiety down. PharmaGABA may influence memory and for this reason should be used as a tool when working the system of the 6 Rs of your program. For long-term sustainable support, maintaining a healthy gut microbiome and supplementing with a 50:50 blend of *Lactobacillus* and *Bifidobacterium* probiotic strains ensure optimal serotonin and GABA expression while optimizing cognition and memory.

Signs of low GABA:

- Compulsive eating
- Cravings or addiction to sweets, alcohol
- Elevated blood pressure
- Feeling buzzing or flighty (not grounded)
- Feeling of physiological tension
- Heart palpitations
- Mental exhaustion from racing thoughts
- Panic attack
- Tightness in the chest

Acetylcholine

This neurotransmitter is primarily thought of as anti-aging due to its protective effects over neurodegenerative diseases such as Alzheimer's and dementia. Acetylcholine is known for its role in memory, concentration, and cognitive reasoning as it signals brain communication as well as synaptogenesis, the process of building new brain synapses or communication channels. All the message-carrying fibers in both the sympathetic and parasympathetic nervous system are protected by a coating called myelin and use acetylcholine as a transmitter. The building block choline and fatty acids in the diet create a fattier myelin sheath for quicker neurotransmitter signal travel.

In anxiety research, lower choline levels trend with high anxiety and panic. Choline has been acknowledged for decades for its role in maternal health, protection from neural tube defects, and support for fetal brain development, but in 1998 it was deemed an essential nutrient by the Institute of Medicine. Choline is a fat-soluble B-vitamin required as a building block for phosphatidylcholine, an integral component of cell membranes, as well as acetylcholine. Choline also plays an integral role in methylation to produce feel-good neurotransmitters and reduce inflammation.

The dietary trend of avoiding saturated fat and dietary cholesterol likely contributed to deficiencies, as the richest forms of this nutrient are egg yolks and liver! Eating 12 to 16 eggs a week from pasture-raised chickens with beautiful orange, nutrient-rich yolks will provide your body with this essential nutrient to protect healthy cells from damage, produce neurotransmitters, and ensure healthy signaling and communication of your neurotransmitters.

Acetylcholine aids as the signal carrier so speed of access to memory, stored information, or sensory reaction can be tied to its activity in the brain. Acetylcholine can actually have both excitatory and inhibitory functions. At the brain and mood level, the primary experience of optimal acetylcholine activity is calm and collected with a clear mind. Peripherally, outside of the brain, acetylcholine activity maintains healthy neuromuscular function and tone as well as digestive and hormonal activity such as peristalsis, the involuntary pumping of the gut that supports bowel regularity.

Low acetylcholine can reduce signaling for mood stability and pleasure such as arousal. As choline plays a primary role in detox, low levels drive sluggish liver function, resulting in toxicity and fatty liver. To add insult to injury, the genetic COMT SNP, discussed in Chapter 5, plays a role in women's ability to convert estrogen into choline, leading to both estrogen dominance and choline deficiency as well as taxing the process of the liver.

It is important to note that an excess of acetylcholine has been demonstrated to drive depression, as it interferes with dopamine expression. For this reason, a choline-rich diet with liver support is a priority for regulation. If you are dealing with significant symptoms, especially memory issues, or elevated liver enzymes, supplementation support may be considered. Phosphatidylcholine and choline bitartrate salts are absorbable safe options for whole-body support of fatty liver and inflammation, but these forms may not cross the blood-brain barrier. CDP-choline and Alpha GPC are two forms that can cross the blood-brain barrier and have a more direct effect on mood and memory, but may interfere more directly with dopamine. For individuals with elevations of dopamine, acetylcholine supplementation may be a powerful tool in regulating neurotransmitter expression.

Signs of low acetylcholine:

- Cognitive decline

- Constipation and gastroparesis

- Fatigue

- Fatty liver or elevated liver enzymes

- Memory loss

- Reduced creativity

- Reduced physical reactivity

- Reduced speed and strength

- Slow mental processing

Epinephrine

The surge when racing to meet a deadline, the primary driver of your stress response, and the bell-and-whistle alarm system of your body also known as adrenaline is a powerful excitatory neurotransmitter, epinephrine. This neurotransmitter can function as lighter fluid to an anxiety fire like a steam train on the tracks without brakes! A balance of epinephrine can aid in creating professional drive and vigor. After all, adrenaline surges can be exciting and invigorating, but an excess can lead to an out-of-body panic and significant anxiety response. Produced by the adrenal glands, epinephrine is a primary responder to HPA-axis stress demands in the body and brain. Epinephrine is built from tyrosine, an amino acid precursor that also builds neurotransmitters norepinephrine and dopamine, collectively known as catecholamines.

Beyond anxiety itself as a stimulant to epinephrine release, bright light, loud noises, and high-intensity activity such as excessive exercise can drive output, which can be expressed in excess. Although this neurotransmitter is not produced in the gut, when dealing with leaky gut or increased food sensitivity to the level of anaphylactic reaction of a food allergy, epinephrine is the go-to drug in the form of EpiPen to deliver adrenaline to stop systemic reaction. Studies demonstrate excessive epinephrine output with both elevated blood pressure and anxiety disorder. On a supplemental level, the best line of defense for reducing epinephrine is through balancing the HPA-axis, specifically focusing on adrenal support and using L-theanine to reduce excess. The formulas discussed in Chapter

6 as nervines and adaptogens would be the go-to tools to reduce stress response and excessive epinephrine output.

Signs of high epinephrine:

- Anxiety
- Elevated blood pressure
- Excessive nerve firing (feeling on edge)
- Hyperactivity
- Incredible hulk mentality
- Insomnia
- Pain
- Panic attack
- Rapid heart rate
- Shortness of breath
- Social anxiety

Norepinephrine

Norepinephrine acts similarly to epinephrine and is also made in the adrenal glands. Like epinephrine, it too has effects in the central nervous system (CNS) and peripheral tissues on an adrenaline-like level; however, norepinephrine seems to have a bidirectional role where it can normalize anxiety activity. Epinephrine is actually made from norepinephrine in the adrenal glands as the attack dog that reacts more aggressively to stress, driving an exaggerated anxiety and stress response, whereas norepinephrine has a more tonifying effect.

Norepinephrine is more acknowledged as a neurotransmitter for mood maintenance and regulation while epinephrine is seen as more reactive or stress responsive in panic or acute anxiety attacks.

Since norepinephrine plays a role in baseline function, many drugs for anxiety as mood stabilizers, as well as drugs for elevated blood pressure and tremors (typically the physical effects of anxiety), have been developed to work on the expression of norepinephrine. Propranolol, for example, is a beta-blocker drug that is targeted for blood pressure through action on both epinephrine and norepinephrine, has influence on performance anxiety, tremors, and migraines.

It is also important to acknowledge that norepinephrine, when too low, can drive flat affect and lack of drive. Drug companies that saw shortcomings in SSRIs developed SNRIs, such as Effexor and Cymbalta, that allow increased concentration of serotonin and norepinephrine. Typically, anxiety is seen with norepinephrine being too high, but social anxiety and withdrawn anxiety symptoms can be seen with values that are too low. Just like a note in the symphony of the brain, something off key on either end can throw the brain signals off, manifesting in anxiety and distress. I suggest using a blend of nervines and adaptogens to tonify stress response in general. A diet rich in tyrosine can be a good foundation and allow the body to use what it needs while preventing excess. Tyrosine, like tryptophan, is found in protein-containing foods and is concentrated in poultry, duck eggs, almonds, avocados, bananas, lima beans, pumpkin seeds, and sesame seeds. Tyrosine supplementation would only be recommended in the case of adrenal fatigue and low catacholamines, along with low cortisol and DHEA, as excess levels can drive stress response. The adaptogenic herbs discussed in Chapter 6 are the best option.

Signs of high norepinephrine:

- Anxiety

- Blood sugar elevation

- Nausea

- Racing thoughts

- Rapid heart rate

- Sweating

- Tremors

Dopamine

This neurotransmitter is typically second in pop culture to serotonin due its association with bliss and reward, but dopamine has a complex relationship with anxiety. Many addictions and self-medication outlets, from drugs and alcohol to caffeine, food, gambling, video gaming, and social media scrolling, target dopamine release and expression. Getting enough dopamine to feel good about yourself while reducing any excess that can put the mind into overdrive is equally important when managing anxiety. Associated with our pleasure centers in the brain, dopamine has activity in libido and excitement, and motivates performance with complex reward centers; hence, addiction is seen with high release.

Dopamine-blocking medications are strongly acknowledged to have antipsychotic and anxiolytic effects. However, we need some dopamine for the ability to drive confidence and a feeling of self-efficacy, which can in turn reduce anxiety and rumination. In fact, a popular antidepressant, Wellbutrin, increases activity of both norepinephrine and dopamine to enhance feelings of self-worth and purpose, which can reduce social anxiety. But, this drug can cause anxiety by producing excessive dopamine activity, manifesting as racing thoughts and almost a manic creativity.

Although too much dopamine can drive anxiety, compared to other stress-responding neurotransmitters, excess dopamine is less attributed to anxiety. For this reason, when looking to balance neurotransmitters for mood stability, it would be reasonable to stimulate dopamine only or prevent dopamine breakdown into norepinephrine and epinephrine to prevent their more anxious reactivity. (Remember norepinephrine is made from dopamine and epinephrine is made from norepinephrine, so rather than concentrating on production of dopamine, which can in turn increase the other two, blocking its breakdown can be the best approach when selecting supplemental support.)

SENSORY OVERLOAD!

Are electronics depleting your dopamine stores? The brain is overburdened with bright blue screen lights and rapid visual effects from electronic monitors flickering quicker than the eye can detect, both driving dopamine dumping. Checking your social media and email, scrolling your digital device, and bombarding the brain with information at a rapid rate can release a surge of dopamine in the brain. This partially explains why we are all so addicted to our smartphones and tablets. Stressful games can drive surges of epinephrine with adrenaline in some, or deplete GABA in the brain's attempt to mellow out the racing brain!

To support your success with the anti-anxiety diet, it is recommended to limit screen time, including phones, computers, and television to five hours/day. If this is not possible due to your field of work, consider blue blocker glasses, which reduce the impact of artificial bright blue light that can throw off your melatonin and serotonin levels, and also drive cortisol release.

For mood stability with anxiolytic effects, compounds that inhibit the breakdown of dopamine are preferred. Phosphatidylserine is a component of cell membranes that functions to balance nutrients and waste in the brain. It has been shown to increase dopamine levels while reducing excessive cortisol and ACTH, thus supporting memory, concentration, and positive feedback signals of dopamine without the stress response of adrenaline. The Calm and Clear formula I use in clinic is a foundational tool to modulate neurotransmitters, as it includes activated B vitamins, nervines, adaptogens, phosphatidylserine, and L-theanine (to be discussed).

Dopamine isn't able to cross the blood-brain barrier. However, L-dopa, its precursor made from L-tyrosine, is often prescribed to support production in conditions such as Parkinson's disease. This approach can be used with anxiety via the use of *Mucuna pruriens*, also known as the velvet bean, that has naturally occurring L-dopa. *Mucuna pruriens* is also being studied for memory and mood stability, and research for Parkinson's has shown it to have more beneficial effects with less side effects than pharmaceutical synthetic L-dopa. However, in high dosage and if taken out of balance, it can drive a too-low blood pressure as well as drug interactions with many Parkinson's drugs, so is not advised without review from your healthcare practitioner.

Lifestyle supporters of dopamine boost include movement, meditation, ample sleep of 7–9 hours per night, listening to music, and experiencing touch by both humans and animals, which all stimulates your dopamine output, giving your brain a feel-good boost! Research has found overeating and obesity associated with people that have less dopamine receptors, so if you are looking for weight loss as well, participating in other lifestyle support (see Chapter 8) and considering supplementation may be key.

Signs of low dopamine:

- ADHD
- Anxiety
- Boredom
- Depression
- Difficulty multitasking
- Fatigue
- Lack of focus
- Low libido

- Parkinson's disease

- Procrastination

- Seeking external pleasures (drug, alcohol, food addiction)

Glutamate

Typically discussed as the counterpart to GABA, glutamate is the primary excitatory neurotransmitter in the CNS, involved in all pathways of anxiety and distress signaling. Carrying messages of stress, memory, and information processing to the brain, too much glutamate with not enough GABA creates excitatory information overload and mood instability, which can be a significant driver for panic attacks or generalized anxiety disorder.

Glutamate excitotoxicity is often caused by the consumption of processed foods such as aspartic acid in aspartame diet sweeteners or glutamate flavor enhancers such as glutamic acid and monosodium glutamate (MSG), which stimulate glutamate activity. (In an excitotoxicity state, excessive excitatory activity can drive inflammation in the cells, eventually leading to cellular death.)

One way the body copes with excessive glutamate is to produce more opioid compounds to try to counteract the excitatory influences. The restriction of gluten and casein-containing dairy in the anti-anxiety diet will aid with reducing the excessive opioid reactivity, which can cause brain fog, rage, and anxiety. The body will also try to counteract glutamate excess in the brain with glutathione, the master antioxidant, which over time will get depleted, leading to more inflammation and cell damage. Supporting the body with a gluten and casein-free diet that is free of preservatives, artificial sweeteners, and flavor enhancers, yet rich in antioxidants, healthy fats, and diverse proteins will be a huge foundation in regulating harmony with glutamate and GABA balance.

GABA is produced from glutamate as a building block, so the ability to balance out glutamate is focused in the conversion pathway. If there is too much stimulation in stress response or the pathway is faulty, often glutamate will be produced without healthy conversion to GABA. Vitamin B6, the same cofactor in regulation of serotonin build in the brain, plays a great role in supporting GABA conversion from glutamate. Driving enzyme function to convert GABA from glutamate is a more sound approach than restricting L-glutamine in whole foods or therapeutic supplement if needed for other demands such as leaky gut or immune distress.

As you may recall, glutamine is the fuel source and building block for gut cells as a tool to support gut lining and reduce food sensitivity. Also, glutamine stores tend to get depleted under stress and can cause sore muscles and reduced immune function. In this sense, optimizing glutamine from glutamine-rich foods, including bone broth, sun-dried tomatoes, mushrooms, miso, and other umami (savory salty) flavors in natural unprocessed forms would be recommended if supporting the body with B6 and reducing inflammation to optimize conversion. If you are dealing with excess glutamate, especially in the form of headaches, you may consider reducing these foods or holding L-glutamine supplementation until it is better managed. Beyond its influence on gut and immune function, glutamine can cross the blood-brain barrier and contribute toward reducing buildup of the toxic by-product ammonia in the brain, as well as providing support for memory, learning, and cognitive processing. L-glutamine can be used as a powerful tool to battle addiction to sugar, drugs, and alcohol.

You may read online that L-glutamine can increase blood sugar levels as it can convert to glucose and play a role on the pancreas; however, research supports its ability to aid in burning body fat, supporting lean mass, reducing blood sugars, and regulating insulin sensitivity. As noted with glutamate foods, if you are experiencing significant symptoms of excessive glutamate, I would not recommend the use of L-glutamine or glutamine-based supplements. However, when reviewing hundreds of studies, the benefits of glutamine in the body are widespread beyond neurotransmitter function for digestive, immunological, growth, and development reasons. In fact, over 50 percent of the amino acids in breast milk, nature's perfect food, come from glutamate and glutamine.

Signs of excessive glutamate:

- Anxiety

- Difficulty focusing

- Headaches

- Hypoglycemia

- Insomnia

- Pain

- Restless leg

- Sensitive to emotions; tearful and quick to laughter

Signs of low glutamate:

- Brain fog

- Delayed eye movements

- Flat affect or limited emotions

- Low appetite

- Sugar cravings

- Delayed eye movements

Neurotransmitter Symptoms and Supplementation

Serotonin		
Symptoms of deficiency	• Anxiety • Poor sleep • Depression or flat affect • Ruminating thoughts • Anticipatory distress • Aches throughout the body (muscular, fascia related)	• Joint pain • Constipation • Tinnitus • Lack of pleasure
Symptoms of excess	• Mania • Agitation • Confusion • Rapid heart rate • Heavy sweating	• Diarrhea • Muscle rigidity • Headaches • High fever
Nutrients of focus	• Tryptophan foods: poultry and all proteins, pumpkin seeds. After 12 weeks, chickpeas and dairy, if tolerated • Folate (methylfolate form): liver, leafy greens, cruciferous vegetables	• Probiotics: cultured vegetables, pickles, kraut, kombucha. After 12 weeks, raw aged cheeses, yogurt, kefir, raw milk, ghee, grass-fed butter, if tolerated
Supplement to consider	• 50–200mg 5-HTP • If there is no impact from 5-HTP after 6 weeks, can try 1–2g of tryptophan per day, taken separately from food	• 50–100mg B6 in activated form P5Ps

Neurotransmitter Symptoms and Supplementation

GABA		
Symptoms of deficiency	• Feeling of physiological tension • Feeling buzzing or flighty (not grounded) • Tightness in the chest • Cravings or addiction to sweets, alcohol	• Compulsive eating • Elevated blood pressure • Heart palpitations • Panic attack • Mental exhaustion from racing thoughts
Symptoms of excess	• Edgy • Anxious • Amplified pain • Restlessness • Inability to focus	• Distrust of others • Increased worry • Diminished memory • Sleepiness and inability to feel awake
Nutrients of focus	• *Lactobacillus*-fermented foods: kimchi, sauerkraut, kefir, miso	• Bone broth, grass-fed whey, and cabbage • Green tea and matcha
Supplement to consider	• L-theanine, taurine, lemon balm, passion flower, and B6 • GABACalm chews. Start at 100–200mg pharma-GABA, working upward to 400–500mg as needed. If negative effects are seen, discontinue. • Meditation and yoga	

Neurotransmitter Symptoms and Supplementation

Acetylcholine		
Symptoms of deficiency	• Memory loss • Cognitive decline • Slow mental processing • Fatty liver or elevated liver function tests (LFTs) • Reduced creativity • Fatigue	• Reduced physical reactivity • Reduced speed and strength • Constipation and gastroparesis • Flushed skin
Symptoms of excess	• Confusion • Blurred vision • Irritability • Headache • Dry mouth	• Stomach problems • Nausea and vomiting • Pain • Muscle twitching and paralysis
Nutrients of focus	• Egg yolks • Liver from grass-fed or pasture-raised sources	• Cruciferous vegetables, including broccoli and cauliflower
Supplement to consider	• Alpha GPC and Citicoline at 300–900mg, after 6 weeks reduce baseline to half dosage	• B-complex with choline as ongoing daily maintenance

Neurotransmitter Symptoms and Supplementation

Epinephrine		
Symptoms of deficiency	• Depression • Low professional drive • Low vigor or passion • Flat affect	• Lack of focus • Difficulty processing information or thinking
Symptoms of excess	• Anxiety • Rapid heart rate • Shortness of breath • Panic attack • Social anxiety • Insomnia	• Hyperactivity • Elevated blood pressure • "Incredible Hulk" mentality • Excessive nerve firing (feeling on edge) • Pain
Nutrients of focus	• Remove caffeine from the diet, avoiding coffee and espresso if levels are in excess • If levels are low, focus on chocolate and tyrosine-rich foods, including all proteins and beans, if tolerated	• Also apply norepinephrine rules
Supplement to consider	• Nervines, adaptogens, L-theanine, and phosphatidylserine as found in Calm and Clear can reduce excess while allowing for rebound if deficient.	• In surges of high epinephrine, GABACalm chews may be considered to aid in "landing gear" to intensive anxiety-stress-panic response

Neurotransmitter Symptoms and Supplementation

Norepinephrine		
Symptoms of deficiency	• Depression • Lethargy • Inattention • Inflammation and pain	• Low libido • Low professional drive • Reduced socialization
Symptoms of excess	• Anxiety • Tremors • Rapid heart rate • Sweating	• Blood sugar elevation • Nausea • Racing thoughts • Irritability
Nutrients of focus	• Avoid aspartame and diet sweeteners containing L-phenylalanine	• If levels are low, tyrosine-rich foods, including eggs (especially duck eggs) and all proteins; beans, if tolerated
Supplement to consider	• Nervines, adaptogens, L-theanine, and phosphatidylserine as found in Calm and Clear can reduce excess while allowing for rebound if deficient	• Zinc aids in maintaining dopamine without metabolism into norepinephrine

Neurotransmitter Symptoms and Supplementation

Dopamine		
Symptoms of deficiency	• Anxiety • Low libido • Depression • Procrastination • Boredom • Fatigue	• Seeking external pleasure • Drug and/or alcohol addiction • ADHD • Difficulty multitasking • Parkinson's disease • Lack of focus
Symptoms of excess	• Aggressive • Overly competitive • Lack of impulse control	• Thrill seeking • Paranoia • Psychosis
Nutrients of focus	• Caffeine and sugar can drive excessive dopamine surges; they should be avoided	• If levels are low, tyrosine-rich foods, including eggs (especially duck eggs) and all proteins; beans, if tolerated
Supplement to consider	• *Mucana pruriens*, to support optimal dopamine when low	• L-tyrosine, to produce L-dopa • CAUTION: Wellbutrin and ADHD drug Ritalin work on dopamine receptors. Do not supplement with these compounds if taking one of these medications.

Neurotransmitter Symptoms and Supplementation

Glutamate		
Symptoms of deficiency	• Sugar cravings • Brain fog • Low appetite • Flat affect or limited emotions • Delayed eye movements • Addictive tendencies	• Difficulty with comprehension and learning • Sore muscles • Poor immune function • Leaky gut • Food sensitivity
Symptoms of excess	• Anxiety • Insomnia • Hypoglycemia • Restless leg • Headaches • Pain	• Panic attacks • Skin flushing, rashing • Difficulty focusing due to overactive mind • Sensitive to emotions; tearful and quick to laughter
Nutrients of focus	• Monosodium glutamate (MSG) can create excessive glutamate expression. Avoid products with "natural flavors" or "yeast," which may contain MSG • Bone broth, grass-fed whey, asparagus, and cabbage	• Pickle fermented red cabbage, (submerged in apple cider vinegar and kept at room temperature for 3 to 5 days, then stored in fridge), used as a glutamine- and probiotic-rich condiment
Supplement to consider	• L-glutamine can be supplemented as an amino acid alone if dealing with muscle recovery and mental health symptoms only; however, if dealing with leaky gut and food sensitivity, look for a formula providing 2–5g of L-glutamine paired with mucilaginous herbs, such as DGL and aloe in the GI Lining Support.	

Balancing Out the Complex Symphony in Your Brain

Excess or deficiency in any one neurotransmitter can lead to the paralyzing effects of anxiety, and even a borderline imbalance can drive panic and racing thoughts. So, how to address this spectrum and support without overshooting?

The first place to start on a foundational level is meeting your ideal protein range and providing your body with probiotics. Note: If probiotics are not tolerated, it is strongly recommended to do a gut bacteria reset cleanse as discussed in Chapter 3. On a supplemental level, I recommend starting with addressing the neurotransmitters. Adaptogens and nervines (discussed in Chapter 6), a quality B vitamin, and the anti-anxiety diet protocol is truly the safest, most broad focus of approach for successful outcomes in establishing a mellow, balanced mood and mind. The one amino acid I do recommend supplementing with for neurotransmitter support across the board is L-theanine.

L-Theanine: The Balancing Block for Your Brain

Found in matcha, or powdered green tea, L-theanine is a modulator for the brain's neurotransmitters, aiding in balancing out both excess and deficiency. As it doesn't drive one pathway, its effects are tonifying to the system, with limited risk, and safe with medication use. L-theanine does cross the blood-brain barrier and can influence the central nervous system by enhancing levels of dopamine, GABA, and serotonin; however, L-theanine effects are balancing and won't overproduce one given neurotransmitter. Beyond its role in enhancing the relaxing and rewarding neurotransmitters in the brain, L-theanine can increase alpha brain waves which are elevated during deep meditation, artistic and creative expression, relaxation, and REM cycles of sleep. Interestingly enough, L-theanine also enhances focus, so it can provide clarity and concentration without agitation or anxiety while preventing drowsiness. In research, L-theanine supplementation has been shown to reduce secretory IgA, which is associated with stress response and leaky gut.

Matcha as Medicine?

Matcha is a powdered form of a Japanese green tea that is grown in shade to increase certain properties and make the taste more smooth with a less astringent aftertaste. Because the ground powder of the entire tea leaf is wholly consumed rather than steeping the leaf and discarding, matcha allows for about 10 times the nutritional boost. The use of shade in the growing process increases production of caffeine and L-theanine, and together they generate steady energy without the jitters or crash associated with caffeine in coffee and other energy drinks.

Matcha can be very supportive of adrenal function for stress response. It provides a pick-me-up with caffeine to stimulate and support healthy mood, while delivering the L-theanine to regulate stress hormones. It also aids in balance, while providing antioxidant EGCG and chlorophyll to fight against cellular damage, aging, and free radicals in the body. Basically, it can fuel productivity and a feel-good buzz without the burnout of a stimulant! The phytocompounds in matcha aid in detoxifying the body and reducing free radicals, which can prevent heart disease and cancer while supporting healthy blood pressure. As matcha can aid in fat burn, it can also improve insulin resistance, which can promote stabilized blood sugar, prevent diabetes, and further enhance mood stability.

How Much Is Enough?

One teaspoon per 6 ounces of hot water is deemed a cup of matcha, which is equivalent to about 10 cups of green tea. Research studies support benefits from green tea at 2 to 3 cups per day, so a serving of 1 cup of matcha or a teaspoon in other fun recipes is an ample dose of this powerful prescription.

Matcha has no calories yet provides:

- EGCG catechins, which aid in metabolism
- Chlorophyll to aid in detoxification and antioxidant function
- Caffeine, a natural stimulant and antidepressant
- L-theanine to aid as a natural relaxant while promoting optimal cognitive function

CAN YOU TEST YOUR NEUROTRANSMITTER LEVELS?

Symptoms of neurotransmitter imbalance can often overlap from one chemical imbalance to another—both excess and deficiency of one compound can cause anxiety. In my clinic, we use a Medical System/Toxicity Questionnaire (MSQ) in pre-appointment forms, then walk through a series of screening questions on how stress response is seen in the body and how anxiety is experienced. When an individual is struggling with significant chronic anxiety or mood imbalance, I will often order a urinary neurotransmitter assessment in combination with assessments of salivary cortisol and hormones.

Studies have demonstrated that specific blood-brain barrier transporters carry neurotransmitters intact from the CNS out to the peripheral tissues, where they are then filtered by the kidneys into urine. Also, animal studies have shown a relationship between presence and level of neurotransmitters in urine to levels in the CNS.

I then use foundational information from the MSQ and initial consultation screening and tie in clinical trends with neurotransmitter imbalance when developing interventions. It is always important to marry the expressed symptoms with lab values when supporting the brain and body.

Other Considerations to Rebalance your Neurotransmitters

Taurine is an amino acid compound made from cysteine, a potent contributor to the detox process and a building block of glutathione. Taurine also contains sulfur and has calming, relaxing properties, functioning as an inhibitory neurotransmitter on both glycine and GABA signaling pathways. Taurine also regulates the conversion of glutamate to GABA. It has diuretic effects, aiding with fluid retention and supporting liver function with bile production to lower excessive estrogen and cholesterol in the body.

Recommended dosage: 500 to 2000 milligrams/day, taken without food, to support anxiety, mood, sleep, and liver function.

Inositol is often not recognized as a B vitamin, but this extended cousin sometimes referred to as B8 has strong stress- and anxiety-managing properties. Similar to choline, inositol has a role in cell membrane function, hormone regulation, and metabolism of fat. As an anxiolytic, inositol aids in mobilizing serotonin signaling and supporting GABA receptor function. Inositol is one of the safest anti-anxiety supplements, along with magnesium, which is why it is featured in my foundational formula, Relax and Regulate. Be mindful when selecting a magnesium and inositol blend that the magnesium is in the form of bis-glycinate, which is more neuro-muscular-focused and absorbable. Beyond mood stability, inositol is well-acknowledged for its ability to aid in insulin sensitivity and hormone regulation with PCOS, thus serving as a great tool for women's health and optimizing fertility. Inositol balances neurotransmitter function versus driving one pathway. Its effects can produce clear cognition, an ability to release racing thoughts, an ability to find a relaxed state at times of stress, and an overall elevated mood.

Recommended dosage: 4 to 12 grams/day.

Melatonin is a hormone regulated by the brain that plays a role with circadian rhythm and sleep cycles. Melatonin levels rise in the evening and reduce in the daytime. Sleeping in a dim lit room or overexposure to electronics can interfere with melatonin production. Known for its role with insomnia and jet lag, melatonin has been used as a supplement for years. However, many do not make the connection that melatonin is produced from serotonin and, thus, made from serotonin's building block, tryptophan. There is a chicken-egg relationship with anxiety and insomnia as racing thoughts can interfere with winding down and falling asleep, and then, a poor night's sleep can reduce GABA and serotonin function driving, more racing thoughts. Use of melatonin to provide a good night's sleep can aid in resetting stress response and reducing stress hormones. Research has now found that melatonin can act as a mood stabilizer, allowing higher levels of serotonin to circulate in the brain.

Recommended dosage: 1 to 3 grams taken at bed, best paired with other nervines as herbal relaxants, such as valerian, skullcap, and passion flower.

Carnitine is an amino acid that functions as a brain booster by enhancing levels of norepinephrine and serotonin. This compound can be used for chronic fatigue and weight-loss support, as it can boost the body's ability to use fat as fuel as well as metabolize fats into energy via the carnitine shuttle.

Recommended dosage: 1 to 4 grams per day.

CBD, or cannabidiol, the non-psychoactive component in cannabis, is making a name in the world of anxiolytics now that it is legal in the United States. When isolated from THC, the psychotropic component that gets you high, CBD holds the power to favorably influence CB1 and CB2 receptors for mood, inflammation, and immune support. Evidence strongly supports CBD as a tool for anxiety ranging from generalized anxiety disorder, panic disorder, social anxiety disorder, obsessive-compulsive disorder, and post-traumatic stress disorder. The endocannabinoid is the largest neurotransmitter system of the body, with endocannabinoids as the highest expressed compounds beyond that of serotonin, GABA, norepinephrine, and dopamine! As an anti-anxiety supplement, CBD is an exciting addition with effects that are still being discovered. Prior funding issues arose surrounding the legality of the controversial compound from which it is expressed.

CBD dosing is difficult to recommend, as it is still so new in clinical experimentation and research. Also, there is a suggested bell curve at which efficacy is seen and then tops off and becomes ineffective. Dosing instructions include consideration of the constituent formula and delivery as a capsule, tincture, or inhalant.

Food as Medicine to Rebalance Your Neurotransmitters

Achieving protein intake to your goal range (page 126) will be the first focus to provide support for neurotransmitter balance. Amino acids serve as neurotransmitter building blocks, and B vitamins serve as cofactors or activators to neurotransmitter action. Get a good dosage of B vitamins along with meeting your protein needs by selecting dark poultry (which is more nutrient rich as opposed to white meat), grass-fed meats, fish, and eggs. The featured recipes in this section provide tryptophan, tyrosine, and antioxidants to protect cells from damage, supporting optimal cellular communication. Work to incorporate matcha into your diet for the balancing influence of L-theanine, and try blending it into a green smoothie. Crunch on salty seaweed for a thyroid-supporting boost of tyrosine, providing bliss expression in the brain. Use nuts and seeds to maintain satiety and gain the support of fats, fiber, and antioxidants to balance mood and hormones.

Rebalance Your Neurotransmitters

❖ *Pumpkin Nut and Seed Bars, page 200*

❖ *Matcha Green Smoothie, page 207*

❖ *Roasted Almonds with Nori and Sesame, page 215*

❖ *Seaweed Turkey Roll-Ups, page 233*

❖ *Sweet and Sour Pork Meatballs, page 235*

❖ *Mediterranean Tuna Salad, page 237*

❖ *Truffled Egg Salad, page 238*

CHAPTER 8

Applying the Anti-Anxiety Diet

Applying the anti-anxiety diet includes a jumpstart into anti-inflammatory eating focused on reducing carbohydrates, ensuring ample amounts of biological protein, and providing an abundance of healthy, brain-supporting fats. The anti-anxiety diet employs tenets of each of the 6 Foundational Rs, focusing on removing inflammatory foods, resetting your gut microbiome, repairing your GI lining, restoring your micronutrient status, rebounding your adrenals, and rebalancing your neurotransmitters.

The program kicks off with ketosis, a very-low-carbohydrate approach to eating that promotes the production of ketones to reduce anxiety and promote grounding mental stability. As you've learned, carbohydrates are broken down to glucose, and sugar fuels imbalanced bacteria, so this will be an optimal time to plow the fields of your gut microbiome and reset your GI tract for healthy bacterial balance! Be sure to take the Gut Bacteria Balance Quiz (page 47), and if your score exceeds 15, consider the gut reset protocol discussed in Chapter 3. If your gut bacteria is not a contributor to your anxiety, you will not need to remove probiotic foods or take the antibacterial and antifungal supplements; however, you may consider consuming one probiotic-rich food per day immediately to aid in maintaining optimal balance.

For 12 weeks, your diet will be free of grains, refined carbohydrates, gluten, corn, soy, sugar, and dairy to balance blood sugar levels and support a more even-keeled mood and energy level. During the first six weeks, it is recommended to stick to Phase 1, ketogenic eating, where you will reduce total carbohydrate intake to 30 grams per day via residual carbs in your non-starchy vegetables and healthy fats. As an example, half an avocado has 6 to 8 grams of carbs, so as you can see, this 30 grams can add up quickly! To stick within the 30-gram limitations, in Phase 1 you will be eliminating all starchy vegetables, legumes, and fruits. After a couple days of this restriction, your body will be forced to manufacture ketones as an alternative energy source to glucose or blood sugar.

As mentioned in Chapter 7, the anti-anxiety diet should be predominantly fat (>50 percent), followed by protein (15 to 30 percent), and moderate carbs (5 to 20 percent) as a baseline. The more aggressive ketogenic phase, Phase 1, will be 70 to 85 percent fat, 15 to 20 percent protein, and 5 to 10 percent carbs.

Understanding Macronutrients

All foods are broken down into carbohydrates, proteins, and fats—these nutrient categories are collectively known as macronutrients. Foods have varied metabolic effects based on the distribution of these categories. Macronutrient ranges can be recommended based on gram or percent calorie distribution.

Carbs

The anti-anxiety diet focuses primarily on restricting carbohydrates to regulate blood sugar levels, reducing spikes of highs or drops of lows, and in the case of Phase 1, reducing carbohydrates further to induce ketosis and support a bacteria cleanse if warranted.

Protein

Protein ranges are emphasized in Chapter 7 where a protein equation is provided to determine levels of individual need. Generally, protein intake is moderate in the anti-anxiety diet, focusing on providing ample amounts needed for neurotransmitter production yet preventing excess, which can drive cortisol release.

Fats

Fats provide the majority of calories in both phases of the anti-anxiety diet. It aids in neurological function, which supports the signaling of neurotransmitters, adrenals (reducing stress), leptin, and sexual hormone reset, and when paired with fibers of a whole foods–based diet, fat provides beneficial bacterial activity. Fats also provide a sustained source of energy and fuel typically experienced as a grounding sense of energy and emotional state.

Calories

This is not a weight-loss plan, so caloric ranges will not be recommended. However, distribution of macros tends to yield more successful changes metabolically when choosing to restrict calories below metabolic output. In up-to-date research, we know people are more of a complex chemistry equation than a simple calculator, so calories in and calories out alone will not yield body composition change. However, a low-glycemic diet leads to muscle-sparing benefits, which aid in metabolic rate increasing caloric burn and supporting optimal metabolism required for weight loss and sustainable maintenance. I often categorize weight loss as a pleasant "side effect" of participating in the anti-anxiety diet program, as mood stability, sleep, and cognition improve along with the shifts in microbiome, reduced inflammation, and restored nutrient status. On top of this, the body sheds excessive body fat, providing favorable composition change. Feeling good in your body and toned or more fit can have a beneficial influence on mood stability with improved confidence and self-worth, which further supports the lifestyle change.

Use the Exchange List on page 262 to aid in navigating serving sizes of particular foods to achieve recommended macronutrient ranges, whether in Phase 1 or Phase 2 of the anti-anxiety diet.

Two-Week Preparation Phase: Cleaning Up and Getting Set!

Prior to starting the diet, it is recommended to kick off with two weeks of removal. This will transition the body and brain by reducing inflammation and regulating blood sugar balance. If you are already coming from a paleo or grain-free, processed-food-free diet, you may decide to jump right into the ketosis Phase 1 plan. But if you are coming from a diet that includes breads, pasta, and ice cream, it is recommended to first remove the five inflammatory foods (see page 20), and then, once those refined carbs and irritants are eliminated, to start to correct blood sugar imbalances and provide more nourishing substitutions. Once you have started to make these shifts, at two weeks in, your body will better be able to handle the stricter ketogenic protocol.

Anti-Anxiety Diet Guidelines

• Eat real foods in their most whole, unprocessed form.

• Aim for organic or local and sustainable whenever possible.

- Prioritize removing the Environmental Working Group's list of the most pesticide-laden items, the Dirty Dozen Plus (see page 266).

- Consume 2 to 3 cups of leafy greens daily.

- Select from a variety of seasonal produce, ideally in wild or heirloom varieties, such as rainbow chard, mizuna, dandelion greens, lacinato kale, etc. Also, consider sprouts as a nutrient-dense option—⅛ cup is equivalent to 1 cup of greens!

- Prioritize fats as the highest contributor in macros. This goes for both Phase 1 and Phase 2 of your anti-anxiety diet, with healthy fats driving the caloric distribution.

- Consume protein in all meals. Use the calculator of your protein needs on page 126 to determine your daily total.

- Get four to five colors on your plate throughout the day. This is one way to ensure full-spectrum antioxidant coverage and a variety of vitamins and minerals!

- Have a cultured food at least four times per week. This includes ⅛ cup of cultured vegetables such as kraut, kimchi, or pickles, 4 to 6 ounces of kombucha, and 6 ounces of homemade coconut yogurt.

- Aim to have 6 to 8 ounces of bone broth four times per week. This can be used as a sipped beverage in the evening or in the base of soups, stews, or as a liquid to aid in braising and sautéing.

- Eat in a relaxed state focused on nourishment with silence, music, or conversation. No screens, working, or driving during meal time. Focus on breath and getting into rest-and-digest mode at meal times to promote digestive enzyme release and optimize absorption of nutrients and reduce gastric stress.

- Listen to signs of physical hunger and don't eat if you aren't hungry. *Hara hachi bu* is a Confucian phrase that translates to "Eat until only 80 percent full." It is used by the Okinawan people who are said to be the longest lived (upward of age 100), healthiest, and happiest people on the planet. Stop before you get full to prevent distress to the digestive tract and engage in mindless overeating.

Phase 1: Ketogenic Protocol

- In ketosis, carbohydrate choices come from residual carbs in non-starchy vegetables, avocados, nuts, and seeds.

- Reduce total carbohydrate intake to 30 grams per day. This means no fruit or starchy vegetables; be mindful of carbohydrate-containing foods.

- Follow for weeks 1 through 6 at minimum! You may follow for weeks 1 through 12+.

Macronutrient % distribution:

- 5 to 10% carbs

- 15 to 30% protein

- 60 to 75% fat

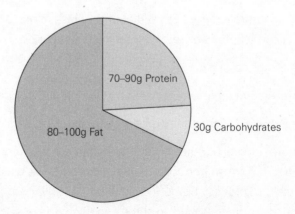

70–90g Protein

80–100g Fat

30g Carbohydrates

Ketosis macronutrient distribution in Phase 1 (relative gram amount is based on a 1200–1400-calorie diet)

During your ketogenic Phase 1 it is important to ensure electrolyte stability. When reducing carbohydrates to less than 30 grams per day, the body will experience a shift in fluid status and thus electrolytes, which are carried with water. The body tends to wring out this excess fluid in the first three to five days of ketosis, which is where many people experience increased urinary output and a whoosh of weight loss on the scale. This will recalibrate over time, but it is important to assist your body during the transition and ensure optimal hydration and electrolyte support.

If you are not looking to lose weight, it is possible to maintain a healthy weight and even gain weight if needed while implementing the ketogenic diet. Often, malnourishment is due to a state of gut distress along with foods that lack nutrient density, both of which are addressed with the anti-anxiety diet.

Who Should Not Do Phase 1?

Depending on where you are with your current diet and your medications, a ketogenic diet may be too drastic and you may choose to stay within the low-glycemic Phase 2 protocol to kick off your anti-anxiety diet. Do not do Phase 1 if you fall under any of the following:

• Uncontrolled medicated diabetic, unless managed with a certified diabetes educator or medical practitioner

• History of eating disorder

• Pregnant, unless monitored by OBGYN and pregnancy team

• Adrenal fatigue that worsens with diet

Note: If the adrenal output is extremely low, you will not have DHEA, a stress hormone made by the adrenals used in the production of ketones. Some individuals with advanced adrenal fatigue need to practice two to three months of Phase 2 eating prior to implementing Phase 1 and may need to supplement with adrenal compound or DHEA.

If adrenal excess is seen, ketosis is a great tool to regulate the elevated DHEA and neurotransmitters to support a rapid reduction in anxiety, as long as it is paired with adaptogenic herbs for resilience to avoid burn out.

Phase 2: Low-Glycemic Protocol

Follow for weeks 7+, to intermittently to cycle out of ketosis, or ongoing according to need.

Macronutrient % distribution:

- 15–25% carbs
- 25–35% protein
- 40–60% fat

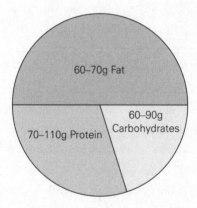

(Relative gram amount is based on a 1200–1400-calorie diet)

If using a tracker or application such as MyFitnessPal, you can enter these macro percentages and then, based on your weight, the program will provide gram recommendations per macro.

Note: Carbs and protein are 4 calories per gram, whereas fat is 9 calories per gram, so you may be fat dominant in macros percent by caloric distribution but the numbers in grams of protein and fat may be closer to equal value.

After six weeks of tight ketosis and allowing your body to convert fat as fuel instead of sugar, you will have an opportunity to transition or intermittently cycle the less-restrictive Phase 2, which is low-glycemic with an upper limit of 90 grams of carbs. It is appropriate to fully transition to Phase 2 if you are feeling low energy on Phase 1 or if you are having unfavorable weight loss or symptom shifts.

In Phase 2, choose carbohydrates in the form of fruits and starchy vegetables to provide dietary variety, beneficial fibers, support of serotonin expression, and a reset in leptin response. Phase 2 eating is one approach to carb cycling while maintaining ketosis the majority of the time. Carb cycling may be done in times of progesterone shifts to offset the physiological hormone demand for a cycling female or once a week or every other week on a Saturday to create a sustainable approach and more social freedom. Favorable effects such as improved ketone production, hormone balance, and reduced stress response can be seen when cycling carbs after becoming adapted to using fat as your primary fuel. If you notice a decline in your progress when you transition to Phase 2, you may consider going back to Phase 1 for an additional four to six weeks prior to advancing again, if desired. Phase 2, low-glycemic eating, can also be done cyclically every quarter or so, where an individual does a ketogenic phase 1 diet for 10–12 weeks and a phase 2 low-glycemic diet for 7–10 days. Interestingly enough, once you get keto-adapted, many people feel so fantastic they choose to stay fat-fueled and don't look back; however, others thrive with this approach of flexibility and see metabolic and hormonal benefits from cycling the two phases.

If you experienced beneficial mood-stabilizing outcomes from the Phase 1 ketogenic approach, consider holding off on transitioning to Phase 2. Men and some women are able to stay in Phase 1 for extended periods of time and continue to reap the benefits; however, often, women, due to hormonal demands, will over time get imbalances in leptin hormone response and, thus, sexual hormone dysfunction. When cycling carbs, the starchy vegetable or fruit choice should be consumed in the evening to enhance serotonin and melatonin function in the brain.

For women who are menstruating, carb cycling (using Phase 2) should be considered at ovulation and menstruation (typically days 1 to 2 and days 17 to 18 of their cycle) to support hormonal influences on mood, cravings, anxiety influence.

There is no right or wrong approach to this. You may notice you feel better in ketosis during certain seasons, levels of stress demand, variance in exercise output, and lifecycle demands, whereas there will be other times when maintaining low-glycemic Phase 2 lifestyle feels appropriate. Listen to your body and remember, if you hold virtue and rigidity as priorities in your diet, you will often fall off or get disconnected with your body. One of the mantras I use in clinic with clients when recalling the downslide of my vegan diet on my body is, "Doctrine creates Disconnect." If you allow principle to override intuition, you will likely not get favorable outcomes or sustainable results.

The most important thing to understand is that your body is healing and it is dynamic. Be sure to listen to feedback from your body during the process and adjust as needed. Resist getting dogmatic with macros, following inflexible guidelines on numbers and percentages. Focus on the primary tenets of the anti-anxiety diet by using food lists, recipes, and food-as-medicine support as priorities to yield best outcomes. Then, if wanting to get more aggressive, play with Phase 1 and Phase 2 variances. The recipes in this book are indexed as KF, or ketosis friendly, if they are supportive of the ketogenic diet.

When transitioning into ketosis, you may experience symptoms of the "keto flu," a collection of flu-like symptoms including headaches, body aches, bowel impact, and fatigue. Both the Anti-Inflammatory Electrolyte Elixir (page 204) and the Electrolyte-Boosting Avocado with a Spoon (page 209) recipes will help ameliorate these undesired side effects when transitioning into a very low carbohydrate diet. Once the body converts to the use of ketones as a primary fuel source, these symptoms of the keto flu resolve.

Carbohydrate-Containing Foods

These foods are only allowed at portions noted below in Phase 2. The carbohydrate items in this section will raise your blood sugar levels and are not appropriate in the ketogenic diet as focused foods; however, you may be able to incorporate small amounts in featured recipes as long as your daily total carbohydrate intake stays below 30g. For blood sugar balance and optimal satiety, be sure to pair them with a protein or healthy fat.

Each serving from this list contains 15 grams of carbohydrates and 80 calories. Aim to select items that are single ingredient whole foods. Focus primarily on starchy vegetables and fruits. Soak beans and grains to limit phytates, lectins, and other inflammatory antinutrients. Avoid refined processed foods and starches made with flour at all costs, along with gluten-containing grains and their products. Nut flours such as almond flour, hazelnut meal, and coconut flour are acceptable in larger portions than in they are in the Phase 1 ketogenic protocol and continue as the preferred "flour" choice.

Starchy Vegetables

In general, a single serving of starchy vegetables is ½ cup unless noted.

• Beets

• Carrots (look for heirloom purple and rainbow carrots)

• Parsnips

• Plantain, ripe: ⅓ cup

• Potato (purple, red, Yukon Gold, heirloom)

• Pumpkin: 1 cup puree, or almost 2 cups chopped

• Sweet potato

• Taro root

• Winter squash (acorn, butternut, delicata)

• Yam

• Yucca: ⅓ cup

Fruit

Avoid canned fruit and fruit juices. In general, a single serving of fruit is as follows:

• ½ cup of fresh, unsweetened fruit (such as berries) or 1 small piece of fruit (such as an apple)

• 2 tablespoons of dried (organic, sulfite-free) fruit

• Apple: 1 medium

• Applesauce: ½ cup

- Apricots: 3 medium
- Banana: ½ medium (about 3 inches long)
- Blackberries: ½ cup
- Blueberries: ½ cup
- Cantaloupe: 1 cup
- Cherries: 15
- Dates: 2
- Figs: 2
- Grapefruit: ½
- Grapes: 15 small
- Guava: ½ cup
- Honeydew: 1/4 small
- Kiwi: 1
- Mango: ½ small
- Orange: 1 small
- Papaya: ½
- Peaches: 2 small
- Pear: 1 small
- Pineapple: 3/4 cup
- Plums: 2 small
- Pomegranate: 1 medium
- Raspberries: ½ cup
- Strawberries: 1 cup
- Tangerines: 2 small
- Watermelon: 2 cups

Once you have completed the first 12 weeks of the anti-anxiety diet program, your gut may be in a state of resilience where it can tolerate the occasional consumption of grains, beans, and dairy. To ensure you are nonreactive, follow the elimination diet reintroduction guidelines on page 32. Even if tolerated, try to limit grains and beans as occasional sides due to lectins and other inflammatory digestive disturbing compounds. Soaking both grains and beans aids in reducing the anti-nutrients and binding compounds that block mineral and vitamin absorption. When soaking, there is an enzyme activation and many of the common irritants are reduced.

Cereal and Grains (Presoaked 8 to 12 hours)

In general, a single serving of cooked grain is ⅓ cup.

• Amaranth

• Buckwheat

• Rice (basmati, brown, wild)

• Millet

• Teff

• Quinoa

Beans, Pea, Lentils (Presoaked 8 to 12 hours)

In general, a serving size of cooked beans is ½ cup.

• Beans: black, cannellini, chickpeas, kidney, lima, navy, pinto, white

• Lentils: brown, green, yellow, red

• Peas: black-eyed, split

Using kombu, a seaweed found in the Asian section of your grocery store, in your cooking process aids in further reduction of phytates, which not only enhances mineral and vitamin absorption but also reduces the gas and bloating that can follow bean consumption.

Dairy

As a liquid, lactose has carbs. Cheeses are also listed under this section, but you should keep them out for at least three months of your anti-anxiety diet, as they tend to be the most concentrated in casein, the protein of concern for mental health. Once you reach the 12+ week mark, your gut lining is likely more resilient, so it may be appropriate to test the reintroduction of cheese. As you may recall from Chapter 2, dairy intolerance is tied to both lack of enzyme lactase as well as low stomach acid with excessive stress or use of PPI. Consider taking a digestive enzyme with lactase, HCl- to support stomach pH, and DPPIV to reduce the casein hit. See the Appendix's Supplement Support for the 6 Foundational Rs section for detailed suggestions.

Follow guidelines in Chapter 2 on elimination reintroduction by consuming cheese three days in a row, increasing the portion per day. Observe shifts in sleep, cognitive function, mood, energy, thought processing, and anxiety. For example, consume 1 ounce, 2 ounces, then 3 ounces, increasing the serving size each day.

In general, a single serving of dairy is as follows:

- Cream cheese: 1 tablespoon

- Cultured sour cream: 2 tablespoons

- Hard/semi-hard cheeses (best raw/aged), such as blue, cheddar, Colby Jack, Gouda, Monterey Jack, Parmesan, Reggiano, Swiss: 1 ounce

- Heavy cream: 2 tablespoons

- Kefir, unsweetened: 1 cup

- Milk, raw or non-homogenized, pasture-raised/grass-fed, whole fat: 1 cup

- Soft/semi-soft cheeses, such as boursin, Brie, Colby, fresh mozzarella, paneer, ricotta: 1 ounce

- Yogurt, plain or Greek, whole fat: 2/3 cup

- Grass-fed whey: 1 scoop or 2 tablespoon, yielding around 20–24g protein

2-Week Meal Plan

Here is a 2-week meal plan providing structure and guidelines to help you visualize and bring your food-as-medicine anti-anxiety diet to life. Phase 1: Ketogenic Protocol falls within the guidelines to consume less than 30 grams of carbs to support ketone production, and Phase 2: Low-Glycemic Protocol, falls within a more liberal approach of less than 90 grams of carbohydrates.

Portions are noted to distribute macronutrients within their given category of protein, carbs, and fats; however, based on individual need you may increase or reduce these portions for your body weight, physical activity, true hunger, and need.

Phase 1: Ketogenic Protocol (7 Days)

Day 1

7:30 a.m.   2 eggs, ½ cup bell peppers, ¼ cup sautéed onion, 1 cup baby spinach, cooked in 1 to 2 teaspoons coconut oil, topped with ½ avocado

10 a.m.   10 roasted macadamia nuts with 2 tablespoons shredded coconut flakes. (Try freezing the nuts for a creamy indulgence that slows down the crunching!)

2 p.m.	4 to 5 ounces roasted chicken pulled from rotisserie, 5 olives, ½ cucumber, sliced, 3 tablespoons Cashew Cheeze Dip (page 218), 6 flax crackers
7 p.m.	5 ounces wild salmon cooked with 1 to 2 teaspoons avocado oil and topped with tarragon, served with 1 cup Asian Braised Bok Choy (page 216)

Day 2

7:45 a.m.	2 Caramelized Onion, Turkey, and Kale Egg Muffins (page 192)
12 p.m.	1 cup Whole Roasted Cauliflower (page 213) served over 2 cups greens tossed in 2 teaspoons each of lemon and olive oil, with one 4–7 ounces roasted chicken thigh
3 p.m.	1 ounce prosciutto with 13 Marcona almonds
7 p.m.	5 ounces sirloin steak with Bacteria-Battling Chimichurri (page 248), with 1 cup roasted yellow summer squash sautéed in 2 teaspoons olive oil and sprinkled with sea salt

Day 3

7:30 a.m.	Morning shake: ½ cup water, ½ cup full-fat coconut milk, 1 tablespoon almond butter, 2 teaspoons cacao powder, pinch of sea salt, 1 to 2 cups of greens, 2 scoops of collagen, and ice (optional)
10 a.m.	2 to 3 Walnut Maca Caramels (page 258)
1 p.m.	6 ounces grass-fed burger patty on lettuce wrap, with ½ avocado, ⅛ cup kimchi, and 1 cup kale chips
4 p.m.	6 ounces Gut-Restoring Chicken Bone Broth (page 223) with 1 tablespoon chopped mint or basil

7:30 p.m.   2 grilled wild shrimp kabobs with zucchini and red onion, ½ cup cauliflower rice served with ½ cup Roasted Colored Peppers (page 220)

Day 4

7:30 a.m.   3 ounces chicken sausage link, ¼ cup sautéed onion, ½ cup kale sautéed in 1 teaspoon coconut oil, served with ¼ cup live active sauerkraut

11:30 a.m.   8 ounces Grass-Fed Beef Knuckle Bone Broth (page 221) with 3 ounces wild cod, ½ small avocado, cubed, and 2 tablespoons scallions

3 p.m.   1 serving Matcha Coconut Gummies (page 261) + 5 to 6 raspberries

7:30 p.m.   1 serving Warming Chicken Thighs with Braised Greens (page 231)

Day 5

7:30 a.m.   2 pasture-raised eggs, 2 slices bacon, cherry tomatoes tossed in 1 teaspoon olive oil with basil, coarse salt, and black pepper

12 p.m.   1 serving Creamy Green Chile Chicken Soup (page 225) over 2 cups baby spinach

3 p.m.   2 to 3 Lime in the Coconut Fat Bomb (page 254) and 6 ounces low-sugar kombucha

7:30 p.m.   ½ cup purple cabbage slaw with 4 to 6 ounces white fish broiled with chili powder seasoning and 2 teaspoons avocado oil, topped with crushed almonds, 2 teaspoons herbs, served in lettuce cups

Day 6

7:30 a.m.	1 serving Stress-Stabilizing Steamer (page 205) with 1 scoop protein (grass-fed whey or collagen)
12 p.m.	2 to 3 Greek Deviled Eggs (page 210) over 2 cups spinach and arugula, with ¼ cup cultured probiotic vegetables
4 p.m.	3 stalks celery cut into 3- to 4-inch pieces, with 1 to 2 tablespoons tahini nut butter spread and ½ cup cherry tomatoes
7 p.m.	5 to 6 ounces Herb-Crusted Pork Tenderloin (page 239) with 1 cup roasted Brussels sprouts
9 p.m.	6 ounces bone broth plus 2 tablespoons cultured veggies such as kimchi, added after soup is removed from heat to retain probiotic cultures

Day 7

7:30 a.m.	2 Prosciutto Egg Cups (page 196) served with a simple arugula salad, seasoned with 1 teaspoon lemon, 1 teaspoon olive oil, coarse black pepper, and truffle salt
12 p.m.	1 to 2 servings Seaweed Turkey Roll-Ups (page 233) with 1 Pumpkin Nut and Seed Bar (page 200)
4 p.m.	½ avocado with juice of ½ lemon, pinch of sea salt, red pepper flakes (optional), and ½ orange bell pepper
7:30 p.m.	4 to 6 ounces Simple Salt and Pepper Scallops (page 249) over 1 cup spiralized zucchini "noodles" with pesto and ¼ cup blistered cherry tomatoes

Phase 2: Low-Glycemic Protocol (7 Days)

Day 1

7:30 a.m. 1 serving Coconut Chia Seed Pudding (page 255) with 1 scoop of protein (collagen or grass-fed whey) or 1 soft-boiled egg

11:45 a.m. 1 serving Truffled Egg Salad (page 238) in lettuce cups with 1 small piece fruit

4 p.m. 1 to 2 Mango Zen Fuego Nutballz (page 212), plus 6 ounces low-sugar kombucha

7:30 p.m. 1 serving Spaghetti Squash Bolognese (page 246) over 2 cups sautéed rainbow chard

Day 2

7:30 a.m. 1 serving Butternut and Brussels Breakfast Hash (page 190)

12 p.m. 1 serving Zesty Creamy Carrot Soup (page 227) with 4 ounces wild halibut baked in parchment with lemon slices

6 p.m. 1 serving grain-free Carnitas Burrito Bowl (page 244) over a bed of 2 to 3 cups leafy greens

9 p.m. 1 Chia Cherry Thumbprint Cookie (page 250)

Day 3

7:30 a.m. 1 serving Sweet Potato Avocado Toast (page 194)

11 a.m. 1 serving Quick Coconut Yogurt (page 198) topped with ½ cup berries and sprinkle of cinnamon

2 p.m. 1 serving Roasted Almonds with Nori and Sesame (page 215), plus 3 ounces roasted turkey

7:30 p.m.   1 serving Sweet and Sour Pork Meatballs (page 235) with 1 cup Roasted Colored Peppers (page 220)

Day 4

7 a.m.   1 serving Coconut No-Oatmeal (page 202) with organic berries

12 p.m.   4 to 5 ounces wild baked salmon with 1 cup of a variety of simple roasted veggies

4 p.m.   1 serving Citrus Burst Smoothie (page 208)

7:30 p.m.   2 to 3 cups greens and 4 ounces shredded rotisserie chicken, dressed with juice of ½ lime, 1 to 2 tablespoons cilantro, sprinkle of mineral salt, and 2 tablespoons Mellow Mama Dressing (page 219)

Day 5

7:30 a.m.   Paleo Pumpkin Protein Pancakes (page 199)

11 a.m.   4 to 5 ounces bunless grass-fed burger with ½ avocado, 2–3 tomato slices, ½ cup sweet potato wedges, and ¼ cup fermented pickles

2 p.m.   1 serving Turmeric Orange Gummies (page 260)

7:30 p.m.   1 serving Mediterranean Tuna Salad (page 237), served in avocado half over 2 cups mixed greens, with lemon juice, to taste

Day 6

9 a.m.   11 serving Matcha Green Smoothie (page 207) with 1 scoop protein (collagen or grass-fed whey)

1 p.m.   1 serving olive tapenade with 2 hard-boiled eggs, 6 to 8 flax crackers, ⅛ cup kimchi, and ½ cup each of bell peppers, jicama, and snap peas

6 p.m.	1 serving Almond Flour Chicken Piccata (page 240) with 1 cup roasted broccoli cooked with 1 teaspoon coconut oil and 1 clove crushed garlic
8 p.m.	1 serving Grain-Free Low-Carb Peanut Butter Cookies (page 256)

Day 7

7:30 a.m.	1 serving Smoked Wild Salmon Scramble (page 197) served over 2 cups of farmer's market mixed greens
12:30 p.m.	¼ cup guacamole with 8 to 10 plantain chips, ½ cucumber, sliced, 3 to 4 ounces shredded chicken, and 7 to 8 blackberries
6 p.m.	1 serving Naturally Nourished Pot Roast (page 229) with ½ cup sautéed mushrooms
9 p.m.	1 serving Chai Gelatin Panna Cotta (page 252)

Lifestyle Support

The recipes in *The Anti-Anxiety Diet* support your body, providing nourishment along with a functional approach targeted to aid in the remove, reset, repair, restore, rebound, and rebalance phases of mood stability and mental health. The variety in flavor profiles and textures will support sustained outcomes as you will find you can make an anti-anxiety diet alternative to any food craving! As you continue to explore new foods and flavors you will also discover you don't miss prior foods that were causing "yuck" in your body while driving anxiety or lack of clarity in your mind.

Remember, food as medicine is a double-edged sword where removal of inflammatory foods is equally as important as inclusion and abundance of therapeutic foods. Each Foundational R chapter provides a summary of food-as-medicine support. If Phase 1 and Phase 2 macro distribution is overwhelming at this time, start with adding an abundance of featured therapeutic ingredients into your diet, and start playing with the recipes in this book. You will experience the benefits of incorporating healthy fats, anti-inflammatory seasonings, and micronutrient-rich produce and proteins within days of consumption. Once you get rocking with abundance, you may feel more ready and empowered to firmly remove all ingredients suggested in Chapter 2. Then, once you have removed inflammatory foods and continue with nourishing your body and brain, you may decide to take things to the level of exploring ketogenic shifts in metabolism.

For some of you, the benefits of incorporating therapeutic foods will be enough. The tools of applying the anti-anxiety diet will ultimately be implemented in different ways for individuals based on need, ability, and outcomes. Be kind to yourself through the process, and when trying a suggestion, focus on giving yourself a minimum of a three- to four-week commitment to experience shifts in your anxiety level.

As your body is physiologically resetting from foundational drivers that cause anxiety, it is important to have support on what you can do now to accelerate outcome beyond nutrition and supplements. Below are primary lifestyle focuses to aid in anxiety reduction.

Download Drivers of Anxiety

Rumination or overthinking can drive racing thoughts and anxiety. Often, the doubting self will critique and question actions or blow events out of proportion, making the body feel paralyzed from action. When working with clients, I recommend they download, or write down, racing thoughts or patterns of rumination and then rework the script. This allows you to consciously confront the voice in your head that nags at your mind, and empowers you to rework the repeating phrase to something that makes you feel confident and at ease.

An example of this may be:

Download: "I'm not going to get better. I am so tired yet there is never enough time. I am never going to get ahead."

Rewrite: "I am taking steps to get done what is reasonable. I am healing and my body is working toward rebalance."

Surrender to the Flow

Beyond rumination, seeing things as doomed or extreme is another factor in anxiety that can throw day-to-day function off balance. When we mentally battle what needs to get done, such as daily tasks or commitments, it can build up and become overwhelming. The surrender-to-the-flow approach focuses on allowing what is and accepting what needs to be done.

An example of this may be as follows:

A woman working full time as a nurse in the hospital picks up extra shifts as she is getting her master's degree and planning a wedding.

She may get in her head, "I have so much to do; I never have time to get anything done. The last thing I want to do is dishes and laundry. I don't get to do what I want to do, ever. My life is out of my control."

This can be shifted with a surrender-to-the-flow approach: "I am empowering myself with a strong career. I choose this stress, and getting things done makes me feel accomplished." Then, put on your favorite music and channel your mellow while you rock out those dishes!

Reduce and Execute

Following up on surrendering to the flow, reduce pending to-dos; this aids specifically with reducing anticipatory anxiety. Regardless of what is on your to-do list, the more items you can knock out or complete, the more at ease you will feel. This can be applied in simple tasks like rinsing your plate immediately and putting it in the dishwasher, to placing your tennis shoes in your car to motivate walking.

Shawn Achor, author of *The Happiness Advantage*, identifies "the 20-second rule," or taking on 20-second actions that reduce energy toward a positive behavior, as a principle of happiness. For example, he references moving his guitar within arms' reach to practice more often. Also, I look at it as doing something such as putting an item away, writing something down, replacing, or refilling, as these actions can make day-to-day keep-up seem less overwhelming.

For those larger to-dos, taking a look at your list and scheduling pending items by date and time realistically will allow you to release what needs to be done until the day it will be done. It takes "what if" out and translates more to what is, releasing anticipatory anxiety. For instance, rather than worrying about everything that is on your plate, you can compartmentalize this and have an attack plan versus feeling unable to take it all on and paralyzing any action only to perpetuate anxiety!

Practice Mindfulness and Meditation

The mind can be like a wild stallion racing in chaos. Meditation and mindfulness can harness this stallion, aiding to induce deep relaxation from an anxiety state. Using visualization to focus racing thoughts, mantras to counteract mental chaos, or the varied forms of meditation, one can achieve inner peace and a silent space in the mind. These techniques are more powerful when applied proactively and will be a handy tool during times of acute anxiety or panic attack.

A meta-analysis at Johns Hopkins University found evidence that incorporating meditation can reduce anxiety, depression, and pain. Aim to incorporate mindfulness and meditation at least 30 minutes daily!

"Chaos demands our attention. It's like a bratty child, jealous of our peace. Chaos will do everything in its power to suck you in and keep your stress level high. With meditation, you can use the quietness of your mind to surround and subdue chaos. Let it go easily somewhere else, while you apply your energy to reaching out into the universe for answers. Let the answers come to you as easily as you let chaos go."
Source: Ram Das Foundation at ramdas.org

Find Your Breath

Rapid heart rate and shortness of breath are two of the most common physiological responses to anxiety. Interestingly enough, breath is one of the most powerful ways to control the autonomic nervous system, aiding in shifting you from the anxiety and driving sympathetic fight or flight to the parasympathetic relaxed state. Various techniques have been studied as effective, such as pranayamic breathing, which is calming breath in through the nose and out through the mouth, counting to three with inhale, and what some people call belly breathing or yoga breath. To accompany breath as a manager of anxiety during times of acute panic, often it is helpful to focus on purposefully creating tension in muscles of the body to then create more release with exhale, or counting heartbeats and trying to match with the breath.

In my clinic, I typically start with recommending Dr. Andrew Weil's 4-7-8 breathing. Using this type of conscious breath can harness the autonomic nervous system and reduce the vagus nerve excitatory output. Implementing even a few sets can shift your system back into your rest-and-digest parasympathetic balance, which is essential for reducing anxiety response and supporting your metabolic function and health. Two to three cycles should be enough to slow your heart rate, relax you, and create whole-body balance.

Follow these steps for 4-7-8 breathing:

- Close your mouth and inhale quietly through your nose to a mental count of four.

- Hold your breath for a count of seven.

- Exhale completely through your mouth, making a whoosh sound to a count of eight. The exhale should be audible.

According to Dr. Weil, this breathing exercise is a natural tranquilizer for the nervous system. He recommends doing 4-7-8- breathing twice daily at a minimum, and notes the more you practice, the more effective a tool it becomes. Using breath to harness the mind and slash anxiety is a tool that can gain power over time, unlike many drugs that may start as effective but lose their influence.

Get a Good Night's Sleep

One of the most powerful ways to support healthy mood and mind for anxiety reduction is getting quality sleep. In fact, sleep can benefit nearly all systems of the body, preventing adrenal burnout and supporting neurotransmitter function while reducing inflammation. When experiencing restful sleep, the brain gets enhanced neuroplasticity as the neurons of the brain get a chance to shut down and repair themselves or improve function. If you find yourself averaging less than seven hours a night, this will accumulate as sleep debt that can drive anxiety with brain fog, difficulty concentrating, irritability, and confusion.

Focus on setting up your daily routine to wind down with a sleep ritual. Stop screen time at least one hour prior to sleep and keep lights dim to support melatonin production. Consider taking time for journaling or meditation and mindfulness, along with practice of breath. Commit to get an average of seven to nine hours per night, and adjust your schedule to accommodate this need.

Drink Enough Water

Dehydration can cause a multitude of health concerns, and anxiety is no exception. Anxiety may not be driven by dehydration, but it can be exacerbated by it. Dehydration can cause rapid heart rate, dizziness, and shifts in blood pressure, which can make anxiety more expressed. Ample hydration can aid in neurological function, and thus, increasing your intake of water can influence neurotransmitters to favorably reduce anxiety. Also, practicing the healthy habit of drinking water can allow you to take a moment to slow down and process when in social or work situations.

Get at least half of your body weight in pounds as the number of fluid ounces of intake per day, and regardless of weight, drink a minimum of 75 fluid ounces.

Example: A 180-pound person needs at least 90 fluid ounces of water per day.

Move Your Body

Walking while talking to a friend or listening to a podcast is a great way to distract the mind from worry or anxiety-driving self-talk. Movement stimulates blood flow, which helps deliver nutrients throughout the body, relax the vessels, and relax mussels while supporting breath. These benefits can be seen with all forms of exercise, but I love to recommend walking outside where the mind can take in nature's beauty while smells, sounds, and touch can distract the brain from anxious thoughts. Being outside also provides exposure to sun, which can boost vitamin D production in the body as a hormonal supporter of mood and inflammatory regulation.

If you prefer to have a phone conversation or walk with a buddy, this would be beneficial as well, as talking can enhance trust and openness, relieving pent-up energy that will drive anxiety if not released.

When focusing on exercise, I like to use the term gentle movement therapy, defined as walking, yoga, Pilates, stretch, and mild strengthening, as I don't like to provoke stress response to the body and burning out the adrenal glands. There are also benefits to more high-energy output such as dancing, resistance, spin, CrossFit, and HIIT training due to the release of endorphins. Higher output typically drives increased endorphins, which interact with the brain to reduce pain perception, allowing physiological performance at a state of distress. The endorphins released have mood-stabilizing, feel-good properties that can ward off anxiety and give a feeling of bliss. Exercise in all forms can reduce anxiety via modulation of the HPA-axis, release of endorphins, and increase of low levels of brain-derived neurotrophic factor.

Mechanisms of the benefits of exercise are broad and multifactorial. Beyond the chemical and physiological effects, the simple distraction of movement with focused energy can be a great tool for managing anxiety. Aim to incorporate 30 to 60 minutes of movement every day.

Closing

From inflammation in your gut to imbalances in your body's stress axis and beyond, anxiety can be a complex web where the root cause can produce vicious cycles if not addressed. Use the quizzes and popouts in this book to prioritize the greatest area of focus for the foundational root of anxiety in your body. Based on symptoms and scoring, you may consider one to two advanced labs to assess your body's needs on a clinical level. Using the Appendix's Supplement Support for the 6 Foundational Rs section, follow guidance based on your scoring and symptoms of need. You may be a candidate for three to six foundational formulas to start resetting your system and accelerate outcomes as you apply the anti-anxiety diet.

Recipes in this book will support each foundational R and can be used regardless of your anxiety area of focus; however, it is recommended to include the recipes or therapeutic ingredients in your primary root cause R of focus, three to four times per week. Start to break free of the vicious cycle of anxiety by eating positive nutrients in abundance and start to implement lifestyle support as a layering effect. Take the time to prioritize self-care and apply the information in this book into your daily life to free yourself from anxiety for good!

CHAPTER 9

Recipes

The recipes of the anti-anxiety diet are organized into the format of a traditional cookbook, starting with breakfasts and ending with desserts. Each recipe falls within the guidelines of the anti-anxiety diet for removal of inflammatory foods, providing strategic nutrients to replete deficiency and rebalance neurotransmitters as well as ingredients to repair gut lining and rebound adrenal gland function h a high-fat, low-glycemic approach.

All recipes featured are gluten-free, corn-free, soy-free, and sugar-free. Look for tags identifying recipes that fall within the Phase 1 ketogenic guidelines as well as potential allergens or irritants:

(**kf**) ketosis-friendly for the Phase 1 ketogenic guidelines

(**gf**) grain-free

(**df**) dairy-free

(**nf**) nut-free

(**ef**) egg-free

Finally, each recipe will be tagged with its primary therapeutic focus, representing one of the 6 Foundational Rs of the anti-anxiety diet. Note that there is synergistic overlap of many recipes, so you may get benefits of two or three different Rs of focus when consuming a recipe in one category.

Build from the ingredients featured in these recipes, pairing them with new ingredients of focus from the Anti-Anxiety Diet Grocery List on page 266 and the Exchange List on page 262 to provide sustainable variety.

THE 6 FOUNDATIONAL RS OF THE ANTI-ANXIETY DIET

remove	Remove Inflammatory Foods
reset	Reset Gut Microbiome
repair	Repair GI Lining
restore	Restore Micronutrient Status
rebound	Rebound Your Adrenal Glands
rebalance	Rebalance Your Neurotransmitters

View the 2-Week Meal Plan (page 173) to envision a layout of how these recipes could look in a typical week. For smoothies and beverages, there will be an option to add protein to provide as a meal replacement or to provide daily amino acid need. Grass-fed whey has the most bioavailable amino acids and, if tolerated, as a casein-free form of dairy, is recommended. Collagen or gelatin as alternates provide protein and gut support as further discussed in Chapter 4, but are less known for their bioavailability of amino acids.

Breakfasts

Butternut and Brussels Breakfast Hash

FOOD AS MEDICINE   Butternut squash is one of the richest serotonin foods, providing 398mg serotonin per 100g of squash! This mood-stabilizing starch paired with detox-supporting Brussels sprouts makes for an amazing start to the day. Sulforaphane compounds in Brussels sprouts are known to promote anti-inflammatory activity in the cardiovascular system and help repair any damage in the blood vessels. The body is able to use the sulfur to bind with toxic substances and remove them from the body. Sprouts also provide antioxidants such as vitamin C and beta-carotene, which help bind oxidized substances and prevent them from causing damage. Brussels sprouts are also a good source nutrients such as folate, manganese, potassium, phosphorus and omega-3 fatty acids.

restore   (gf) (df) (nf)

Makes: 2 servings   *Prep time:* 10 to 15 minutes   *Cook time:* 30 to 40 minutes

4 slices pasture-raised bacon	½ teaspoon fresh sage, minced
½ yellow onion, diced	½ teaspoon fresh thyme
2 cloves garlic, minced	1 cup Brussels sprouts, halved
1 cup diced butternut squash	4–6 pasture-raised eggs
½ teaspoon sea salt	¼ cup broccoli sprouts, for garnish
¼ teaspoon black pepper	

1. Cook bacon in a medium cast-iron skillet over medium-high heat until crispy.

2. Remove the bacon and set aside on paper towels. Keep bacon grease in the pan and add the onion and garlic. Cook until translucent and starting to brown, about 5 minutes.

3. Add the butternut squash along with the seasonings. Cook, stirring every couple of minutes, until squash has begun to soften, about 15 minutes.

4. Add the Brussels sprouts and mix with the squash. Cook another 10 minutes, stirring occasionally, until both the butternut squash and Brussels sprouts are cooked through and browned.

5. With the back of a spoon, create a one inch well and crack an egg into it. Repeat with the remaining eggs. Turn down the heat to low and cook, covered, about 3 to 4 minutes until egg whites are fully cooked and yolks are to your liking.

6. Chop the bacon into ½ inch pieces and add to the skillet. Top with the broccoli sprouts for serving.

Nutrition facts per serving
Calories: 367   Carbohydrates: 17g   Fiber: 5g   Protein: 27g   Fat: 22g

Caramelized Onion, Turkey, and Kale Egg Muffins

FOOD AS MEDICINE Eggs provide about 7 grams of protein each, as well as choline for brain development and omega-3s for heart health. Cooking your onions may reduce the vitamin C content in them; however, you will not lose too much of the key polyphenols quercetin and glutathione. These two super antioxidants reduce histamine activity and free radical overload. If you don't have the patience to caramelize the onions, sautéing them will work fine in this recipe. These egg muffins are a great make-ahead breakfast and can even be frozen and reheated throughout the week.

remove (gf) (df) (nf)

Makes: 6 (2-muffin) servings   *Prep time:* 10 minutes, or 40 to 45 minutes with caramelization   *Cook time:* 30 to 35 minutes

1 tablespoon ghee

1 onion, thinly sliced

½ pound ground organic turkey thighs (80/20 blend of lean/fat)

1 bunch lacinato kale, cut into thin strips

12 pasture-raised eggs

1 teaspoon sea salt, plus more to taste

¼ teaspoon black pepper, plus more to taste

1 teaspoon paprika

1 tablespoon fresh chopped sage

1 tablespoon thyme, leaves removed from stalk (about 5 sprigs)

1. Preheat oven to 350°F.

2. Coat a muffin tin with coconut oil or use parchment muffin liners for easy cleanup.

Feeling zen? Start with caramelizing the onions:

1. Heat the ghee in a cast-iron skillet over medium-low heat.

2. Add the onion and a pinch of salt and stir to coat.

3. Cook for 30 to 45 minutes, stirring only every 10 minutes or so to prevent burning.

4. Move on to step 3 below.

Need to knock it out? Start with a quicker sauté:

1. Heat the ghee in a cast-iron skillet over medium-low heat. Add only half the onion and a pinch of salt, and stir to coat.

2. Allow to sauté for about 3 to 5 minutes before stirring, and let cook for another 3 minutes.

3. Turn the heat up to medium and add the ground turkey with an additional pinch of salt and pepper. Stir every couple of minutes until turkey is cooked through and browned.

4. Fold the kale into onion and turkey mixture and allow to cook down, about 2 to 3 minutes. Then turn off heat.

5. Crack the eggs into a large bowl and whisk. Add the sea salt, black pepper, paprika, sage, and thyme; stir until incorporated.

6. Divide the turkey, kale, and onion mixture between the muffin tins, then fill with the egg mixture.

7. Bake for 30 to 35 minutes or until the eggs rise and are cooked through with the center of each muffin no longer jiggly.

Nutrition facts per serving
Calories: 300   **Carbohydrates:** 8g   **Fiber:** 6g   **Protein:** 28g   **Fat:** 17g

Sweet Potato Avocado Toast

Sweet potatoes come in about 400 varieties and two main hues, with either cream- or orange-colored flesh. When you have removed grains from your diet and are looking for something hearty to sink your teeth into, these sweet potato toasts are sure to tame sugar cravings while keeping your blood sugar stable!

FOOD AS MEDICINE   Sweet potatoes are rich in beta-carotene (which the body converts to vitamin A) and are also good sources of vitamin C, manganese, copper, vitamin B6, potassium, iron, and dietary fiber. Antioxidant compounds in sweet potatoes have anti-inflammatory effects and can target brain and blood vessel health.

remove

Makes: 4 servings   *Prep time:* 5 to 10 minutes   *Cook time:* 15 minutes

1 medium sweet potato, sliced vertically in ¼-inch slices	4 slices pasture-raised bacon, chopped or torn
1 tablespoon avocado oil	4 eggs, prepared as desired
1 medium avocado	1 teaspoon red pepper flakes
1 teaspoon lemon juice	sea salt, to taste
8 to 10 cherry tomatoes, sliced	

1. Preheat the oven to 400°F.

2. Brush the sweet potato slices lightly on both sides with the avocado oil.

3. Place the slices on a baking sheet and roast for about 15 minutes, until potato slices are cooked through and lightly browned but not mushy.

4. While the sweet potato slices are roasting, mash the avocado with a fork and sprinkle with sea salt and lemon juice.

5. Remove the sweet potato slices from the oven and spread the avocado mixture over the slices. Top with the tomato slices and bacon pieces.

6. Add a fried or poached egg for protein, and sprinkle with pepper flakes and salt to garnish.

Nutrition facts per serving

Calories: 294   Carbohydrates: 22g   Fiber: 7g   Protein: 10g   Fat: 20g

Prosciutto Egg Cups

FOOD AS MEDICINE   Eggs are a nutritionally dense food, providing about 7 grams of protein each, as well as choline for brain development and omega-3s for heart health. Eggs are also high in sulfur, which supports detoxification as well as cysteine and Vitamin D. Choose pasture-raised eggs and always eat the yolk—this is where the nutrients are most concentrated!

Makes: 6 servings   *Prep time:* 10 minutes   *Cook time:* 15 to 20 minutes

    12 thin slices prosciutto

    12 pasture-raised eggs

    2 tablespoons fresh chopped chives

1. Preheat oven to 350°F.

2. Line 12 muffin tins with one slice each of prosciutto, making sure it is covering the entire surface. This will replace your muffin liner and requires no greasing of the tin!

3. Carefully crack one egg into each tin. Bake for 15 to 20 minutes, until yolks are set to your liking (I like them a little runny). Remove from the oven and sprinkle with the chives.

Nutrition facts per serving
Calories: 210   **Carbohydrates:** 0g   **Fiber:** 0g   **Protein:** 20g   **Fat:** 14g

Smoked Wild Salmon Scramble

FOOD AS MEDICINE   Salmon is one of the best sources of cardioprotective omega-3 essential fatty acids. Omega-3 fatty acids are responsible for reducing inflammation in the body and preventing plaque buildup in the arteries, as well as promoting healthy cognitive function and skin health. I also love the omega-3s from salmon because they are said to increase metabolism and decrease fat cell size—particularly belly fat! Choosing wild caught over farmed salmon ensures you are getting all the omega-3 salmon naturally has to offer minus harmful chemicals and hormones sometimes found in farmed salmon.

remove

Makes: 2 servings   *Prep time:* 10 to 15 minutes   *Cook time:* 4 to 5 minutes

4 pasture-raised eggs	1 tablespoon grass-fed butter
2 tablespoons coconut milk (optional)	2 tablespoons fresh chopped chives
pinch sea salt	2 tablespoons fresh chopped dill
pinch black pepper	2 teaspoon capers
4 ounces wild caught smoked salmon, torn into 1 inch pieces	

1. Whisk the eggs, coconut milk, sea salt, and pepper in a medium bowl. Add the smoked salmon pieces.

2. Heat a cast-iron skillet over medium-low heat. Once heated, add the butter.

3. Pour the egg mixture into the skillet and cook, stirring gently to scramble, about 3 minutes.

4. Once cooked, fold in the chives, dill, and capers.

Nutrition facts per serving
Calories: 288   Carbohydrates: 5g   Fiber: 0g   Protein: 19g   Fat: 17g

Quick Coconut Yogurt

FOOD AS MEDICINE Probiotics mean "for life," and you want to support your gut with as much beneficial life as you can tolerate, ideally with one probiotic-rich food per day! When removing dairy during the anti-anxiety diet, the reduction of yogurt consumption can unfavorably reduce probiotic intake. This recipe gives you the benefits of probiotics without the hit of casein or lactose. Also, coconut milk provides a rich source of beneficial fats to reduce inflammation as well as compounds to reduce yeast activity in the body. I recommend Native Forest Simple brand, which has only coconut and water as ingredients, with no binders or fillers. This rich, creamy yogurt goes great with a ⅛ to ¼ cup of fruit or mixed into a savory sauce with curry powder, or stands alone as a balanced snack!

reset

Makes: 3 (6-ounce) servings *Prep time:* 5 minutes, 36 to 48 hours to ferment

1 (16-ounce) can full-fat coconut milk

½ teaspoon gelatin

2 Naturally Nourished Restore Baseline probiotic capsules, each providing 15 billion CFU of a 50:50 blend of *Lactobacillus* and *Bifidobacterium* strains

2 teaspoons vanilla extract

1. Shake can of coconut milk vigorously and pour contents into a clean, 1-liter jar.

2. Whisk in gelatin. If you are not able to make a smooth texture, blend mixture on high in blender.

3. Return mixture to jar and add in powder from opened probiotic capsules, discarding capsule exterior. Stir in the powder with a wooden spoon and top the jar with a cheesecloth, securing with a rubber band on top.

4. After 36 to 48 hours, stir the yogurt and add in vanilla. Eat immediately or place a lid on the jar and refrigerate for 5 to 7 days.

Nutrition facts per serving
Calories: 209   Carbohydrates: 4g   Fiber: 1g   Protein: 2g   Fat: 20g

Paleo Pumpkin Protein Pancakes

FOOD AS MEDICINE   Just 1 cup of cooked pumpkin offers 200% of your daily needed vitamin A in the form that best protects your vision. The soluble fiber and zinc in pumpkin play a role for blood sugar and insulin regulation while the phytosterols in the seeds aid in lowering bad cholesterol levels. The abundance of antioxidants serve to scavenge free radicals while protecting against oxidative damage and decrease inflammation in the body.

remove

Makes: 2 (3-pancake) servings   *Prep time:* 5 to 10 minutes   *Cook time:* 5 to 10 minutes

¼ cup coconut flour	pinch sea salt
½ teaspoon cinnamon	4 eggs
¼ teaspoon nutmeg	½ cup pumpkin puree
¼ teaspoon ground ginger	1 teaspoon vanilla extract
¼ teaspoon ground cloves	2 tablespoons maple syrup
1 scoop grass-fed whey protein powder	1 tablespoon butter or ghee

1. In a large bowl, the coconut flour, cinnamon, nutmeg, ginger, cloves, whey protein, and sea salt.

2. In a medium bowl, whisk together the eggs, pumpkin puree, vanilla, and maple syrup.

3. Add the wet ingredients to the dry and mix until well combined.

4. Melt butter or ghee in a medium skillet over medium heat. Pour about ¼ cup of batter into the skillet to create a 3-inch pancake. Cook until bubbles begin to appear, then carefully flip and cook until golden brown, about two more minutes. Repeat for remaining batter.

Nutrition facts per serving
Calories: 355   Carbohydrates: 28g   Fiber: 8g   Protein: 26g   Fat: 12g

Pumpkin Nut and Seed Bars

FOOD AS MEDICINE   Pumpkin seeds and flesh provide support for inflammation, cancer, and eye health. Pepitas, or pumpkin seeds, contain a compound called phytosterols, which have been shown to help lower the bad cholesterol levels in your blood. The flesh is high in vitamin A, an antioxidant that promotes healthy immune system and skin. Additional antioxidants in pumpkin, such as vitamin C, beta-carotene, and vitamin E, help bind to damaging free radicals in the body and protect against further damage and inflammation. This no-bake bar is a great low-glycemic blend that will provide healthy fats while filling the flavors of fall without the excess sugar!

rebalance

Makes: 12 (1-bar) servings   *Prep time:* 15 to 20 minutes, 4 hours to set

⅓ cup pumpkin seeds

½ cup walnuts

½ cup pecans

4 pitted dates, chopped

½ teaspoon sea salt, plus more to taste

2 tablespoons pumpkin puree

⅓ cup cashew butter

2 tablespoons coconut oil

1 teaspoon cinnamon

1 teaspoon maple syrup (optional)

1 scoop collagen peptides

1 teaspoon vanilla extract

1 to 2 teaspoons water, as needed

1. Place the pumpkin seeds, walnuts, and pecans in the food processor. Pulse with six to eight turns of your "s" blade.

2. Add the dates and sea salt and pulse until combined and in small pieces, about 20 pulses. The mixture should be very textured with small pieces of each ingredient. Place mixture in a medium bowl and set aside.

3. Place the pumpkin puree, cashew butter, coconut oil, cinnamon, and optional maple syrup in a small saucepan over medium-low heat. Stir frequently, until combined. Add a pinch of salt to taste depending on the cashew butter you are using.

4. Turn off the heat. Add the collagen peptides and vanilla extract, and stir. Add the water as needed to achieve a maple syrup viscosity.

5. Once a creamy, pourable thickness is achieved, pour the liquid mixture into the bowl with the nut, seed, and date pieces, and combine.

6. Press the mixture into a pan lined with parchment paper. Place in the refrigerator for at least 4 hours before cutting into bars. These store best in the fridge or freezer.

Nutrition facts per serving

Calories 196   Carbohydrates: 13g   Fiber: 4g   Protein: 7g   Fat: 15g

Coconut No-Oatmeal

FOOD AS MEDICINE   This grain free "oatmeal" uses shredded coconut instead of oats, making it a great low-carb alternative to traditional oatmeal that is equally satiating and delicious when you're craving a warm breakfast. Coconut contains medium-chain fatty acids (MCTs), which work to tonify the adrenal glands, aid in sleep regulation, reduce stress, and boost the metabolism. While saturated fat once got a bad rap, we are now learning that eating this type of fat can aid in weight loss and appetite regulation and even be heart protective! Coconut also contains lauric and caprylic acids, which have antibacterial, antifungal, and antiviral benefits. Caprylic acid also has the unique ability to combat yeast overgrowth in the body. The addition of whey protein supports lean body mass and cognitive function, making this a balanced breakfast!

rebalance

Makes: 4 servings   *Prep time:* 5 minutes   *Cook time:* 10 minutes

1 cup shredded unsweetened coconut

2 tablespoons almond flour

½ cup coconut milk

½ cup filtered water, plus more as needed

½ teaspoon ground cardamom

1 teaspoon ground cinnamon

½ teaspoon ground ginger

1 teaspoon vanilla extract

pinch sea salt

2 scoops grass-fed whey protein powder

berries and nuts of your choice, to serve

extra cinnamon and coconut shreds, to serve

1. Place all ingredients except the protein powder and toppings in a small saucepan over medium heat. Cook, stirring occasionally until the mixture begins to thicken and coconut starts to soften and absorb the liquid, about 10 minutes. You can add more filtered water as needed to thin out the mixture.

2. Remove from heat and stir in the whey protein powder. Spoon into a bowl and top with berries and nuts and sprinkle with cinnamon and coconut. You can make this ahead of time and

store individual servings for up to three days in mason jars—it only gets better with time!

Nutrition facts per serving

Calories: 262   Carbohydrates: 7g   Fiber: 4g   Protein: 15g   Fat: 19g

Beverages

Anti-Inflammatory Electrolyte Elixir

FOOD AS MEDICINE   This recipe provides the anti inflammatory benefits of turmeric while stabilizing electrolytes as you transition into ketosis or a lower carbohydrate diet. It also makes a great post-workout recovery beverage and supports the adrenals, as vitamin C is most concentrated in this tiny stress gland.

rebound

Makes: 6 (1-cup) servings   *Prep time:* 10 minutes

2-inch turmeric root, peeled and chopped

3 lemons, peeled, with white pith intact

5 cups of filtered water

1 cup coconut water, unsweetened

1 teaspoon sea salt or Himalayan salt

1. Place the peeled and chopped turmeric in the blender with remaining ingredients. Blend on high until completely broken down.

2. If desired, strain for a smooth texture and discard pulp.

3. Place in mason jar and shake to distribute all ingredients. Serve 1-cup portions on ice and store in fridge for up to 7 days.

Nutrition facts per serving
Calories: 11   Carbohydrates: 3g   Fiber: 0g   Protein: 0g   Fat: 0g

Stress-Stabilizing Steamer

FOOD AS MEDICINE   This beverage tonifies the immune system, nervous system, and adrenal glands, which in turn can balance mood and hormonal expression. Rich in vitamin D, omega-3 fatty acids, and adaptogenic herbs, this beverage is indulgent yet grounding and tonifying for your body.

Adaptogenic herbs help your body to be more resilient to stress demands without getting depleted or having anxious reactivity or thoughts. Ashwagandha and maca aid in supporting stress response while preserving primary stress glands, the adrenals, the pituitary, and the thyroid. Look for maca in the supplement section of your natural food store, by the superfoods and smoothie add-ins. Ashwagandha can be used in bulk powder from a natural foods or herb store, or purchased as pure capsules and opened for this recipe.

rebound

Makes: 1 (12-ounce) serving   *Prep time:* 10 minutes

½ cup full-fat canned coconut milk

½ cup water

1 pasture-raised egg yolk

1 teaspoon maca powder

1 teaspoon ashwagandha

pinch salt

pinch cayenne

1 scoop collagen peptides

1 date, pitted and chopped (omit to make KF)

½ teaspoon cinnamon, plus more to serve

1. In a small pot, warm the coconut milk and water on the stovetop over medium heat until it begins to simmer. Then, lower heat and slowly whisk in egg yolk, continuously whisking to avoid scrambling.

2. Move the mixture to a blender and add the other ingredients. Blend until smooth and creamy.

3. Pour into a mug and top with a pinch of cinnamon. Sip and savor this luscious beverage!

Nutrition facts per serving

Calories: 305   Carbohydrates: 11g   Fiber: 3g   Protein: 14g   Fat: 23g

Almond Collagen Hot Cocoa

FOOD AS MEDICINE   This hot chocolate has the decadent taste of Nutella without any of the artificial flavors and preservatives! When choosing a chocolate bar, always look for at least 70 percent cacao, but when you are using raw cacao powder you are getting 100 percent pure cacao. The antioxidants in cacao exceed those in red wine and even green tea. Cacao is high in magnesium, which can help to lower blood pressure and relax muscles, and it provides theobromine, a bitter alkaloid that supports healthy serotonin levels. The addition of collagen supports a balance of carb-to-protein ratio while providing gut, hair, skin, and nail support!

repair   (ef)

Makes: 2 (8-ounce) servings   *Prep time:* 10 to 15 minutes

1 cup full-fat coconut milk

½ cup filtered water

3 tablespoons raw cacao powder

2 tablespoons almond butter

1 date, pitted (omit to make KF)

2 teaspoons vanilla extract

¼ teaspoon sea salt

2 scoops collagen peptides

1. In a small pot, heat coconut milk and water to a low simmer on the stovetop, and slowly whisk in cacao and almond butter until well combined.

2. Remove from heat. Add to blender along with date, if using, vanilla, and sea salt.

3. Blend on high for 45 to 60 seconds until well incorporated.

4. Add collagen and mix again for about 15 to 30 seconds. Pour into 2 mugs.

Nutrition per servings

Calories: 432   Carbohydrates: 20g   Fiber: 4g   Protein:16g   Fat: 32g

Matcha Green Smoothie

FOOD AS MEDICINE Matcha is a powdered form of a Japanese green tea that is grown in shade to increase levels of medicinal properties and make the taste more smooth with a less astringent aftertaste. Matcha is a ground powder of the entire leaf of tea, which is consumed whole rather than steeping the leaf and discarding, allowing for about 10 times the antioxidant boost. The use of shade in the growing process increases production of caffeine and L-theanine, a natural mood stabilizer. Matcha can be a therapeutic intervention for depression, anxiety, and adrenal fatigue as well as diabetes, heart disease, cancer, and more. L-theanine is a modulator for neurotransmitters, aiding to promote production of those that are low while supporting excretion to those that are elevated. It supports the alpha brain waves which are seen during REM cycles of sleep, meditation, creative process, and concentration.

rebalance

Makes: 2 (8-ounce) servings   *Prep time:* 15 minutes

1 teaspoon matcha

8 ounces non-dairy milk of choice

¼-inch fresh ginger root

1 frozen banana

2 cups leafy greens of choice, the darker the better

½ avocado, cubed

1 scoop grass-fed whey protein powder or 1 to 2 scoops collagen peptides (optional)

1. In a blender, mix the matcha, milk of choice, ginger, and banana.

2. Blend in the leafy greens. Once incorporated, add avocado to create a nice, creamy finish.

3. If desired, add in protein powder at the end, with just a brief mix so as not to over-fluff.

Nutrition per serving, without protein added
Calories: 150   Carbohydrates: 21g   Fiber: 8g   Protein: 4g   Fat: 7g

Citrus Burst Smoothie

This recipes provides a bright start to the morning or serves as a nice midday pick-me-up with a creamy, indulgent, dairy-free base.

FOOD AS MEDICINE   Citrus is a rich source of bioflavonoids such as nobiletin (found in the peel), which can promote detoxification, reduce inflammation, and fight against cancer. Be sure to include the white furry pith of the orange in this recipe, as it supports these antioxidant properties. Many ingredients in this recipe are rich in vitamin C, which plays a crucial role in stress response. Our adrenal glands are our most concentrated storage tissue for vitamin C, and they use the vitamin to regulate cortisol. Winter provides the sweetest citrus, which is quite a blessing since vitamin C can also support mood stability, aiding in seasonal depressive disorder!

Makes: 2 (12-ounce) servings   *Prep time:* 10 minutes

1 cup frozen mango	4 ounces water
½ cup raspberries	2 tablespoons hemp seeds
whole orange, peeled	1-inch turmeric root
juice of ½ lemon	1 scoop grass-fed whey protein powder
6 ounces full-fat coconut milk	

1. Place mango, raspberries, orange, lemon juice, coconut milk, and water into a blender and mix on high for about 2 minutes until smooth.

2. Add hemp seeds and turmeric root and mix until well blended.

3. When all ingredients in smoothie are combined and creamy, pulse in the scoop of whey for 2 seconds. You want to incorporate it into the smoothie, but not overmix it, since doing so will create foam.

Nutrition facts per serving
Calories: 360   Carbohydrates: 29g   Fiber: 6g   Protein: 18g   Fat: 20g

Snacks/Appetizers

Electrolyte-Boosting Avocado with a Spoon

FOOD AS MEDICINE   Avocados have more potassium than bananas without the high blood sugar spike while providing more bacteria building fiber. Avocados provide neurotransmitter supporting B-vitamins and methylation support as a rich source of folate and glutathione! This is a great snack to aid in electrolyte balance when transitioning into ketosis or a lower carbohydrate diet.

restore   (kf) (gf) (df) (nf) (ef)

Makes: 2 servings   *Prep time:* 15 to 20 minutes

1 lemon

1 avocado, halved, pit removed

½ teaspoon sea salt or pink Himalayan salt

pinch red chile flakes, sesame seeds, or dulse flakes, to serve

1. Juice lemon and splash on avocado halves.

2. Sprinkle on salt and optional toppings. Eat with a spoon for a quick grounding boost of fats, fiber, and electrolyte stability in time of transition.

Nutrition facts per serving
Calories: 122   Carbohydrates: 8g   Fiber: 5g   Protein: 2g   Fat: 11g

Greek Deviled Eggs

Deviled eggs are an easy party favorite or a quick snack packed with protein and healthy fats that will help to curb carb cravings. This Greek twist on the traditional provides a unique briny flavor that pairs well with a side salad or grilled veggies.

FOOD AS MEDICINE Eggs are a simple biological protein providing a rich source of B vitamins that aid in methylation. The yolk is high in sulfur and the antioxidant cysteine, which supports detoxification. Choose pasture-raised eggs and always eat the yolk—this is where the nutrients are most concentrated! Sourcing is important as those produced from pasture-raised chickens will have higher amounts of vitamin D and omega-3s!

restore   (nf)

Makes: 6 servings   *Prep time:* 15 to 20 minutes

6 large eggs

3 tablespoons avocado- or olive-based mayonnaise free of soybean oil or added sugars (I use Simple Olive Oil Mayonnaise)

1 teaspoon Dijon mustard

2 tablespoons chopped kalamata olives

1 teaspoon olive juice

pinch black pepper

½ teaspoon paprika, plus more to serve

fresh basil or oregano, destemmed and leaves chopped, to serve

1. Fill a medium saucepan with enough water to cover the eggs by 1 inch. Bring to a boil, then gently lower in the eggs. Reduce heat to a medium boil and cook for 10 minutes. Remove from the heat and drain the water.

2. Place the eggs into a bowl of cold water and allow to cool completely before peeling. Once peeled, slice the eggs in half lengthwise and carefully scoop out the yolk with a small spoon. Place the whites on a plate and set aside.

3. In a medium bowl, combine the egg yolks, mayonnaise, mustard, olives, olive juice, black pepper, and paprika. Mash the yolks until smooth and evenly distributed.

4. Scoop the filling into the hollows of the egg whites, then sprinkle with additional paprika and the chopped herbs. Refrigerate until ready to serve.

Nutrition facts per serving

Calories: 129   Carbohydrates: 1g   Fiber: 0g   Protein: 6g   Fat: 11g

Mango Zen Fuego Nutballz

FOOD AS MEDICINE   This recipe provides a kick of antioxidants to light your inner fire while cooling down your system. The curry powder provides spice from cayenne, which includes capsaicin, which has turmeric, with curcumin, both potent anti-inflammatory compounds to cool and soothe your system. This salty, spicy, crunchy snack satisfies while packing a powerful punch of vitamins, minerals, and antioxidants.

remove

Makes: 12 (2-ball) servings   *Prep time:* 15 to 20 minutes, 30 minutes to chill

2 cups cashews

⅓ cup toasted coconut

¼ cup dried mango, torn into 1-inch pieces

¾ teaspoon sea salt

1 tablespoon plus 1 teaspoon curry powder

¼ teaspoon black pepper

3 tablespoons brown rice syrup

⅓ cup chopped dry roasted pistachios

¼ cup sesame seeds

1. Place cashews and coconut in food processor. Run "s" blade for about 45 to 60 seconds until finely blended to a meal.

2. Pulse in torn mango pieces until well incorporated.

3. Add sea salt, curry powder, and black pepper, and pulse until well blended.

4. While mixing, pour in brown rice syrup until a rollable texture forms.

5. Add chopped pistachios and pulse them slightly to keep texture. Once mixed in, scrape sides of food processor and scoop 1½-tablespoon portions.

6. Roll into balls, and then roll each ball in sesame seeds. Set in the refrigerator for 30 minutes before eating.

Nutrition facts per serving
Calories: 205   Carbohydrates: 12g   Fiber: 4g   Protein: 7g   Fat: 15g

Whole Roasted Cauliflower

FOOD AS MEDICINE   Cauliflower has a mild and sweet flavor and can be prepared in a variety of ways, including roasted, sautéed, steamed, or even chopped as a rice substitute or mashed as a potato substitute. Cauliflower has a variety of nutritional benefits, one of them being cancer prevention. The indole-3-carbinol (I3C) compound in cruciferous and sulfur-containing veggies has been found to prevent cancer and inhibit the growth of tumors in the body. Cauliflower also contains active compounds needed for both Phase 1 and Phase 2 detox activities, as well as glucosinates that help to activate enzymes needed for detoxification.

restore   (kf) (gf) (df) (nf) (ef)

Makes: 6 servings   *Prep time:* 10 minutes   *Cook time:* 40 to 50 minutes

1 whole cauliflower	1 teaspoon turmeric
2 tablespoons coconut oil, melted	¼ teaspoon cayenne
1 teaspoon cumin	½ teaspoon sea salt
1 teaspoon paprika	green onion and cilantro, to serve

1. Preheat the oven to 400°F.

2. Using a paring knife, cut the core out of the cauliflower head and remove the leaves, keeping the head intact.

3. Mix the coconut oil with the spices and sea salt. Rub the cauliflower all over with the oil and spice mix, ensuring all sides are coated.

4. Place the cauliflower in a cast-iron skillet. Bake for 40 to 50 minutes until the cauliflower is fork tender and spices have created a golden brown crust on the outside.

5. Top with sliced green onions and chopped cilantro. Let cool 5 minutes before slicing and serving.

Nutrition facts per serving
Calories: 84   Carbohydrates: 8g   Fiber: 4g   Protein: 3g   Fat: 5g

Curry Roasted Cauliflower

This is a crunchier variation of the recipe on page 213, but just as nutritionally beneficial!

FOOD AS MEDICINE   There are nutritional benefits to cauliflower; it contains the detoxifying sulfur compound, I3C, which is known to help prevent breast cancer, as well as other sulfur compounds like glucosinolates that help to activate enzymes needed for liver detox and methlyation as discussed in Chapter 5. Cauliflower also works as a prebiotic fiber, supporting a healthy gut microbiome and helping to remove toxins in a bacteria reset.

    reset (kf) (gf) (df) (nf) (ef)

Makes: 4 (⅔-cup) servings   *Prep time:* 5 minutes   *Cook time:* 20 minutes

1 head cauliflower, cored and chopped into 1- to 2-inch pieces	2 tablespoons turmeric
¼ cup avocado oil	1 tablespoon curry powder
	1 teaspoon sea salt

1. Preheat oven to 400°F.

2. On a baking sheet, spread out cauliflower pieces and drizzle with avocado oil.

3. With your hands, rub cauliflower to evenly distribute the oil so all pieces are coated evenly. You may need more oil depending on the size of your cauliflower head.

4. Sprinkle turmeric, curry powder, and sea salt over the coated cauliflower. Rub in seasonings with hands until distributed.

5. Place in oven on low rack and roast for 20 minutes. Check at 15 minutes and shake pan to prevent sticking. Pieces should be nice and roasted with a crunch!

Nutrition facts per serving
Calories: 167   Carbohydrates: 7g   Fiber: 4g   Protein: 3g   Fat: 14g

Roasted Almonds with Nori and Sesame

FOOD AS MEDICINE Sea vegetables have 10 to 20 times the minerals as land vegetables due to the mineral deficiency in our soils. Rich in the trace mineral iodine, which many people are deficient in, sea vegetables aid in tonifying the thyroid gland, which can help with weight loss and optimizing metabolic function. They also help reduce inflammation.

rebalance

Makes: 12 servings   *Prep time:* 5 minutes   *Cook time:* 12 to 15 minutes

2 sheets nori

2 cups almonds

2 tablespoons kelp powder

3 tablespoons sesame seeds

1 teaspoon sea salt

1 teaspoon turmeric

1 teaspoon chili powder

pinch of cayenne

2 tablespoons sesame oil

2 tablespoons coconut aminos

1–2 teaspoons honey (exclude for KF)

1. Preheat the oven to 350°F.

2. Tear the nori into small pieces and place in a medium bowl along with the almonds.

3. In a separate bowl, combine the kelp powder, sesame seeds, sea salt, turmeric, chili, and cayenne.

4. Combine the sesame oil, coconut aminos, and honey, if using, with the almonds. Sprinkle with the dry mixture and toss to coat.

5. Place on a baking tray lined with parchment paper in a single layer. Bake 12 to 15 minutes until liquid is absorbed. Cool and store in mason jars.

Nutrition facts per serving
Calories: 187   Carbohydrates: 7g   Fiber: 4g   Protein: 7g   Fat: 17g

Asian Braised Bok Choy

FOOD AS MEDICINE   The savory and rich umami profile is typically associated with Asian flavors; however, often these foods are loaded with preservatives and mood-disturbing compounds such as MSG. This dish evokes the nostalgia of take-out yet provides a nice brightness of flavor with fresh ingredients that serve to detoxify your body rather than weigh it down. Bok choy is a flavor sponge and has a less bitter flavor than the other cruciferous vegetables, yet it provides the same beneficial detoxifying properties to support healthy methylation and over 70 antioxidants to support optimal cell function and messaging.

Ingredient note: Tamari is a great pantry staple as a gluten-free alternative to soy sauce. It is an aged version of soy in a traditional form, which has some health-supporting compounds allowable in the anti-anxiety diet; however, if looking to be 100 percent soy-free, you can substitute an equal amount of liquid coconut aminos.

restore

Makes: 4 (½-cup) servings   *Prep time:* 5 minutes   *Cook time:* 25 minutes

1 tablespoon sesame oil	½ teaspoon hot chili sesame oil
1 to 2 bunches bok choy, about 3 cups total of chopped white parts and leaves, divided	1 teaspoon fish sauce
	½ teaspoon tamari
½ yellow onion, peeled and chopped	1 inch turmeric, chopped
	1 inch ginger, chopped

1. Heat a cast-iron or stainless-steel pan on medium heat and add sesame oil until warm, then add in the white parts of the bok choy and onion.

2. After 4 to 5 minutes, once the vegetables start to soften, add the hot chili sesame oil, fish sauce, tamari, turmeric, and ginger.

3. Stir, then allow to sit in pan over medium-low heat until softened and flavors are combined, about 4 to 5 minutes.

4. Add the leaves and turn off the heat. Stir to combine.

5. Serve immediately or within 15 minutes of completion for best texture.

Nutrition facts serving

Calories: 68   Carbohydrates: 3g   Fiber: 1g   Protein: 2g   Fat: 6g

Cashew Cheeze Dip

When removing inflammatory foods from your diet it is important to find enjoyable replacements. This dip may not make you forget about cheese but it will help you fill the void of savory creamy goodness, and the brightness of the lemon zest will have you smiling. The soft spread goes great on cucumber slices or raw vegetables as well as on top of a Bolognese or to crumble up as a boost to a salad.

remove

Makes: 6 (¼-cup) servings *Prep time:* 15 minutes, 4 to 12 hours soak time in advance, 2 to 4 hours to set

1 cup raw cashews, soaked for at least 4 hours (up to 12 hours or overnight is fine), drained

zest of 1 lemon

2 teaspoons lemon juice, plus more to taste

2 tablespoons tahini

1 tablespoon thyme

¾ teaspoon sea salt, plus more to taste

½ teaspoon truffle salt

¼ teaspoon white pepper

1. In a food processor with the "s" blade, blend cashews, lemon zest, and lemon juice. Scrape sides of processor with spatula and pat down mixture if needed to keep dense enough to mix into a wet ball.

2. Add in tahini, thyme, and sea salt, and mix well. After scraping sides again, add truffle salt and white pepper, pulsing until well combined.

3. Taste and add more lemon or salt as needed. The texture should be dense but similar to a soft cheese.

4. Enjoy immediately or store in fridge for 2 to 4 hours to set. This dish will keep for 5 to 6 days airtight in fridge.

Nutrition facts per serving
Calories: 162   Carbohydrates: 11g   Fiber: 2g   Protein: 5g   Fat: 12g

Mellow Mama Dressing

FOOD AS MEDICINE   Pulling from the inspiration of a green goddess dressing, this blend will channel your inner mellow mama! Avocados are a great source of vitamins E, K, and B6, as well as natural folate. The combination of B vitamins and fatty acids help to manage stress response and reduce excess cortisol stress hormone. Tahini adds to the creaminess while providing a nice boost of minerals including magnesium and calcium for relaxation. Garlic and basil kick up the flavor and provide an antioxidant punch! This recipe can be kept thicker to use as a dip or thinned as desired with water.

| restore | |

Makes: 8 (2-tablespoon) servings   *Prep time:* 15 minutes

2 tablespoons chopped fresh basil

2 cloves garlic, smashed

¼ cup tahini

¼ avocado

⅓ cup lemon juice

1 tablespoon Bragg Raw Apple Cider Vinegar

2 tablespoons chopped fresh rosemary

1 teaspoon sea salt

2 tablespoons water, plus more as needed to thin

3 tablespoons olive oil

1. Blend all ingredients except olive oil in blender. Increase speed to high until well combined and getting creamy, adding an additional teaspoon of water at a time as needed.

2. Once incorporated and desired texture is achieved, drizzle in olive oil while motor is running to emulsify and create an even creamier texture.

3. Once blended, ensure texture is as desired to pour or scoop, adding a couple teaspoons of water if needed to thin.

4. Serve immediately. Store leftovers up to 7 days in a Mason jar in the fridge.

Nutrition facts per serving
Calories: 184   Carbohydrates: 4g   Fiber: 2g   Protein: 5g   Fat: 17g

Roasted Colored Peppers

FOOD AS MEDICINE   Peppers are a great bright vegetable side to accompany any protein. Bell peppers actually have more vitamin C than citrus fruits by weight and provide a nice boost to support adrenal health and cortisol regulation. This recipe can be done with any vegetable, from broccoli to asparagus. Consider topping these vegetables with my Bacteria-Battling Chimichurri (page 248). Learn more simple roasted vegetable options on my blog at alimillerRD.com.

rebound kf gf df nf ef

Makes: 4 (⅔-cup) servings   *Prep time:* 25 to 35 minutes

4 colored bell peppers, sliced into 6 to -8 large pieces

½ red onion, sliced ½ inch thick

2 tablespoons olive oil

1 tablespoon avocado oil

1 teaspoon sea salt

1. Preheat the oven to 400°F.

2. On a baking sheet, spread out pepper and onion pieces. Liberally drizzle olive oil and avocado oil on top. Rub peppers and onions with hands until all pieces are glistening.

3. Sprinkle with sea salt and place in oven. After 15 to 20 minutes, shake pan to shift pieces around, then place back in oven.

4. Bake an additional 10 to 15 minutes, until pieces start to slightly brown for a nice roasted flavor.

Nutrition facts per serving
Calories: 102   Carbohydrates: 3g   Fiber: 1g   Protein: 0g   Fat: 11g

Lunch/Dinner

Grass-Fed Beef Knuckle Bone Broth

FOOD AS MEDICINE   Bone broth contains the amino acid glutamine, which aids in rebuilding the gut, where most of the immune system is regulated. Bone broth is like a facelift for the gut, as the glutamine sealant is paired with collagen, which tightens gut junctions to aid in repair from leaky gut while supporting improved ability to absorb nutrients. Beef bones contain more of the collagen and gelatin that we are looking for than chicken, making it a more therapeutic option for those dealing with digestive distress or food sensitivities.

repair   (ef)

Makes: 6 (12-ounce) servings   *Prep time:* 70 minutes   *Cook time:* 24 to 48 hours to simmer

5 to 8 pounds grass-fed beef bones

gallon freezer bag full of vegetable scraps (carrot peelings, onion tops, celery leaves, etc. Don't use brassicas or beets as they contribute an off taste to the broth!)

6 stalks celery, cut into chunks

2 carrots, cut into chunks

2 tablespoons black peppercorns

1 tablespoon sea salt

2 tablespoons Bragg Raw Apple Cider Vinegar

2 to 3 bay leaves

filtered water to fill stockpot (fully cover all bones and veggies)

1. Preheat the oven to 400°F.

2. Rinse bones and pat dry, then place in a roasting pan. Bake in a preheated oven for about an hour until the bones are well-browned and fragrant.

Note: Roasting the bones ensures a good flavor in the resulting beef stock. Failure to do so may lend a sour or off taste to the end product.

3. Once the bones are browned, drain off any fat. Add the bones to a big pot or slow cooker along with the remaining ingredients. Add filtered water to cover, and bring to a boil.

4. Turn down the heat and simmer for 24 to 48 hours.

5. After simmering for 1 to 2 days, turn off heat and allow to slightly cool. Then filter through a fine-mesh sieve and bottle in mason jars.

6. The stock should set just like gelatin, and the fat should rise to the top. Upon using in recipes or eating, pick off the fat (this is tallow) and reserve it for cooking, then scoop out the gelled stock and reheat to use in soup or broth in any cooking dish or to sip on 6 ounces daily.

7. Store in the fridge for up to 1 week or freeze in mason jars with ample space for expansion once fully cooled. The broth can also be frozen in ice cube trays so that you can quickly add a small portion to sauces or use a couple cubes to deglaze a pan!

Nutrition facts per serving
Calories: 118   Carbohydrates: 0g   Fiber: 0g   Protein: 10g   Fat: 7g

Gut-Restoring Chicken Bone Broth

FOOD AS MEDICINE   Chicken soup has long been promoted as a "cure" for the common cold, and University of Nebraska researchers validate that claim. They tested 13 brands and found that all but one (chicken-flavored ramen noodles) blocked the migration of inflammatory white blood cells. Cold symptoms result from an accumulation of these cells in the bronchial tubes, so the ability to block the build up will block symptoms or advancement of illness. The amino acid cysteine, released from chicken during cooking, chemically resembles the bronchitis drug acetylcysteine. Chicken broth has another amino acid, glutamine, which aids in rebuilding the gut where most of the immune system is regulated. Use sea salt to create a nice salty broth, which keeps mucus thin the same way cough medicines do. Give your soup a boost with garlic, onions, carrots, and celery, all of which can increase immune-boosting power.

If you'd like, you can use the bones of a rotisserie chicken instead of a raw chicken, and begin this recipe at step 4.

repair

Makes: 16 (8-ounce) servings   *Prep time:* 1½ hours   *Cook time:* 1½ hours, plus 24 to 36 hours to simmer

1 pasture-raised raw chicken

1½ tablespoons ghee or grass-fed butter

1½ tablespoon sea salt, divided

2 tablespoons black peppercorns

1 yellow onion with skin, quartered and then chopped in half

1 red onion with skin, quartered and then chopped in half

3 carrots, chopped in 2–3-inch pieces

1 full celery bunch, leaves on, chopped

1 bunch fresh rosemary

6–7 cloves garlic, skinned, smashed

1–3 cups vegetable scraps (onion skins, chard stems, carrot tops, etc.)

2 tablespoons Bragg Raw Apple Cider Vinegar

2 tablespoons turmeric, ground or freshly chopped

2–3 bay leaves

water

1. Preheat the oven to 350°F.

2. Coat the inside (cavity) and outside of the chicken with ghee, half of the sea salt, and black pepper.

3. Roast the chicken for 1½ hours until the juices run clear. Remove and discard the skin. Remove and reserve meat for chicken salad or soup (or eat for dinner).

4. Put the carcass into 4-quart pot or slow cooker and pour in the liquid from roasting pan. Add the onions, carrots, celery, rosemary, garlic, and vegetable scraps to the pot or slow cooker. Cover all bones and veggies with water and put on stove.

5. Bring the pot to a boil and then reduce heat to a slow simmer. If using a slow cooker, run on high for first 4 hours. Add vinegar, turmeric, remaining sea salt, and bay leaves. Let simmer with lid on until bones are soft and broth is a rich yellow hue, 24 to 36 hours. Do not agitate or stir broth once cooking to allow optimal collagen formation in broth; allow it to gel. If looking to make a more concentrated stock, remove lid for last 4 to 6 hours to condense liquid.

6. Discard bones and vegetables. If not using within 5 days, cool slightly and strain the stock into a freezer-safe container. If using a glass container, be sure to leave 1–2 inches of room for expansion; if using plastic, cool completely in fridge in glass first.

Nutrition facts per serving
Calories: 40   Carbohydrates: 0g   Fiber: 0g   Protein: 3g   Fat: 3g

Creamy Green Chile Chicken Soup

FOOD AS MEDICINE   This soup will kick up some heat in your belly while supporting metabolism with capsaicin from the Hatch peppers. Balancing out the spice, avocado works to cool things down while providing a nice source of potassium, B vitamins, and fiber. The jicama is a potent prebiotic fiber that fuels good bacteria, maintaining healthy growth of probiotics for a symbiotic gut. Serving as a fertilizer for the gut, the prebiotics in this soup are further supported with the base of bone broth, which protects and lines the GI tract and promotes relaxation.

reset   (kf) (gf) (df) (nf) (ef)

Makes: 8 (2-cup) servings   *Prep time:* 30 to 40 minutes   *Cook time:* 25 to 30 minutes

1½ tablespoons avocado oil

1 red onion, chopped

3 cloves garlic, crushed

2 tablespoons cumin

1 teaspoon sea salt

1 yellow bell pepper, chopped

2 cups medium spicy Hatch chiles

8 cups Gut-Restoring Chicken Bone Broth (page 223)

1¼ cups full-fat coconut milk

3 avocados, divided

1 cup chopped jicama, divided

2 cups shredded rotisserie chicken

1 bunch cilantro, leaves chopped

1. In a large stockpot, heat avocado oil over medium-high heat and then add in onion to sauté.

2. Once onion is softened, about 4 to 5 minutes, add garlic and cumin. Stir to combine.

3. Season with sea salt and add bell pepper pieces. Sauté an additional 4 to 5 minutes.

4. Add Hatch chiles and bone broth to the pot and stir to combine, bringing liquid to a simmer.

5. Once simmering, add in coconut milk and allow soup to thicken slightly, about 10 minutes of simmering.

6. Transfer a little over half of the soup in 2 batches of 3 cups each to a blender and puree. In each batch, mix in 1 avocado and ¼ cup jicama. This allows a predominantly creamy soup while still allowing some texture.

7. Return both pureed soup mixtures back to the stockpot and stir all soup to combine. Add in ¾ of the remaining jicama, along with shredded chicken. Bring back up to a simmer for 15 to 20 minutes.

8. Ladle into soup bowls and top with 2 tablespoons each chopped avocado, jicama, and cilantro.

Nutrition facts per serving
Calories: 275   Carbohydrates: 12g   Fiber: 5g   Protein: 16g   Fat: 20g

Zesty Creamy Carrot Soup

FOOD AS MEDICINE   This soup pairs a base of nourishing bone broth with antioxidant-rich carrots. Since it is a root vegetable, I don't peel organic choices to retain their soil-based minerals and microbes for healthy gut bacteria support. Carrots are also a great source of vitamins A, K, and C, a benefit which is further enhanced with the addition of orange juice and zest. This soup has a nice zing from the anti-inflammatory and digestion-supporting ginger but is also reminiscent of a Creamsicle with the blend of coconut milk.

Makes: 6 (1½-cup) servings   *Prep time:* 30 to 40 minutes   *Cook time:* 5 to 30 minutes

2 tablespoons coconut oil

1 yellow onion, chopped

2 teaspoons sea salt, divided, plus more to taste

1½ cups carrots, chopped in 1-inch pieces

6 cups Gut-Restoring Chicken Bone Broth (page 223)

3 inches ginger, peeled and cut into 5 to 6 pieces

juice and zest of 1 orange

Himalayan pink salt, to taste

12 ounces full-fat coconut milk

chopped mint, to serve

chopped basil, to serve

black pepper, to taste

1. Heat stock pot over medium-high heat and add coconut oil until melted and hot, then add chopped yellow onion and stir to coat, adding 1 teaspoon of sea salt.

2. Allow onion to heat undisturbed for 3 to 4 minutes then stir and allow to sit for another 3 to 4 minutes to create golden browning. Once onion is softened, add carrots and remaining teaspoon of sea salt. Stir until coated and allow to cook about 4 to 5 minutes, then add broth and ginger pieces. Place lid on pot and simmer for 20 minutes.

3. Stir orange juice and zest into soup.

4. Allow flavors to combine for about 3 to 5 minutes with lid off, then add additional salt and pepper to taste and then add coconut milk.

5. Allow flavors to combine for a couple of minutes more, and then transfer in two batches to your blender to puree into a velvety texture.

6. Plate desired servings and top with fresh chopped mint and basil.

Note: If desired, or if your blender is not able to completely incorporate mixture, consider straining soup through a cheesecloth, gauze, or a fine sieve; however, it is optimal to maintain all elements to retain the fibers.

Nutrition facts per serving
Calories: 125   Carbohydrates: 6g   Fiber: 1g   Protein: 12g   Fat: 6g

Naturally Nourished Pot Roast

FOOD AS MEDICINE   This pot roast recipe is a great make-ahead, one-pot meal, and the leftovers get better each day! Chuck or rump roast will be a more affordable option and is made tender by braising in the slow cooker with aromatic herbs, bone broth, and vegetables. Grass-fed beef is rich in anti-inflammatory and heart-healthy omega-3 fatty acids and CLAs and is free from added hormones and antibiotics found in CAFO-raised animal products.

| repair | (kf) (gf) (df) (nf) (ef)

Makes: 10 (6-ounce) servings   *Prep time:* 25 to 30 minutes   *Cook time:* 6 hours

4 pounds grass-fed chuck roast

2 teaspoons sea salt, plus more to taste

1 teaspoon coarse ground black pepper, plus more to taste

4 tablespoons grass-fed tallow, divided

2 yellow onions, peeled and quartered

1 bunch carrots, unpeeled, cut into 2-inch pieces

1½ cups red wine

2 bunches curly kale, stems removed and torn into 2-inch pieces

½ pound Yukon gold or red potatoes, cut into quarters

10 cups Gut-Restoring Chicken Bone Broth (page 223) or Grass-Fed Beef Knuckle Bone Broth (page 221)

2 tablespoons tomato paste (optional)

6 sprigs fresh rosemary

4 sprigs fresh thyme

sea salt, to taste

1. Generously salt and pepper the chuck roast and bring to room temperature.

2. In a hot cast-iron skillet, add 2 tablespoons of tallow and begin to pan sear each side of the roast, browning on 4 to 6 sides for 3 to 4 minutes each, for a total of 15 to 20 minutes. Once browned, place in slow cooker on high heat.

3. Add remaining 2 tablespoons of tallow along with onions and carrots to pan. Sauté for about 4 minutes and then add the

wine to reduce browned bits from pan. Add this mixture to slow cooker, placing it around the roast. Mix in raw kale and potatoes, distribute evenly around the roast, and combine well with carrot-onion mixture.

4. Pour in bone broth mixed with optional tomato paste. Add rosemary, thyme, and additional salt and pepper to taste.

5. Place lid on slow cooker and leave on high setting for first 4 hours, then switch to simmer or low for remaining 2 hours. The roast is ready when it is tender and easily pulls apart using two forks.

6. Place roast on a plate and shred with forks, then return to slow cooker to mix with broth and vegetables, and serve into bowls.

Nutrition facts per serving
Calories: 331   Carbohydrates: 11g   Fiber: 3g   Protein: 40g   Fat: 10g

Warming Chicken Thighs with Braised Greens

FOOD AS MEDICINE   This recipe uses dark meat, which contains a wealth of nutrients and helps to balance out amino acids in the body that can get thrown off with excessive consumption of lean meats. Dark meat delivers more anti-anxiety-supporting zinc and selenium and is also abundant in the nutrient taurine, which supports GABA production for relaxation. This recipe pairs a nourishing protein with leafy greens and antioxidant-rich seasonings to enhance neurotransmitter balance and provide methylation support.

| restore | | | | |

Makes: 8 servings   *Prep time:* 5 to 10 minutes   *Cook time:* 30 to 40 minutes

2 pounds chicken thighs	1 tablespoon turmeric
1 teaspoon sea salt, plus more to taste	1 tablespoon cardamom seeds
1 teaspoon black pepper	1 bunch collard greens, cut into thin strips
2 tablespoons ghee, divided	¾ cup coconut milk
5 tablespoons grainy mustard	½ cup Gut-Restoring Chicken Bone Broth (page 223)
1 yellow onion, diced	chopped cilantro, to serve
5 cloves garlic, chopped	

1. Season chicken thighs with 1 teaspoon each sea salt and black pepper.

2. Heat a cast-iron skillet to medium-high heat and add 1 tablespoon ghee until melted, then add in thighs and allow to brown slightly for about 4 to 5 minutes before flipping to brown on other side, 3 to 4 minutes. After the second half is browned, remove from heat and set on plate.

3. Spread grainy mustard over the chicken thighs with a brush Meanwhile, preheat oven to 400°F.

4. Reheat pan and add additional tablespoon of ghee. Then add onion and stir to coat with ghee. Sprinkle with sea salt.

5. After 3 to 4 minutes, add chopped garlic and stir to combine. After another 2 to 3 minutes when onion is softened, add turmeric and cardamom seeds.

6. Allow flavors to combine for a minute or so, then add chopped greens, coconut milk, and bone broth, stirring to combine.

7. Return chicken thighs to the pan on top of greens and liquid. Place in oven to bake for 20 minutes at 400°F.

8. Remove from oven, top with chopped cilantro, and serve.

Nutrition facts per serving
Calories: 227   Carbohydrates: 2g   Fiber: 1g   Protein: 24g   Fat: 13g

Seaweed Turkey Roll-Ups

FOOD AS MEDICINE   Nori is a great source of tyrosine, an amino acid used as a building block in the production of neurotransmitters, including dopamine, norepinephrine, and epinephrine. Combining the amino acid tyrosine, found in seaweed, with the tryptophan in turkey is a way to support a blissful state and aid in a mellow mood. The red pepper provides a boost of vitamin C for adrenal support beyond its antioxidants and fiber to contribute a nice crisp crunch.

rebalance

Makes: 4 servings   *Prep time:* 15 to 20 minutes

4 nori sheets

1 avocado, halved and pitted

2 teaspoons lemon juice

¼ teaspoon sea salt

½ pound "in-house" roasted turkey or nitrite-free, stabilizer-free deli turkey

1 red bell pepper, sliced into matchsticks

2 cups leafy greens of choice

warm water

1. Lay out nori sheets with shiny side down.

2. In a bowl, mash avocado with lemon juice and sea salt.

3. Spread the avocado on each nori sheet with a spatula.

4. Lay out 2 to 3 slices of turkey and 2 to 3 slices of bell pepper horizontally at the bottom quarter of each sheet of nori.

5. Gently roll 1 sheet at a time, starting at the bottom, and stopping once past the red pepper to add a handful of greens on top of the turkey in remaining space.

6. Continue to roll past peppers and over greens until final inch is exposed.

7. Wet your index and middle finger in warm water and run over exposed edge of nori sheet.

8. Immediately seal the sushi roll, using additional water as needed to bind.

9. Using a sharp knife, cut into slices as desired.

Nutrition facts per serving
Calories: 153   Carbohydrates: 9g   Fiber: 5g   Protein: 17g   Fat: 6g

Sweet and Sour Pork Meatballs

FOOD AS MEDICINE   Pasture-raised pork is an excellent source of B vitamins and is high in anti-inflammatory, heart healthy, and cancer-fighting omega-3 fatty acids as well as conjugated linoleic acids (CLAs). Pork is also an excellent source of the amino acid tryptophan, which we usually associate with our Thanksgiving turkey. The body uses tryptophan as a precursor to serotonin.

rebalance

Makes: 4 (3-meatball) servings   *Prep time:* 15 to 20 minutes   *Cook time:* 50 to 60 minutes

For the meatballs:

1 yellow onion, quartered

2 cloves garlic, smashed and peeled

1 pound ground pork

1 large egg

1 teaspoon sesame oil

1 teaspoon fresh ginger

1 teaspoon sea salt

For the sauce:

1 cup fresh or frozen pineapple, cubed

3 tablespoon tomato paste

¼ cup honey

⅓ cup coconut aminos

1 tablespoon Bragg Raw Apple Cider Vinegar

To garnish:

¼ cup green onions, roughly chopped

1 tablespoon sesame seeds

1. Preheat the oven to 375°F.

2. Place the onion and garlic in the food processor and pulse until roughly chopped. Add the pork, egg, sesame oil, ginger, and sea salt. Continue to pulse until all ingredients are incorporated and evenly distributed.

3. Wet both hands and shape the pork mixture into 1-inch meatballs. Place on a baking sheet lined with parchment paper. Bake 25 to 30 minutes, until internal temperature reaches 145°F.

4. While the meatballs are baking, make the sauce. Combine pineapple, tomato paste, honey, coconut aminos, and vinegar in the blender or clean food processor and blend until smooth. Adjust seasoning to taste.

5. Pour the sauce mixture into a small sauce pan and bring to a boil, then reduce the heat to a simmer. Cook, stirring frequently until the sauce thickens, 8 to 10 minutes.

6. When the sauce is honey-thick and meatballs are cooked through, place the meatballs in the sauce and coat thoroughly. Sprinkle with green onions and sesame seeds to serve.

Nutrition facts per serving
Calories: 312   Carbohydrates: 30g   Fiber: 6g   Protein: 29g   Fat: 11g

Mediterranean Tuna Salad

FOOD AS MEDICINE   Fatty fish like tuna and salmon are some of the best sources of omega-3 fatty acids. Omega-3 fatty acids are responsible for reducing inflammation in the body and preventing plaque buildup in the arteries as well as promoting healthy cognitive function and skin health. Due to the concerns with mercury in tuna, I opt for wild canned skipjack, which is a smaller fish that will have less chance for bioaccumulation or buildup of harmful heavy metals and toxins. I prefer to buy Wild Planet Canned Skipjack.

rebalance   (kf) (gf) (df) (ef)

Makes: 2 (½-cup) servings   *Prep time:* 10 to 15 minutes

- 1 can skipjack tuna
- ⅛ cup Kalamata olives, chopped, plus 1 tablespoon olive brine
- ¼ small red onion, finely chopped
- 1 stalk celery, chopped
- 2 tablespoons fresh chopped parsley
- ½ cup cherry tomatoes, quartered
- 1 tablespoon red wine vinegar
- 1 tablespoon olive oil
- juice of ½ lemon
- sea salt and black pepper, to taste
- 1 whole avocado, pitted and halved

1. Place the canned skipjack in a large bowl and break up with a fork until flaky. Add the olives, onion, celery, parsley, and cherry tomatoes and mix until just combined.

2. Whisk together the vinegar, olive oil, lemon juice, and olive brine and a pinch of salt and pepper. Pour the dressing over the tuna mixture and toss to combine. Serve in an avocado halves for a quick and easy meal.

Nutrition facts per serving
Calories: 296   Carbohydrates: 11g   Fiber: 3g   Protein: 20g   Fat: 20g

Truffled Egg Salad

FOOD AS MEDICINE   Eggs help liver function, support cognitive function, and provide acetylcholine to enhance neurotransmitter signaling. Eggs also provide a great source of omega-3s, B-vitamins, and vitamin D, all of which support mood stability and a grounded mind. Hard-boiled eggs are a great weekly staple for any meal and this recipe kicks up egg salad to something gourmet and extremely satisfying.

rebalance

Makes: 4 servings   *Prep time:* 10 to 15 minutes   *Cook time:* 10 minutes

8 eggs

3 tablespoons avocado mayonnaise

1 tablespoon Dijon mustard

juice of ½ lemon

1 teaspoon truffle oil

½ cup finely chopped red onion

2 tablespoons fresh chopped chives

½ cup chopped celery

2 tablespoons fresh chopped parsley

1 tablespoon fresh finely chopped dill

½ teaspoon sea salt

¼ teaspoon black pepper

butter or romaine lettuce, for serving

1. Fill a pan large enough to fit the eggs in a single layer with 2 inches of water. Bring to a boil. Gently lower the eggs into the boiling water and boil for 10 minutes. Drain and run under cool water.

2. When cool enough to handle, peel the eggs and place in a bowl. Mash with a fork, then add the mayonnaise, mustard, lemon juice, and truffle oil.

3. Fold in the chopped onion, chives, celery, parsley and dill. Season to taste with the salt and pepper and additional truffle oil if needed. Serve over butter or romaine lettuce.

Nutrition facts per serving
Calories: 235   Carbohydrates: 3g   Fiber: 1g   Protein: 13g   Fat: 10g

Herb-Crusted Pork Tenderloin

FOOD AS MEDICINE   Pork is an excellent source of B vitamins and if pasture-raised will be free of added toxins and a rich source of anti-inflammatory omega-3 fatty acids as well as CLAs. Although turkey usually takes the lead, pork is also a rich source of the amino acid tryptophan, which is a precursor or building block to produce serotonin. This recipe is a great and quick weekday option with very little prep and fuss (and makes great leftovers in a salad, lettuce wrap, or stir fry)!

restore

Makes: 4 (6-ounce) servings   *Prep time:* 5 minutes active   *Cook time:* 40 minutes

1 to 1½ pounds pork tenderloin	½ teaspoon smoked paprika
1 tablespoon cumin	1 teaspoon sea salt
1 tablespoon dried oregano	1 teaspoon black pepper
1 teaspoon dried fine garlic granules	

1. Preheat grill to medium heat around 425°F. Pull pork tenderloin out on countertop while you mix seasonings.

2. Combine cumin, oregano, garlic, paprika, salt, and pepper in a small bowl.

3. Using your hands, rub the seasoning mixture onto the pork tenderloin, coating completely.

4. Place seasoned tenderloin on the grill for 20 minutes, flipping at 10 minutes into the process.

5. At 20 minutes, move from grill and check temperature to meet 145 to 155°F internally. Allow to sit for 8 to 10 minutes prior to slicing and serving.

Nutrition facts per serving
Calories: 165   Carbohydrates: 4g   Fiber: 1g   Protein: 29g   Fat: 4g

Almond Flour Chicken Piccata

FOOD AS MEDICINE   This quick and easy chicken piccata is breaded with almond flour, which is high in monounsaturated fats and vitamin E, making it heart healthy and anti-inflammatory. The use of ghee helps to build a delicious, rich sauce that is also high in anti-inflammatory, anti-tumorigenic, and heart disease–preventing CLAs. Ghee is clarified butter, which is able to tolerate higher heat treatments and has the milk solids removed. Along with the glutamine-rich bone broth, ghee can help to repair the gut lining and contains butyric acid to nourish the cells of the intestines.

remove

Makes: 4 servings   *Prep time:* 10 minutes   *Cook time:* 15 to 20 minutes

4 skin-on pasture-raised boneless chicken breasts (about 5–6 ounces each)

2 eggs

½ cup almond flour

2 tablespoons grass-fed ghee

1 clove garlic, minced

2 tablespoons capers, drained

⅓ cup white wine

⅓ cup Gut-Restoring Chicken Bone Broth (page 223)

juice of 1 lemon

2 tablespoons fresh chopped parsley

sea salt and black pepper, to taste

1. Lay the chicken breasts between two sheets of parchment paper and pound with a cast-iron skillet until flattened, about ¼ inch thick.

2. Beat the eggs with a pinch of sea salt in a shallow bowl. Combine the almond flour, a pinch of salt, and a pinch of pepper in a separate bowl. Dip each chicken breast in the egg mixture, then coat each side with the almond flour.

3. Melt the ghee in a large cast-iron skillet over medium heat. Add the chicken and cook for about 3 minutes per side until it reaches an internal temperature of 165°F.

4. Once cooked, transfer the chicken to a plate. Add the garlic and capers to the skillet and cook for 1 minute. Deglaze the pan

with the wine and the stock, then add the lemon juice. Bring to a boil, then cook over medium heat until reduced by about half, 8 to 10 minutes. Season to taste with salt and pepper.

5. Add the chicken to the sauce and allow to heat through, 2 to 3 minutes. Sprinkle with parsley and serve with the pan sauce and a side of sautéed veggies.

Nutrition facts per serving
Calories: 374   Carbohydrates: 3g   Fiber: 1g   Protein: 41g   Fat: 20g

Slow Cooker Carnitas

Pair with a side of seasoned grilled zucchini, onions, and summer squash. Or, try the Carnitas Burrito Bowl (page 244).

FOOD AS MEDICINE   This healthy slow cooker carnitas recipe is seared with lard or bacon grease before being added to the slow cooker. Lard or bacon fat can be a healthy choice! Lard is a type of fat that is 45% monounsaturated, 39% saturated, and 11% polyunsaturated, making it relatively stable and tolerable to moderate-high heat. Quality saturated fats are necessary for a balanced diet. Saturated fat plays a role in cellular membrane health, brain function, nerve function, and can reduce your risk of heart disease—yes, reduce! The addition of saturated fat to the diet reduces the levels of a substance called lipoprotein (a) that correlates strongly with risk for heart disease.

Buy real lard that is only made up of a single ingredient. Pasture-raised animals are less inflammatory than those raised in confined animal feeding operations (CAFOs) that are not able to roam and are fed a diet of GMO corn/soy along with hormones and excessive antibiotics.

restore	

Makes: 12 (2/3-cup) servings   *Prep time:* 10 to 15 minutes   *Cook time:* 12 to 18 hours

1 pasture-raised pork shoulder or rump roast (3 to 4 pounds)

2 tablespoons lard or bacon fat

2 teaspoons olive oil

4 cloves garlic, crushed

1 bunch green onions, chopped

1½ cups minced fresh cilantro

1 cup tomatillo salsa

½ cup chicken broth, plus more as needed

½ cup tequila (optional)

1 chopped jalapeño or 2 roasted Hatch chiles

fresh cilantro leaves, sliced red onion, and chopped tomatoes, to serve

2 (10-ounce) tubs mixed greens

sea salt and black pepper, to taste

1. Sprinkle the roast with salt and pepper on all sides.

2. Heat cast-iron pan and put a bit of pasture-raised lard or bacon grease at the bottom. Sear all sides of roast for about 3 to 4 minutes per side.

3. While the roast is searing, mix together the oil, garlic, salt, and pepper. Once the searing is completed, rub the oil mixture onto the roast and return it to the slow cooker.

4. Add the onions, cilantro, salsa, broth, tequila, if using, and chiles to the slow cooker. Cover and cook on low for 12 to 18 hours or until meat is tender; you should be able to pull the meat off bone or shred meat simply with a fork.

5. Remove meat; cool slightly. Shred with two forks and return to the slow cooker; heat through for another 10 to 20 minutes to bring back to the desired temperature and allow flavors to meld.

6. Serve with chopped tomatoes, onions, and cilantro over a bed of greens.

Nutrition facts per serving
Calories: 287   Carbohydrates: 5g   Fiber: 0g   Protein: 42g   Fat: 11g

Carnitas Burrito Bowl

FOOD AS MEDICINE   This Carnitas Burrito Bowl uses Slow Cooker Carnitas over a bed of leafy greens to add volume and nutrient density. Volumetrics is the principle of getting the most volume out of the least amount of calories. This concept can also be referred to as the energy density or caloric density of a food. When we break down foods into their macronutrients, we know that fat at 9 calories per gram is more than twice the energy density of proteins and carbohydrates at 4 calories per gram. Foods that are high in fiber and water tend to be the best option when applying volumetrics. Fresh fruits and vegetables, which are 80% to 90% water by weight, are the best choices. This approach has dual strength as water has an energy density (or caloric impact) of zero and the sensation of hunger is often confused with that of thirst, so it will rehydrate your body while providing satiety.

restore

Makes: 4 (6-ounce) servings   *Prep time:* 15 to 20 minutes   *Cook time:* 15 to 20 minutes

1 tablespoon avocado oil

1 onion, sliced

2–3 bell peppers, sliced

¼ recipe Slow Cooker Carnitas (page 242)

8 cups romaine or butter lettuce, chopped

1 avocado, quartered and sliced

1 cup pico de gallo

1 handful cilantro, chopped

1½ tablespoons olive oil or avocado oil, plus more to drizzle

lime wedges, for serving

1. In a cast-iron skillet, heat the avocado oil over medium heat. Add the sliced onions and cook, stirring occasionally, until translucent and beginning to cook down.

2. Once the onions are cooked down, add the sliced bell peppers and cook, stirring occasionally until softened, about 5 minutes. Once cooked, set aside.

3. In the same skillet, heat the carnitas until just heated through.

4. Place the lettuce in the bottom of a large bowl. Add the carnitas, then top with the sautéed onions and bell peppers. Top with the avocado slices, pico de gallo, cilantro, a drizzle of olive or avocado oil, and a squeeze of lime.

Nutrition facts per serving
Calories: 411   Carbohydrates: 13g   Fiber: 6g   Protein: 24g   Fat: 27g

Spaghetti Squash Bolognese

FOOD AS MEDICINE   Grass-fed beef is rich in anti-inflammatory and heart-healthy omega-3 fatty acids and CLAs and is free from added hormones and antibiotics found in conventionally raised animal products. For meats, eggs, and dairy, there are significant nutritional differences in pastured animal products resulting in increased amounts of CLAs, which are omega fatty acids with research supporting efficacy as cancer fighting, aiding in weight loss, and supporting insulin sensitivity to promote blood sugar regulation. These CLAs are found 5 times higher in pastured grass-fed products which are also higher in amounts of omega-3 fatty acids, vitamin E, B vitamins, calcium, magnesium, and potassium, with ⅓–½ less fat and ⅓ less cholesterol than conventional products.

restore

Makes: 4 servings   *Prep time:* 40 to 50 minutes   *Cook time:* 30 to 35 minutes

1 large spaghetti squash	½ pound grass-fed ground beef
1-2 tablespoons ghee or grass-fed butter	½ pound pasture-raised ground pork
1 onion, finely diced	½ cup full-fat coconut milk or heavy cream
1 carrot, finely diced	⅓ cup tomato paste
1 stalk celery, finely diced	½ cup dry white wine or beef broth
2 cloves garlic, minced	sea salt and black pepper, to taste
4 slices pasture-raised bacon, chopped	chopped basil for serving

1. Preheat the oven to 375°F.

2. Slice the spaghetti squash in half lengthwise. Place both halves face down on a baking sheet and add about 1 inch of water. Roast for 30 to 45 minutes until skin can be pierced with a fork and flesh is translucent.

3. Allow to cool, then scoop out seeds and discard. Using a fork, scrape out the flesh of the squash. Season with salt and pepper and set aside.

4. In the meantime, heat ghee or butter in a large cast-iron skillet or Dutch oven over medium heat. Add onions, carrots, celery and a generous pinch of sea salt. Sauté until translucent, about 5 minutes. Add garlic and cook one more minute.

5. Add the chopped bacon and cook, stirring occasionally until it begins to brown. Add the ground beef and pork and break up with a wooden spoon. Cook, stirring occasionally until all meat is browned. Add the coconut milk or cream, tomato paste, and wine or broth, and simmer on low heat for 30 minutes. Add salt and pepper to taste. Serve over the spaghetti squash and top with chopped basil.

Nutrition facts per serving
Calories: 354   Carbohydrates: 10g   Fiber: 5g   Protein: 23g   Fat: 24g

Bacteria-Battling Chimichurri

FOOD AS MEDICINE   Fresh herbs are a great way to provide a punch of flavor and nutritional density! Parsley, oregano, and basil have properties that can aid in antimicrobial, antibacterial, and antifungal support to the remove bad bacteria. Combine with garlic and olive oil as other potent fighters to make a dip with a kick to reset your microbiome. Use as a spread on roasted proteins such as lamb or beef or on roasted vegetables such as carrots. This recipe also serves nicely as a dip for raw veggies and can be mixed into scrambled eggs or added on top of an avocado half.

If you are including vinegar and probiotics at this time, try swapping 1 tablespoon lemon juice for 1 tablespoon Bragg Raw Apple Cider Vinegar to benefit from the probiotic yeast strains.

reset   (kf) (gf) (df) (nf) (ef)

Makes: 6 (¼-cup) servings   *Prep time:* 10 to 15 minutes

¼ cup freshly chopped parsley

¼ cup freshly chopped basil

2 tablespoons dried oregano

5 cloves garlic, smashed

2 tablespoons lemon juice

½ cup extra-virgin unrefined olive oil

2 teaspoons sea salt, plus more to taste

¼ teaspoon white pepper

2 teaspoons red chile flakes

1. In a food processor, using the "s" blade, combine parsley, basil, oregano, garlic, and lemon juice on high speed.

2. After a minute or so, use a spatula to scrape sides, and mix again for 1 minute.

3. Scrape sides again, then while blade is running, pour in olive oil at a constant drizzle. Then sprinkle in salt, pepper, and chile flakes.

4. Adjust flavors to taste, adding additional salt as needed.

Nutrition facts per serving
Calories: 168   Carbohydrates: 2g   Fiber: 1g   Protein: 0g   Fat: 18g

Simple Salt and Pepper Scallops

FOOD AS MEDICINE   Scallops are a quick and easy omega-3 rich shellfish that has low toxicity due to its size. As a quick protein that can be thought of as elegant, scallops provide a potent dosage of vitamin B12 and selenium along with other mood-stabilizing minerals. If you haven't made scallops at home this is a simple, non-intimidating approach that can be dressed up by any sauce or sides you like.

| restore | (kf) (gf) (df) (nf) (ef)

Makes: 4 servings   *Prep time:* 1 minute   *Cook time:* 6 to 10 minutes

1 pound wild scallops	½ teaspoon sea salt
1½ tablespoons lard	½ teaspoon black pepper

1. Rinse scallops and pat dry with a cloth towel; set aside.

2. Heat a stainless-steel pan or cast-iron skillet to medium-high heat and add ghee.

3. As ghee is melting in pan, sprinkle scallops on both sides with salt and pepper.

4. Place scallops in heated pan with melted ghee and allow to sit for 3 to 5 minutes undisturbed to create a nice sear.

5. Flip once, then sear another 3 to 5 minutes on the other side. You will know they are done when they are all white and no longer translucent when viewed from the side.

Nutrition facts per serving

Calories: 151   Carbohydrates: 3g   Fiber: 0g   Protein:18g   Fat: 6g

Desserts

Chia Cherry Thumbprint Cookies

FOOD AS MEDICINE Chia seeds are packed with anti-inflammatory omega-3 fatty acids as well as a substantial amount of fiber. They are a great addition to smoothies, breakfasts, and desserts, providing a gel-like jam for fruit puree. Although this recipe is an indulgence, the higher fiber and healthy fats from almond flour and coconut oil help stabilize blood sugar and create a feeling of satiety, keeping you full for longer. Beyond satisfying a sweet tooth, this recipe supports relaxation as the red and purple pigmentation in cherries, known as anthocyanin, helps regulate blood flow. In addition, cherries provide a rich food source of melatonin for improving quality of sleep, resetting one's circadian rhythm, and reducing anxiety throughout the following day.

remove   (ef)

Makes: 12 (1-cookie) servings   *Prep time:* 15 to 20 minutes   *Cook time:* 10 to 12 minutes

For the jam:

¾ cup dried cherries (unsulphured, with no added sugar), soaked in ¼ cup warm water

1 tablespoon dark amber maple syrup

1 to 2 tablespoons filtered water, divided

3 tablespoons chia seeds

For the cookies:

1½ cups almond flour

¼ cup coconut flour

2 tablespoons almond butter

1 teaspoon baking soda

⅓ cup coconut oil, melted

2 tablespoons dark amber maple syrup

½ teaspoon vanilla extract

½ teaspoon almond extract

¼ teaspoon sea salt

1. In a food processor using the "s" blade, combine the soaked cherries with their soak water, maple syrup, and 1 tablespoon of the filtered water. Process until smooth, adding the rest of the water as needed.

2. Pulse in the chia seeds. Scoop out into a small bowl and allow to sit for at least 15 minutes while you make the cookies. This allows your "jam" to gel.

3. Preheat the oven to 350°F. Line a baking sheet with parchment paper.

4. Combine the almond flour, coconut flour, almond butter, baking soda, coconut oil, maple syrup, vanilla extract, almond extract, and sea salt in a food processor with the "s" blade. Mix until a uniform dough forms into a ball.

5. Scoop out the dough one heaping tablespoon at a time and roll into smooth balls between the palms of your hands. Place on the baking sheet and use your thumb to create a well in the middle for the jam. Scoop out one teaspoon of the chia jam into each cookie.

6. Bake for 10 to 12 minutes until the tops begin to brown. Remove from oven and let cool at least 15 minutes before serving, to set.

Nutrition facts per serving
Calories: 155   Carbohydrates: 14g   Fiber: 4g   Protein: 3g   Fat: 10g

Chai Gelatin Panna Cotta

Sourcing of your gelatin is important! Be sure to use a pasture-raised or grass-fed form of beef gelatin for the most therapeutic effects. CAFO (concentrated animal feeding operation) animal farms can add toxicity to the gelatin, as seen in processed fruit-flavored gelatin products seen in most hospitals and grocery stores.

FOOD AS MEDICINE   Gelatin is comprised of glycine and proline, two amino acids that are generally limited in the American diet as they are found mostly in organs, bones, and fibrous animal tissues that don't often get eaten. Glycine can aid in relaxation and support GABA production. Gelatin can also aid in mood stability, as well as contribute to healthy skin and promote collagen formation for strong bones, joints, hair, and nails. In addition, gelatin has the ability to line the GI tract and reduce inflammation caused by food sensitivity, or inflammatory bowel disease, thus helping to repair your gut lining.

Makes: 4 (6-ounce) servings   *Prep time:* 10 minutes, 2 hours to set

1 can full-fat coconut milk

4 black tea bags (I use 2 Earl Grey and 2 of a black blend with complementary flavors)

1 tablespoon grass-fed beef gelatin

2 teaspoons almond extract

1 teaspoon vanilla extract

1/4 teaspoon ground cardamom

1 teaspoon ground cinnamon

¾ teaspoon ground ginger

1 to 2 tablespoons dark amber maple syrup (optional)

1. In a medium saucepan, heat the coconut milk to a low simmer and then remove from heat. Steep tea bags in this mixture for 5 to 6 minutes. Squeeze the tea bags into milk and then discard.

2. Allow the mixture to cool to room temperature, then add the cooled tea coconut milk to a blender along with remaining ingredients.

3. Blend on high for 45 to 60 seconds, until well incorporated.

4. Allow to sit in blender for 5 minutes to bloom the gelatin, then blend on high for 1 minute and pour mixture into 4 glass jars or containers with lids.

5. Set jars in fridge to allow gelatin to set for at least four hours before serving.

Nutrition facts per serving
Calories: 194   Carbohydrates: 3g   Fiber: 0g   Protein: 4g   Fat: 19g

Lime in the Coconut Fat Bomb

FOOD AS MEDICINE   A fat bomb is a high-fat, low-carb sweet tooth treat typically made with coconut oil, grass-fed butter, and other flavors of choice. This version is dairy-free and uses coconut butter (pure coconut including some flesh as opposed to just pure oil separated out in coconut oil). Coconut has beneficial fat-burning and immunological properties. Coconut oil for example is high in lauric acid, which boosts the immune system and can kill harmful pathogens like bacteria, viruses, and fungi. Coconut oil is made of medium-chain triglycerides (MCTs), which do not require the enzyme lipase in order to be digested, helping to achieve optimal absorption and increasing the body's production of ketones as fuel. This recipe is a bright way to start or end your day, incorporating the zing and brightness of lime zest with a nice creamy coconut crunch!

Makes: 6 fat bombs   *Prep time:* 10 minutes active, 5 hours to freeze

3 tablespoons coconut butter

3 tablespoons coconut oil

2 tablespoons coconut shreds, divided

1 teaspoon lime extract

1 tablespoon lime zest

⅛ teaspoon sea salt

1. Blend coconut butter, coconut oil, 1 tablespoon coconut shreds, lime extract, lime zest, and salt in a food-processor with an "s" blade.

2. Chill in freezer until firm, about 1 hour.

3. Mix remaining coconut shreds on a plate, then roll fat bomb mixture into a ball and roll into the coconut shreds.

4. Place on plate or in glass container in freezer to set for at least 4 hours and store in freezer until ready to eat, if desired!

Nutrition facts per serving
Calories: 125   Carbohydrates: 2g   Fiber: 1g   Protein: 2g   Fat: 15g

Coconut Chia Seed Pudding

When looking to support restoration of your gut bacteria, consume fiber in adequate amounts to fertilize the beneficial probiotic strains. Chia seeds provide a soothing gel-like soluble fiber that supports healthy gut lining function and healthy gut bacteria. Fiber is not only important for colonization of probiotics, it also helps with detoxification to aid in binding toxins and excreting these toxins through the colon while supporting healthy motility, preventing constipation. Coconut milk provides a creamy base to this pudding, which can be served as a parfait with fresh or sautéed fruit. If looking to make this a light meal, consider adding a scoop of protein such as grass-fed whey or collagen to ensure ample amino acid intake.

 reset (gf) (df) (nf) (ef)

Makes: 6 servings   *Prep time:* 5 minutes, plus 6 to 8 hours to set

2 cups full-fat coconut milk (choose a brand that is simple without guar gum and stabilizers)

½ cup chia seeds

⅓ cup large coconut shreds

1 tablespoon vanilla extract

½ teaspoon ground cinnamon

⅛ teaspoon ground cardamom

2 tablespoons dark amber maple syrup

2 scoops collagen peptides (optional)

1. In a bowl, whisk together all ingredients until well-combined.

2. Separate into 6 glass jars with lids and place in fridge.

3. After an hour, stir the mixture 2 to 3 times to create best texture. Keep refrigerated 6 to 8 hours or longer for pudding to set.

Nutrition facts per serving
Calories: 247   Carbohydrates:14g   Fiber: 7g   Protein: 5g   Fat: 18g

Grain-Free Low-Carb Peanut Butter Cookies

FOOD AS MEDICINE   Peanut butter often gets a bad rap, much of it having to do with the way peanuts grow. As a legume versus a tree nut like most counterparts, peanuts are at higher risk for toxicity and mold. Be sure to choose organic peanut butter and rotate your nut butters in general for best nutritional variety. Peanuts are popular for their flavor but they also provide quite a punch of nourishment. Rich in minerals including copper, manganese, molybdenum, and vitamins niacin (B3) and biotin, peanuts can support a healthy mood while serving in this recipe to provide fat and protein to balance out blood sugar levels. This low-carb cookie uses a natural maple syrup rather than a processed sugar alcohol or refined sugar, providing a nice chewy mouthfeel and satisfying sugar cravings while preventing blood sugar spikes and crashes.

restore

Makes: 21 servings   *Prep time:* 10 minutes   *Cook time:* 10 to 13 minutes

1½ cups natural organic peanut butter made with peanuts, salt, and no added oils (For best outcome, choose a liquidy brand such as Kirkland.)

2 tablespoons coconut oil, melted

½ cup dark amber maple syrup

1 tablespoon vanilla extract

1 large egg, whisked

½ teaspoon sea salt

1 teaspoon baking soda

3 to 5 tablespoons almond flour

⅓ cup chocolate chips, ⅓ cup large coconut shreds, or ¼ cup chia seeds (optional)

1. Preheat oven to 350°F.

2. In a large bowl, stir together peanut butter, melted coconut oil, maple syrup, and vanilla until combined.

3. Incorporate whisked egg, salt, and baking soda.

4. Add 1 tablespoon of almond flour at a time as needed to achieve a spoonable texture.

5. Scoop 2 tablespoon portions onto a baking sheet lined with parchment paper. Gently press down each spoonful with 2 fingers to flatten.

6. Bake for 10 to 13 minutes, being sure to check for doneness at 10 minutes.

7. Allow to cool prior to serving for best texture.

Nutrition facts serving
Calories: 158   Carbohydrates: 9g   Fiber: 1g   Protein: 4g   Fat: 7g

Walnut Maca Caramels

FOOD AS MEDICINE   Walnuts are a rich source of omega-3s to reduce inflammation and anxiety. Beyond omega-3s, walnuts are a great source of polyphenols, antioxidants that have disease-fighting properties; however, these are found primarily in the skin, so be sure to buy walnut halves that have not been peeled or blanched. When consuming the skin, be mindful—they may be more bitter, as most foods high in tannins are. This property has an antimicrobial and antiparasitic role, aiding in resetting the microbiome as well as reducing inflammation. Luckily, this recipe balances out the bitterness of the skin with vanilla, salt, and dates.

Another potent anti-anxiety player in this treat is maca. Maca is a Peruvian root vegetable that has adaptogenic properties. Adaptogens aid in stress response, preventing stress-induced fatigue and adrenal distress. As the adrenals are preserved other glands in the body have the ability to shine, which means more balanced thyroid and sexual hormones too!

Makes: 16 servings   *Prep time:* 10 to 15 minutes

1½ cups walnuts	3 to 9 dates, chopped, divided
1 teaspoon sea salt	shredded coconut flakes, cacao nibs or powder, or hemp seeds, for garnish
2 tablespoons maca powder	
1 tablespoon vanilla extract	

1. In a food processor using the "s" blade, combine walnuts and sea salt.

2. Blend until combined into a fine meal and a thin line of nut butter starts to form on the side of the container.

3. Scrape sides of food processor container with a spatula and add maca and vanilla.

4. Blend another 15 to 20 seconds and scrape sides again, then add 3 pitted chopped dates, about 3 tablespoons.

5. Blend for another 20 to 30 seconds, scrape sides, and taste. Adjust by adding more dates and sea salt if needed.

6. With your hands, roll mixture into balls of 1 to 2 tablespoons per ball. Store in fridge.

7. Optionally, roll in shredded coconut flakes, cacao nibs or powder, hemp seeds, or other tiny texture and flavor enhancers of choice!

Nutrition facts per serving
Calories: 97   Carbohydrates: 5g   Fiber: 1g   Protein: 2g   Fat: 8g

Turmeric Orange Gummies

FOOD AS MEDICINE   The combination of anti-inflammatory turmeric and ginger balanced with electrolytes and the natural sweetness of vitamin C–rich orange coconut water creates a great blend of cooling support to heal leaky gut and boost antioxidant intake. This recipe is very child friendly and a great support to cool bowel inflammation, provide connective tissue support, and aid in relaxation and adrenal rebound.

rebound

Makes: 6 servings   *Prep time:* 5 minutes, plus 4 hours to overnight to set

2 tablespoons pasture-raised, grass-fed gelatin, such as Vital Proteins

½ cup coconut water

1 cup fresh-squeezed orange juice

2 teaspoons dried turmeric powder

½ teaspoon dried ginger powder

1. Activate the gelatin by adding it to the coconut water and stirring until dissolved. The mixture may start to thicken.

2. Heat remaining ingredients in a small saucepan over medium-low heat until just simmering. Pour the heated liquid into the bloomed gelatin and stir to combine.

3. Pour into silicone molds or into a shallow 8 × 8-inch glass baking dish. Refrigerate for 4 hours or overnight, then pop out of molds or cut into fun shapes with cookie cutters!

Nutrition facts per serving
Calories: 36   Carbohydrates: 7g   Fiber: 0g   Protein: 1g   Fat: 1g

Matcha Coconut Gummies

FOOD AS MEDICINE   Matcha provides the highest source of L-theanine, which aids in stabilizing and balancing neurotransmitters while supporting alpha-brain waves for concentration, creativity, and focus, and mimics activity seen during deep meditation. By reducing stress, the adrenals get a chance to rebound with less distress or demand. The addition of ginger and coconut provide a zingy kick with a creamy finish to serve as a balanced snack or a fun way to end a meal while supporting gut integrity and serving as a mid-day brain boost.

 rebound kf gf df ef

Makes: 12 servings   *Prep time:* 10 to 15 minutes, plus 4 to 8 hours to set

1 cup coconut water

3 tablespoons pasture-raised, grass-fed gelatin, such as Vital Proteins

1 cup full-fat coconut milk

1 tablespoon honey or maple syrup

1 teaspoon vanilla extract

2 teaspoons matcha powder

1. Place the coconut water in a small bowl and add the gelatin. Mix until combined and allow to "bloom" while you do the next steps.

2. In a small saucepan, bring the coconut milk to a simmer over low heat. Once heated, place in the blender and add the gelatin and coconut water mixture, honey, vanilla, and matcha. Blend on high for about 30 seconds, or until color is uniform throughout.

3. Tap the blender on the counter to break up any bubbles. If you have created a lot of foam, you may want to skim this off before proceeding or use a fine mesh strainer for best results.

4. Pour into silicone molds or into a shallow 8 × 8-inch glass baking dish. Refrigerate for 4 hours or overnight, then pop out of molds or cut into fun shapes with cookie cutters!

Nutrition facts per serving
Calories: 76   Carbohydrates: 3g   Fiber: 0g   Protein: 6g   Fat: 5g

Appendix

Exchange List

To truly understand the two phases of the anti-anxiety diet, it is important to familiarize yourself with exchanges of foods in their whole form to master the variance between ketogenic and low-glycemic structure. The foods below are organized in categories and provide exchange sizes that correspond with certain amounts of macronutrients. They can be included in both Phase 1 and Phase 2 of the anti-anxiety diet. Carbohydrate-Containing Foods (page 168) are consumed more abundantly in Phase 2, so it is important to separate those from the foods you want to be more mindful of, and to stay within 30 or 90 grams.

Non-starchy vegetables: Choose organic/sustainably grown, local, and seasonal when possible.

Fats: Available in the form of nuts, seeds, fruits, and oils. Choose organic where possible and select options in the most whole form. Store fats in cold, airtight, dark storage. Avoid corn, soy, canola, safflower, and vegetable oils.

Clean proteins: Fats support neurotransmitter balance and regulate blood sugar levels, so it is not recommended to eat only lean options. Select from all categories for best diversity. You will notice the portions will shift based on the category, and items in the high-fat section will be more of an accent to the dish as opposed to a featured protein. For instance, I would not recommend getting a full 4 ounces of your protein needs from bacon, but you could add two slices of bacon to two eggs to meet your total protein needs. All choices should be grass-fed, pasture-raised, wild, and free of growth hormones and antibiotics.

When in Phase 1 of your program, I recommend selecting foods located in this section. The servings are not to mandate how much you eat but instead to understand how much of each macronutrient is in a particular food, so you can empower yourself with the way you comprise your meals, potentially using two to three servings of an item. As fats support neurological function, and both Phase 1 and Phase 2 are fat-dominant, you will likely have two or three servings of fat at meals and snacks. Use the Anti-Anxiety Diet Grocery List on page 266 and the 2-Week Meal Plan on page 173 to get more ideas and shopping structure!

Non-Starchy Vegetables

Each serving contains 5 grams of carbohydrates and 25 calories. In general, a single serving is ½ cup of cooked vegetables or vegetable juice, or 1 cup of raw vegetables.

- Artichoke
- Asparagus
- Bamboo shoots
- Beans (green, wax, Italian)
- Bean sprouts
- Broccoli
- Brussels sprouts
- Cabbage (green, Napa, Chinese)
- Cauliflower
- Celery
- Chives
- Cucumber
- Eggplant
- Garlic
- Greens (bok choy, collard, dandelion, escarole, kale, mustard, Swiss chard, turnip)
- Jicama
- Leeks
- Lettuce, mixed greens (romaine, red/green leaf, endive, spinach, arugula, radicchio, watercress, chicory)
- Mushrooms, all kinds
- Okra
- Onions
- Pea pods, snap peas, snow peas
- Peppers, all varieties
- Radishes
- Sauerkraut, raw, unpasteurized, live
- Sea vegetables (dulse, kelp, nori, hijiki)
- Sprouts and microgreens
- Squash (summer, spaghetti)
- Tomatoes
- Zucchini

Fats: Nuts and Seeds

Each serving contains 3 to 4 grams of carbohydrates, 5 to 8 grams of fat, 70 to 90 calories, and 3 grams of protein. In general, a single serving, unless otherwise noted below, is 2 tablespoons of nuts or 1 tablespoon of seeds.

- Cashews, 6 nuts
- Chia seeds
- Ground Flaxseed
- Macadamia nuts, 5 nuts

- Nut butters, 1 tablespoon
- Peanuts, 10 nuts
- Pistachios, 18–20 nuts
- Pumpkin seeds

- Sesame seeds
- Sunflower seeds
- Brazil nuts, 2–3 nuts
- Pecans, 6–8 halves

- Walnuts, 6–8 halves
- Almonds, 8–10 nuts
- Hazelnuts, 8–10 nuts

Fats: Fruits

Each serving (indicated below) contains 1 to 2 grams of carbs, 5 to 7 grams of fat, and 70 to 90 calories.

- Avocado, medium, ¼
- Coconut milk (full fat), 1 ounce
- Olives, 8 to 10

Fats: Oils

Each serving contains 0 grams of carbohydrates, 5 grams of fat, and 45 calories. In general, a single serving is 1 teaspoon of oil or butter, and 1 tablespoon of salad dressing or dip such as mayo, aioli, chimichurri, pesto. It may be appropriate to have multiple fat servings in meals/snacks based on your needs.

No or Low Heat	Medium Heat	High Heat	Spreads/Sauces
• Extra-virgin olive oil	• Sesame oil	• Avocado oil	• Aioli, mayo
• Flax seed oil	• Walnut oil	• Coconut oil, refined	• Chimichurri, pesto
• Virgin coconut oil		• Ghee, grass-fed	• Salad dressing
• Virgin avocado oil		• Grapeseed oil	
		• Lard, pasture-raised	
		• Peanut oil	
		• Palm oil, sustainable	

Clean Proteins

All animal-based proteins have 7 grams of protein per ounce/portion.

Lean Meats and Proteins

Consume 4- to 6-ounce portions. Unless otherwise noted, each 1-ounce serving contains 0 grams of carbohydrates, 7 grams of protein, 2 to 4 grams of fat, and 45 calories.

- Beef or bison: chuck roast, rump roast, flank or tenderloin steaks, ground 90 to 95% lean
- Deli meats (in-house roast, nitrite-free, free of binders, fillers), 3 grams fat per ounce
- Egg whites, 2 (though whole eggs are preferred!)
- Fish, fresh or frozen: cod, flounder, grouper, halibut, mahi-mahi, salmon, snapper, trout, tuna, etc.
- Pork, lean cuts: tenderloin, chop
- Poultry breast, white meat
- Shellfish: shrimp, crab, clam, oysters, lobster

Medium-Fat Meats and Proteins

Consume 3- to 4-ounce portions. Unless otherwise noted, each 1-ounce serving contains 0 grams of carbohydrates, 7 grams of protein, 5 to 7 grams of fat, and 75 calories.

- Beef or bison: ground <90% lean, prime rib, porterhouse, T-bone steak
- Egg (whole), 1
- Pork: shoulder roast, ribs
- Poultry, skin on, bone in, dark
- Sausage, 4 to 7 grams of fat per ounce

High-Fat Meats and Proteins

Consume 1- to 2-ounce portions. Unless otherwise noted, each 1-ounce serving contains 0 grams of carbohydrates, 7 grams of protein, 8 or more grams of fat, and 100 calories.

- Bacon: pork, 2 slices; turkey, 3 slices
- Cured meats, with 8 grams of fat or more per ounce (nitrite-free): coppa, guanciale, lardo, pastrami, prosciutto, salami soppressata
- Humanely raised pate, terrine, or foie gras
- Sausage, with 8 grams of fat or more per ounce

Anti-Anxiety Diet Grocery List

Use this list to plan your grocery shopping. I noted portions in some sections, such as produce and proteins, to aid in weekly shopping strategy. Choose local, seasonal items whenever possible and experiment with new items from week to week to ensure a variety of different antioxidants, amino acids, and micronutrients.

Foods to Eat

These foods are supportive of your goals in both phases. Look for organic, local products, if possible. Ideally, protein should be wild-caught/humanely raised, grass-fed, and organic.

Fruits and Vegetables

I recommend purchasing fruits and vegetables according to a color spectrum to optimize antioxidant intake. If in Phase 1, choose berries as your only fruits. Quantities below are suggested per week to get widespread support.

❑ 2 bunches leafy greens (kale, chard, red leaf lettuce, etc.)

❑ 2–3 green vegetables

❑ 2–3 red items

❑ 1–2 purple items

❑ 2–3 yellow/orange items

❑ 1–2 white/tan items

❑ 2–3 choices of alliums: onions (yellow, red, white), garlic, shallots, leeks

Prioritize organic produce. If not shopping organic, avoid certain items due to higher toxicity and pesticide residue, according to the 2018 Dirty Dozen Plus list. Items in italics should be consumed only in moderation or during Phase 2.

❑ *Apples*

❑ Bell peppers

❑ Berries

❑ Celery

❑ Cucumbers

❑ *Grapes*

- ❏ Green beans
- ❏ Kale
- ❏ Lettuce

- ❏ *Nectarines*
- ❏ *Peaches*
- ❏ *Potatoes*

- ❏ Spinach
- ❏ Strawberries

Fresh Herbs

Pick two to three fresh herbs per week.

- ❏ Basil
- ❏ Cilantro
- ❏ Ginger
- ❏ Mint

- ❏ Oregano
- ❏ Parsley
- ❏ Rosemary
- ❏ Sage

- ❏ Thyme
- ❏ Turmeric

Clean Proteins

Each week, select 1–2 ground meats for foods like meatballs, hamburgers, tacos, and meatloaf; 1–2 bone-in, skin-on whole cuts of meat for pan-searing, roasting, or grilling; 1–2 chuck, round, or shoulder roasts for searing and slow cooking; and 12–24 eggs. Additionally, each month, select 1 tub of protein for 2 to 5 shakes or smoothies weekly.

- ❏ Beef
- ❏ Pork
- ❏ Chicken
- ❏ Turkey
- ❏ Bacon

- ❏ Lamb
- ❏ Eggs
- ❏ Salt-cured and preservative-free charcuterie

- ❏ Fish
- ❏ Shellfish
- ❏ Collagen peptides
- ❏ Grass-fed whey protein powder

Nuts and Seeds

Select raw or dry roasted, organic nuts and seeds. Each week, choose 2–3 nuts to focus on and rotate, using 1–2 nut butters or nut butter blends. Challenge yourself to buy new nuts and seeds to get more nutritional density and variety beyond almonds, such as pumpkin seeds and Brazil nuts. Always have a nut flour on hand for thickening and making low-glycemic baked goods.

- ❑ Almonds
- ❑ Brazil nuts
- ❑ Chia seeds
- ❑ Coconut flour
- ❑ Flax seeds or crackers
- ❑ Nut butter, fresh ground, with no added oils or sugar
- ❑ Nut flour/meal
- ❑ Pecans
- ❑ Pumpkin seeds
- ❑ Sunflower seeds
- ❑ Walnuts

Fats

Ensure you have 1 cold-pressed extra-virgin oil for salad dressings and raw applications, as well as 1 to 2 high-heat options as refined oils or solid cooking fats. Fats are pantry staples versus weekly buys, so refill when needed.

- ❑ Almond oil
- ❑ Avocado, avocado oil
- ❑ Coconut shreds, coconut butter, coconut oil
- ❑ Ghee
- ❑ Grapeseed oil
- ❑ Lard, pasture-raised for high heat
- ❑ Olives, extra-virgin refined olive oil

Condiments

These condiments are pantry staples versus weekly buys, so refill when needed.

- ❑ Bragg Raw Apple Cider Vinegar
- ❑ Avocado/olive oil–based mayo
- ❑ Balsamic and other vinegars
- ❑ Coconut aminos
- ❑ Fermented pickles
- ❑ Horseradish
- ❑ Hot sauce/sriracha
- ❑ Kimchi
- ❑ Lime/lemon juice, organic

- ❑ Miso (Though made from soy, miso has more health supporting properties.)
- ❑ Mustard
- ❑ Nut cheese
- ❑ Olives
- ❑ Salsa
- ❑ Sauerkraut, live, raw

Drinks

Select quantities per preference and consumption.

- ❑ Black tea (and blends)
- ❑ Green tea (and blends)
- ❑ Kombucha
- ❑ Matcha
- ❑ Red wine (optional; Pinot Noir has a higher concentration of resveratrol.)
- ❑ Rooibos tea
- ❑ Sparkling mineral water
- ❑ Tulsi holy basil tea
- ❑ White tea (and blends)

Baking

These baking items are pantry staples versus weekly buys; refill when needed.

- ❑ Cacao powder, raw
- ❑ Coconut shreds
- ❑ *Coconut sugar*
- ❑ *Dark amber maple syrup*
- ❑ Dark chocolate, 70% or higher
- ❑ *Dates*
- ❑ *Honey, raw, local*
- ❑ Vanilla extract
- ❑ *Sucanat*

Pantry Items

These pantry items are pantry staples versus weekly buys; refill when needed.

- ❑ Coconut milk, canned, full-fat
- ❑ Collagen, grass-fed
- ❑ Fruit, dried, organic
- ❑ Gelatin, grass-fed
- ❑ Jerky, grass-fed, soy and wheat free
- ❑ Kale chips

- ❏ Nori sheets
- ❏ Pork rinds, pasture-raised
- ❏ Tomatoes, glass jar or BPA-free canned
- ❏ Whey protein, grass-fed

Dried Herbs/Spices

Have these on hand and refill when needed.

- ❏ Allspice
- ❏ Black pepper
- ❏ Cayenne
- ❏ Cinnamon
- ❏ Sea salt
- ❏ Chili powder
- ❏ Cloves
- ❏ Cumin
- ❏ Curry powder
- ❏ Dill
- ❏ Fennel
- ❏ Garlic (dried and powdered)
- ❏ Herb and seasoning blends
- ❏ Himalayan pink salt
- ❏ Nutmeg
- ❏ Paprika
- ❏ Red pepper flakes
- ❏ Turmeric

Foods in Moderation

Eat these foods a couple times a week or only in Phase 2 of the program.

Vegetables: All starchy, use within produce guidelines

Fruit: All beyond berries, use within produce guidelines

Beverages: Coffee, 100% juice (limit glycemic index by adding greens or diluting with soda water), alcohol consumed with other clean ingredients and limited to 2 drinks

Quality packaged (limited processing and packaging, no preservatives): Vegetable chips, almond flour or flax grain-free crackers, nut-and-dried-fruit bars

Eat these foods if tolerated after first 12-week elimination period and if not dealing with leaky gut:

Legumes: chickpeas, beans (black, navy, etc.), lentils, peas, hummus

Grains: Amaranth, teff, rice, quinoa, millet, oats, buckwheat

Dairy (unsweetened, full-fat, grass-fed, organic, raw or non-homogenized, probiotic-rich): Milk, cream, Greek yogurt, cheese (hard, aged, raw)

Foods to Avoid

These foods do not support your anti-anxiety diet outcomes.

Grains: All flours (whole and refined), barley, rye, wheat, spelt, couscous, grits, popcorn, pasta, bread and bread products, cereal and cereal products

Processed sweeteners: Table sugar, cane juice, corn syrup, artificial sweeteners, agave, non-caloric sweeteners and sugar alcohols (erythritol, xylitol)

Dairy (nonorganic, less than full-fat, sweetened): 1% or 2% milk, reduced-fat cheese, half and half, coffee creamer, chocolate or flavored milk, sweetened yogurt

Meat (conventionally raised, grain-fed): Fried or mixed with fillers

Beverages (sweetened, colored, processed): Soda, sports drinks, beer

Miscellaneous (foods with unnatural ingredients, prepackaged with preservatives and fillers): Fast food, prepackaged processed snacks and meals, fried foods

Supplement Support for the 6 Foundational Rs

I provide this information with the intention to welcome you into the thought process I use when working with my own patients. Areas of need are divided to address inflammation, dysbiosis, leaky gut, micronutrient deficiency, adrenal fatigue, or neurotransmitter imbalance. You may use this to guide your selection of formulas with understanding of dosage and form of compound to make it functional in your body.

To make it easy, I have provided the name of the private label formula that I have in my clinic. You can view these and the entire Naturally Nourished supplement line on my website at www.alimillerRD .com/store. Please note these are not recommendations for you to take but information for you to discuss with your wellness and healthcare team, providing access to third-party-assessed formulas with quality, potency, and purity at an affordable price.

When using supplements, always respect the mechanism of action and the influence of excess as possibly just as concerning as deficiency. Try to shift no more than two things at a time so if you notice improvement or decline, you can identify the variable and make a further shift. Precaution should be taken with supplementation of amino acids noted in the Rebalance Neurotransmitters section, especially in individuals dealing with schizophrenia, bipolar disorder, or other mental illnesses being monitored by a psychiatrist or physician. It is strongly recommended that this resource be used in conversation with your personal medical team and as a guide to discuss options for mood management support. Anyone currently managed by a medical team for any condition including pregnancy, autoimmune disease, and cancer should discuss any additional formulas to ensure they will not interfere with treatment.

Noticeable changes with supplements can be seen within minutes, hours, or upwards of four to six weeks. If you have an inflammatory, microbiological, or brain chemical imbalance, your anti-inflammatory diet focused on healthy fats and protein will aid in synergizing with supplements as tools to accelerate your anti-anxiety outcomes!

`reduce` inflammation

Omega-3 high-dose EPA-DHA

Dosage: >850mg EPA; >550mg DHA

Naturally Nourished formula: EPA-DHA Extra

How to take: 1–2 gel capsules twice daily with food

Alternatives: Molecularly distilled, third-party assessed EPA and DHA gel capsule for potency and purity. Stabilized with antioxidants. Ensure dosage is potent enough to provide 2g EPA and DHA per dosage to have clinical results.

Anti-anxiety focus: Reduces inflammatory chemicals that interfere with mood stability and drive anxiety response. Unlike anti-inflammatory drugs, EPA-DHA can cross the blood-brain barrier and fuel healthy brain function. A study on high-dose EPA at 2g daily demonstrated significant reduction in anxiety.

`reduce` inflammation

Turmeric

Dosage: 1–3g

Naturally Nourished formula: Super Turmeric

How to take: 1 gel capsule twice daily with food

Alternatives: Curcumin is difficult to absorb, so often it is paired with black pepper or fat. Black pepper can be a digestive irritant so is not preferred. Look for an option with three bioactive, health-promoting curcuminoids: curcumin, bisdemethoxy curcumin, and demethoxy curcumin, along with turmeric oil.

Anti-anxiety focus: Inhibits inflammatory brain signals, reduces cortisol while enhancing serotonin. A research study in 2015 at UCLA demonstrated anti-anxiety effects directly from supplementation of curcuminoids with healthy fats.

`reduce` inflammation
Digestive enzyme with DPP4 and bile

Dosage: >150mg HCl, >150mg digestive enzyme complex, including ox bile

Naturally Nourished formula: Digestaid Enzyme

How to take: 1–2 capsules prior to all meals or prior to dining out

Alternatives: Enzyme formula providing DPPIV, ox bile, lipase, amylase, pepsin, protease, lactase, and HCl.

Anti-anxiety focus: Reduces inflammatory activity of gluten and casein while reducing large particles that could get fermented by dysbiosis and supporting enhanced nutrient absorption.

`reduce` inflammation
Proteolytic enzyme blend with anti-inflammatory herbs

Dosage: Greater or equal to 200mg Proteolytic enzyme blend, 200mg turmeric, 200mg boswellia, and other synergistic botanicals such as ginger, quercetin, rosemary, rutin, and resveratrol.

Naturally Nourished formula: Inflammazyme

How to take: 1–2 capsules aken twice daily without food

Alternatives: A blend of anti-inflammatory tropical enzymes and plants including those listed above, as well as an active proteolytic enzyme blend in a non-GMO formula.

Anti-anxiety focus: Proteolytic enzymes are a second line of defense after EPA-DHA and turmeric, covering foundational needs. Typically thought of as addressing tissue inflammation and structural health, such as recovering from an injury, bromelain and quercetin have been shown in studies to reduce anxiety. Research confirmed quercetin impact on reducing corticotropin releasing hormone (CRH), which directly influences cortisol and anxiety fight-or-flight expression.

reduce inflammation

L-carnitine

Dosage: 2g

Naturally Nourished formula: Boost and Burn

How to take: 1 tsp daily upon rising

Alternatives: Potent source of L-carnitine at 2g dosage blended with other metabolic boosters such as ribose and pantothenate.

Anti-anxiety focus: L-carnitine drives fat metabolism and increases ketone production. When using ketones to support mood stability and reduce excitatory stress response or anxiety, enhancing dietary strategy with supplemental support can accelerate results.

reset gut microbiome

Berberine

Dosage: 400mg

Naturally Nourished formula: Berberine Boost

How to take: 2 tablets twice daily with food during 6-week cleanse; may continue 1 tablet when transitioning to a higher carbohydrate intake or to support blood sugar reduction

Alternatives: A formula that provides a potent dosage of berberine compounds from whole plants and complementary herbs to support liver, reduce yeast, and promote healthy blood sugar metabolism.

Anti-anxiety focus: Berberine has many anti-anxiety effects by reducing CRF and tyrosine hydroxylase, both of which can drive anxiety response. Taking berberine at a high dosage of around 1g daily can support a fungal and bacterial cleanse to combat dysbiosis and support a balanced microbiome for optimal neurotransmitter production.

Aromatic, antimicrobial, and antifungal herbs

Dosage: 400mg blend of oil of oregano, thyme oil, sage oil, and lemon balm

Naturally Nourished formula: CandiActivator

How to take: 1 gel capsule twice daily without food

Alternatives: A formula that suspends the above-mentioned dried herbs and essential oils to optimize the absorption and function of botanicals in order to kill yeast and pathogenic bacteria, and promote healthy digestive function. Look for a product containing a 400mg blend of aromatic herbs safe for oral consumption.

Anti-anxiety focus: Herbs included aid in resetting gut microbiome, supporting a bacteria and yeast cleanse. Beyond dysbiosis, some of the featured herbs such as lemon balm (*Melissa officinalis*) has anxiolytic effects used for hundreds of years to reduce panic and anxiety, and to improve sleep.

`reset` gut microbiome

Botanical blend with antiparasitic, antibacterial, antifungal compounds

Dosage: >600mg tribulus, >450mg caprylic acid, paired with 3–4 other herbs and botanicals at around 1g dosage

Naturally Nourished formula: GI Reset

How to take: 3–4 capsules daily, 2 with food and 1–2 without

Alternatives: Blend of botanical extracts and caprylic acid with clinical evidence for supporting a healthy gastrointestinal microbiome, including wormwood, tribulus, and uva ursi as second line of defense following a berberine and essential oil herbal blend.

Anti-anxiety focus: Tribulus is a nice add-on to a bacterial or yeast cleanse as it has antispasmodic, anti-inflammatory, and analgesic pain-relieving effects aiding in addressing anxiety during cleanse. Ensuring removal of pathogenic bacteria or yeast will ultimately aid in optimal probiotic growth and promote healthy neurotransmitter balance.

Bacteriophage/probiotic combination formula

Dosage: 15–30mg, 5–10 billion CFU blend of *Lactobacillus*, *Bifidobacterium*, and *Streptococcus* paired with a bacteriophage prebiotic

Naturally Nourished formula: GI Cleanup

How to take: 1 upon rising and 1 at bedtime, taken 30+ minutes from food intake

Alternatives: A formula with probiotics and specific bacteriophages (viruses that exclusively infect bacteria to create space for probiotics). Highly specific bacteriophages may be classified as prebiotics since they enhance the growth of beneficial bacteria in the gastrointestinal tract. This formula should be paired with a blend of probiotic strains.

Anti-anxiety focus: The unique cleanup activity of bacteriophages aids in supporting removal of bacteria during a cleanse or weakening overgrowth of bacteria to maintain reduced activity. This creation of space when paired with probiotic cultures in a formula aids in proliferation or growth and development of probiotic strains to support mood stability and reduce anxiety.

Phase 2 liver detox supportive formula

Dosage: Blend of sulfur-containing amino acids, conjugating compounds, and Phase 2 detox drivers

Naturally Nourished formula: Ultimate Detox

How to take: 2 capsules two to three times daily with or without food

Alternatives: Formula that provides L-methionine, MSM, L-glutamine, glutathione, NAC, taurine, calcium d-glucarate, and other Phase 2 liver support

Anti-anxiety focus: Supporting the liver during a bacterial cleanse is important, especially with focus on excretion when buildup of toxic compounds can occur during a microbiome cleanse. Glutathione and NAC can support reduced oxidative stress with detox activity, which has been shown to have anti-anxiety effects.

`reset` gut microbiome

Probiotic

Dosage: 15 billion CFU of 50:50 blend of *Lactobacillus, Bifidobacterium*

Naturally Nourished formula: Restore Baseline Probiotic

How to take: 1–3 capsules at bedtime; consider using with a probiotic challenge. See details on page 57.

Alternatives: A blend that delivers 15 billion CFU with 50:50 blend of lacto and bifido strains that is free of FOS.

Anti-anxiety focus: Probiotics specifically, *Lactobacillus* and *Bifidobacterium* strains, aid in production of serotonin, GABA, and other neurotransmitters that have positive mood-stabilizing effects.

`reset` gut microbiome

High-dose probiotic

Dosage: 60 billion CFU of 50:50 blend of *Lactobacillus, Bifidobacterium*

Naturally Nourished formula: Targeted Strength Probiotic

How to take: 1 capsule at bedtime

Alternatives: A blend that delivers 60 billion CFU with 50:50 blend of lacto and bifido strains that is free of FOS.

Anti-anxiety focus: Probiotics, specifically *Lactobacillus* and *Bifidobacterium* strains, aid in production of serotonin, GABA, and other neurotransmitters that have positive, mood-stabilizing effects. A more potent formula is fitting if recovering from dysbiosis or benefits are seen in probiotic challenge at higher dosage.

`reset` gut microbiome

Broad-spectrum probiotic

Dosage: Full-spectrum probiotic with 7 strains, including *S. boulardii* for full GI coverage and antifungal effects

Naturally Nourished formula: Rebuild Spectrum probiotic

How to take: 1 capsule upon rising and/or 1 at bedtime

Alternatives: A blend that delivers 30 billion CFU with multistrain blend of probiotics, including dose-dependent *S. boulardii*; blend that is free of FOS.

Anti-anxiety focus: Probiotics support production of neurotransmitters that have positive mood-stabilizing effects. A more wide-spectrum formula is fitting if recovering from dysbiosis or following use of antibiotic. Also, this blended formula is fitting for those struggling with yeast or candida overgrowth with presence of *S. boulardii*.

`reset` gut microbiome

Prebiotic fiber blend

Dosage: 6g prebiotic fiber featuring acacia gum, cranberry seed extract, carrot fiber, glucomannan, flaxseed, and prune

Naturally Nourished formula: PhytoFiber

How to take: 1 tbsp daily with food, separately from mineral supplements

Alternatives: A whole food fiber blend of vegetables, roots, seeds, and fruits to support healthy gut bacteria.

Anti-anxiety focus: Prebiotic fibers encourage proliferation of probiotic strains of bacteria. Providing a prebiotic fiber at 5.5g daily aided in reducing a.m. cortisol and regulating mood in a 2015 study.

`repair` GI lining support

L-glutamine

Dosage: 3500mg L-glutamine

Naturally Nourished formula: GI Lining Support

How to take: 1 tsp at bedtime to aid in repairing gut lining and support less inflammation during remove phase, upwards of 3 tsp daily per need

Alternatives: Synergy formula providing L-glutamine and mucilaginous compounds to coat and soothe the GI tract and repair leaky gut.

Anti-anxiety focus: L-glutamine paired with gut lining support aids in repairing GALT, thus reducing inflammation, and signals that drive anxiety response. In neurotransmitter support, L-glutamine oral supplementation can raise GABA, the feel-good mellow-out neurotransmitter, to reduce anxiety without converting into the excitatory glutamate.

GI lining support

Gelatin

Dosage: 10–20g protein from grass-fed gelatin

Naturally Nourished formula: N/A

How to take: Consume a gelatin-based recipe or add gelatin to hot beverages or smoothies a couple times per week

Alternatives: Look for a product that offers grass-fed sourcing and has only gelatin with no additives.

Anti-anxiety focus: Gelatin provides glycine, which promotes relaxation and GABA expression. When converted to gummies, it has mucilaginous compounds that reline the gut to heal leaky gut and reduce inflammation.

restore micronutrient status

Multivitamin

Dosage: Potent, pure, bioavailable nutrients, with broad-spectrum antioxidant blend

Naturally Nourished formula: MultiDefense with or without iron (with iron for women menstruating)

How to take: 1 tablet twice daily with food

Alternatives: Ensure methylated Bs, such as 5-methyltetrahydrofolate versus folic acid, methylcobalamin versus cyanocobalamin; ensure vitamin A is in mixed carotenoid and retinyl blend; ensure it includes choline and inositol, as well as chromium and selenium in >100% DV.

Anti-anxiety focus: Ensuring a foundation of micronutrient support will prevent deficiency of nutrients featured in Chapter 5. Prior to using specific nutrients of focus for anxiety reduction, start with a quality multivitamin.

restore micronutrient status

Magnesium bisglycinate

Dosage: 200–600mg magnesium bisglycinate, 4–12g myo-inositol

Naturally Nourished formula: Relax and Regulate

How to take: 1–2 scoops at bedtime mixed with 3–4 ounces water

Alternatives: Ensure noted active featured ingredients with limited additives and GMO-free, corn-free formula.

Anti-anxiety focus: Magnesium deficiency can drive increased anxiety reactivity and stimulation of cortisol, which further drives anxiety and distress response. Magnesium has been deemed the original "chill pill" as it directly works at the HPA-axis with the ability to suppress cortisol and adrenal output via reduced release of ACTH (adrenocorticotropic hormone) from the pituitary. Inositol scores similarly to fluvoxamine SSRI on improvements on Hamilton Rating Scale for Anxiety scores, agoraphobia scores, and Clinical Global Impressions Scale scores. Inositol was shown to reduce the number of panic attacks per week by 4.0 compared with a reduction of 2.4 with fluvoxamine.

`restore` micronutrient status

Zinc

Dosage: 30mg chelated zinc

Naturally Nourished formula: N/A

How to take: 1 capsule without food and separately from other minerals

Alternatives: Look for a chelated form for most bioavailability: zinc picolinate, zinc gluconate, zinc orotate, or zinc methionate.

Anti-anxiety focus: Zinc both enhances conditions to optimize GABA formation and expression. It also competes with copper, which has been shown to drive excitatory stress hormone output seen in the primal survival part of the brain often overstimulated during times of panic.

`restore` micronutrient status

Calcium

Dosage: 500–1000mg calcium from microcrystalline hydroxyapatite concentrate (MCHC)

Naturally Nourished formula: Osteofactors

How to take: 1 tablet two to three times daily with food

Alternatives: Look for a bone matrix MCHC form to ensure balanced mineral composition and prevent calcification activity.

Anti-anxiety focus: Calcium is required as a mineral to regulate neurological function and deficiency and has been tied to mania, panic, confusion, and chronic anxiety. Calcium like glutamate has excitatory impact on a neurological level and the neuron impact is regulated by magnesium. If supplementing with calcium be sure you are taking a quality magnesium as well.

restore | micronutrient status

Vitamin D3/K2 blend

Dosage: 5000 IU vitamin D, 550 vitamin K

Naturally Nourished formula: Vitamin D Balanced Blend

How to take: 1 capsule at breakfast (meal with fat)

Alternatives: Soy-free formula with K1 and K2 M7 in dosage of D3/K with 10 IU: 1mcg

Anti-anxiety focus: The only vitamin that is a hormone, vitamin D influences genes that regulate the immune system and release neurotransmitters such as serotonin to influence brain function and mood stability. Vitamin D supports brain-derived neurotrophic factor (BDNF) levels, which have been shown, when low, to drive anxiety and depression.

restore | micronutrient status

Methylation supporting B-complex

Dosage: B1 100mg, B2 50mg, B3 50mg, B6 (in P5P and pyridoxine HCl blend) 50mg, folate (in mixed methyl-form) 200 mcg, B12 250mcg, biotin 2000mcg, B5 100mg, TMG 200mg, choline 100mg

Naturally Nourished formula: B-complex

How to take: 1 capsule upon rising or midday, with or without food

Alternatives: Look for a formula with mixed folate in methylated form as opposed to synthetic folic acid, which is not appropriate for individuals with MTHFR gene discussed in Chapter 5. Also a good B-complex will have other methylation supporters, such as choline and glycine, to prevent overmethylation or methyl-trap action, which can drive excessive stress chemical response.

Anti-anxiety focus: Providing activated B vitamins is one way to support optimized function of the HPA-axis and neurotransmitter balance. Methylated B12, folate, and choline have been shown to reduce homocysteine levels to reduce inflammation and support SAM-e production for mood-stabilizing effects while also promoting production of dopamine and serotonin.

`restore` micronutrient status

Methyl B12 lozenge

Dosage: 5000mcg of methylcobalamin

Naturally Nourished formula: B-12 Boost

How to take: Take 1–2 lozenges per day in morning and mid-afternoon

Alternatives: Look for B-vitamins in methylated forms not cyanocobalamin. You may consider a hydroxy or adenosyl form if already using a methyl form without results or experiencing more neurological effects.

Anti-anxiety focus: B-12 is used in red blood cell function and neurological, gastrointestinal, and psychological health. There is importance of vitamin B12, folate, and homocysteine in carbon transfer metabolism (methylation) required for the production of serotonin, other monoamine neurotransmitters, and catecholamines. Agitation, irritability, negativism, confusion, anger, and insomnia can be associated with B12 deficiency, with severe symptoms of panic and psychosis that can be resolved when levels are repleted.

`rebound` adrenals

Nervine and adaptogen blend with L-theanine

Dosage: Blend of B vitamins in active form with nervine and adaptogen herbs, along with phosphatidyl serine, taurine, and L-theanine

Naturally Nourished formula: Calm and Clear

How to take: 1–2 capsules three times daily with or without food

Alternatives: Look for a product that provides methylated B12, but if getting methylated folate in a complex or multivitamin avoid extra folate. Look for a product that has a blend of 3–5 herbs in combination of nervines and adaptogens, such as passion flower, lemon balm, valerian, and ashwagandha. Ideally product also provides L-theanine, taurine, and phosphatidyl serine to regulate neurotransmitters and cortisol levels.

Anti-anxiety focus: Clinical effects of anxiety reduction and stress resilience is seen in use of ashwagandha, a featured adaptogen in this formula. Lemon balm has tonifying nervine effects to aid in relaxation and anxiolytic influence, creating a state of calmness. Taurine plays a role in supporting liver function and modulating both excitatory and inhibitory neurotransmitters, namely GABA. Phosphatidyl serine can blunt excessive cortisol stress-responding effects in the body.

`rebound` adrenals

Adaptogen blend

Dosage: 600mg synergy blend of adaptogens per capsule

Naturally Nourished formula: Adaptogen Boost

How to take: 2–4 capsules daily with or without food

Alternatives: Blend of adaptogenic herbs, including panax ginseng, rhodiola, and cordyceps.

Anti-anxiety focus: Adaptogens aid in responding to stress without depleting the HPA-axis or driving imbalanced action. These herbs can support energy and stress tolerance without depletion. Adaptogens aid in reducing the impact of stress to the adrenal glands by helping the body respond more directly and providing support for energy. Rhodiola in particular can reduce anxiety with dose-dependent reduction in symptoms of panic and distress.

`rebalance` neurotransmitters

Pharma GABA

Dosage: 100–300mg pharma-GABA

Naturally Nourished formula: GabaCalm chew

How to take: 1–3 chews as needed in acute times of anxiety and/or as a base to regulate physiological stress response

Alternatives: Look for a chewable product that has limited binders and fillers, providing 100–200mg pharmaGABA per chew.

Anti-anxiety focus: GABA serves as a critical calming agent for the body, helping to combat stress and anxiety. It has an acute response to stress and is best used when needed per stress-induced demand such as public speaking, performance review, social engagement, and flying. Via influence of the vagus nerve running from the brain through the gut, pharmaGABA has anxiolytic effects to create a sense of peace and calmness with reduced tremors and physiological stress response.

`rebalance` neurotransmitters

5-HTP

Dosage: 50–200mg.

Naturally Nourished formula: N/A

How to take: 50–100mg capsule once or twice daily; without food in the evening to aid with sleep, may be taken in the day as well to support mood stability. WARNING: 5-HTP cannot be combined with an SSRI medication as it can cause serotonin excessive syndrome.

Alternatives: Look for a formula that pairs 5-HTP with B6 and L-theanine to support conversion and modulation of neurotransmitters.

Anti-anxiety focus: 5-HTP has symptom management for pain, mood stability, and sleep support when compared to a placebo.

`rebalance` neurotransmitters

L-theanine

Dosage: 200–1000mg.

Naturally Nourished formula: Calm and Clear

How to take: 1–2 200mg capsules 2–3 times per day without food; This can be taken at rise, mid-day, and bed as it may improve REM cycles with sleep.

Alternatives: Look for a formula that uses suntheanine form with enhanced bioavailability. Matcha is a great food-as-medicine option and provides a potent amount of L-theanine but is not at an effective supplemental level, providing around 20 mg per tsp.

Anti-anxiety focus: L-theanine crosses the blood-brain barrier and can influence the central nervous system by enhancing levels of dopamine, GABA, and serotonin; however, L-theanine effects are balancing and won't overproduce one given neurotransmitter.

L-tyrosine

Dosage: 500–1500mg

Naturally Nourished formula: N/A

How to take: Best taken without food to support use of amino acid influence without competing with protein-containing foods. Best taken during the day. WARNING: Do not combine this supplement with Wellbutrin, Ritalin, or other dopamine reuptake inhibitors.

Alternatives: Be mindful; If not dealing with adrenal fatigue and instead suffering from racing thoughts and excessive adrenaline response, this formula may not be for you as it can increase catecholamine stress chemical responders.

Anti-anxiety focus: L-tyrosine has anti-stress effects that can promote energy and alleviate anxiety. It has been shown to enhance cognition under times of stress and support adrenal output of stress-responding chemicals in a time of adrenal fatigue. This would be a go-to if dealing with fatigue-induced anxiety, but may drive stress chemical response and may need to be paired with GABA, 5-HTP, and/or L-theanine.

rebalance | neurotransmitters

SAM-e

Dosage: 400–1600mg

Naturally Nourished formula: N/A

How to take: 1–2 capsules 1–2 times per day without food.

Alternatives: Look for a formula that combines SAM-e with methylated B12 and methylfolate (5-MTHF) to ensure you can support methylation while reducing the risk of overdriving this pathway.

Anti-anxiety focus: SAM-e plays a role with methylation while preventing overdrive of this metabolic function. It can influence serotonin, melatonin, and dopamine activity while reducing excessive adrenaline. Research suggests that SAM-e can be an effective, well-tolerated, and safe adjunctive treatment strategy as an alternative or in conjunction with SSRI drugs.

Advanced Functional Labs

Now that you understand the Foundational 6 Rs of anxiety, you may want to dig deeper into your body's greatest area of focus. Using the quizzes in this book and symptoms noted, you will be able to prioritize where to start. The labs are ordered as follows: inflammatory, microbiome, leaky gut, micronutrients, and HPA-axis and neurotransmitters.

Inflammatory Assessments

Inflammation may be the root cause of your anxiety! Chemical messengers of inflammation cross the blood-brain barrier and interfere with signaling of feel-good, mellow-out neurotransmitters while increasing sense of panic and distress, fight-or-flight survival response. Here are the panels I recommend:

C-Reactive Protein (CRP)

CRP is elevated in inflammatory disease conditions and can be used as both an acute and chronic marker of inflammatory distress. This marker has been assessed to have a correlation with anxiety and, if found to be elevated above 3.0, it is recommend to proceed with the Mediator Release Test (page 288). If above 1.0, it is highly recommended to add a therapeutic anti-inflammatory supplement to your daily routine, such as omega-3, turmeric, or tropical enzyme support.

Specimen: Blood test

Company: Any, non-specific

Ideal range: HS-CRP <0.8 mg/L

Fasting Insulin

Fasting insulin is a marker of imbalanced blood sugar and elevated levels of blood sugar along with low-grade inflammation. Elevated insulin drives more oxidative stress in the brain and interferes with neurotransmitters. Beyond crashes and mood instability, with blood sugar spikes and drops, insulin has direct anxiety effects.

Specimen: Blood test

Company: Any, non-specific

Ideal range: <8 uIU/mL

Hemoglobin A1C% (HgbA1C%)

HgbA1c% is a 3-month average of how glycosylated or coated in sugar your red blood cells are. When elevated, the quickest way to reduce this value is to reduce reliance on glucose as fuel and help the body to become more fat-adapted. Following Phase 1 of the anti-anxiety diet would be recommended to accelerate your blood sugar reduction with a ketogenic diet.

Specimen: Blood test

Company: Any, non-specific

Ideal range: 4.5–5.4%

Ferritin

This is a marker of iron storage and too low of a value can drive issues with thyroid hormone, hair loss, brain fog, and anemia. Too high of a value can be an acute phase reactant to inflammation seen with autoimmune disease, liver disease, cancer, and other non-specific inflammation.

Specimen: Blood test

Company: Any, non-specific

Ideal range: 70–200

Mediator Release Test (MRT)

The Mediator Release Test (MRT), also known as the MRT Inflammatory Food Panel, looks at the release of inflammatory chemicals in your blood when certain foods or chemicals hit it. In this sense, it assesses how your body responds to foods and chemicals and the level of leaky gut status based on reactivity. Food sensitivity symptoms are often chronic because the chemical mediators that make us feel sick are released every time you eat your unknown reactive foods. Also, to add complexity, your body may react up to 72 hours post consumption, and the reaction may be dependent on a synergy of ingredients. Certain foods may be moderately inflammatory and on their own tolerated, but if you have meals or snacks that are in higher amounts of moderate foods, their impact can accumulate, and if in a given window, drive increased inflammatory response such as diarrhea, joint pain, skin flares, anxiety, and panic! The MRT test helps you determine a starting point for identification of dietary and chemical irritants, allowing for an elimination diet to reset the system, and your immune system and inflammatory pathways to cool and reset.

Specimen: Blood test

Company: Oxford Biomedical

Ideal range: No severe RED reactions, <5 moderate YELLOW reactions

Microbiome

As serotonin and GABA are manufactured by healthy gut bacteria, dysbiosis (the imbalance of bad bacteria or yeast) may be the root cause of your anxiety! Assessing your levels of bacteria, both good and bad, can be helpful in determining if you need to proceed with a bacterial cleanse or simply a flourish of probiotics. Here are the panels I recommend:

Comprehensive Digestive Stool Analysis

Stool analysis is gold standard for assessing the microbiome. This panel specifically identifies both positive and negative bacteria strains to determine state of gut symbiosis. The three-day stool collection assesses bacteria, yeast, and parasites, both active and in dormant form. If a pathogen is found, this panel provides therapeutic guidance on what natural and pharmaceutical compounds will be most successful in eradication through a cleanse. Beyond microbiome assessment, this panel provides information on digestive function including pH, enzymes, and malabsorption status, as well as state of gut inflammation and damage.

Stool test should include:

- Beneficial, commensal, and pathogenic bacteria, yeast culture
- Parasite assessment: ova and active parasites
- Digestive/Absorptive markers: elastase, fat, carb, protein malabsorption
- Inflammatory bowel markers: calprotectin, lactoferrin, white blood cells, mucus, lysosome
- Leaky gut markers: calprotectin, secretory IgA
- SCFA (short chain fatty acids) and their distribution

Specimen: Stool 1 or 3 day collection

Company: Doctor's Data or Genova Diagnostics

Ideal range: Beyond 30 markers, needs to be reviewed with practitioner

Breath Test

The breath test is the gold standard for upper intestinal imbalance or small intestinal bacterial overgrowth (SIBO). Although the testing can be time consuming and unreliable based on exhale, it is the best way to determine action in the small intestines and stomach. Most panels will include a base collection followed by drinking a solution with testing in 15–30 minute increments for up to 4 hours.

Specimen: Breath

Company: Any, non-specific

Ideal range: *H. pylori* negative, hydrogen within normal limits (WNL), methane WNL, fructose, other sugars WNL

Organix Dysbiosis

The Organix Dysbiosis test looks at organic acids in the urine as a marker of metabolism of microbes in the biome. The results are able to determine yeast and pathogenic bacteria activity with presence of particular compounds absorbed along the small intestine. This test can be used to confirm yeast overgrowth and SIBO, but may overlook microbes in the colon.

Specimen: Urine

Company: Genova Diagnostics

Ideal range: Arabinose <29 mmol/mol creatine, benzoate <1.3 mmol/mol creatine, benzoate, and all other markers WNL

Leaky Gut

If your gut is in a state of increased permeability, you will have less micronutrient absorption and more inflammation. As both nutrient deficiency and inflammation are drivers of anxiety, leaky gut may be your root cause. If you score high on the Anti-Anxiety Leaky Gut Quiz (page 68) you may want to run advanced labs to get a baseline read; however, you will want to run the MRT test regardless to get the information of what to do to start healing your leaky gut! When looking to heal leaky gut, it is most important to understand what needs to be removed so you can put the fire out before you start rebuilding the house. Here are the panels I recommend:

Zonulin Protein

Zonulin is a protein that functions with tight junctions of the gut lining, essentially working as the gatekeeper to your gut lining on the gut-blood barrier. Both gluten and gut bacteria imbalance can increase zonulin, which releases the seal on the gut, driving leaky gut reactivity of inflammation, mood disturbances, and autoimmune disease.

Specimen: Serum or stool

Company: Doctor's Data and Genova Diagnostics

Ideal range: Within normal limits (WNL) per lab

Secretory IgA

Secretory IgA (sIgA) is the first line of defense lining our mucosal membranes in the mouth, nose, respiratory tract, sexual orifices, and gut. An elevation of secretory IgA is seen with stress response from bacteria imbalance, infection, food particle insult, or mental stress. Low secretory IgA is indicative of prolonged distressed state and, often, immune insufficiency or chronic illness.

Specimen: Saliva, serum, or stool

Company: Doctor's Data, Labrix, Genova Diagnostics

Ideal range: WNL per lab

Calprotectin

Calprotectin is a protein that drives white blood cell action in intestinal lining and is used as the primary indicator to distinguish between irritable bowel syndrome (IBS) and inflammatory bowel disease (IBD) such as colitis and Crohn's disease. It is the primary marker to establish remission of IBD conditions and monitor flares of disease presence.

Specimen: Serum or stool (stool is superior)

Company: Any, non-specific

Ideal range: WNL, ranges, shifts based on lab company

Mediator Release Test (MRT)

See page 288 for details.

Specimen: Blood test

Company: Oxford Biomedical

Ideal range: No severe RED reactions, <5 moderate YELLOW reactions

Micronutrients

If you are low in key nutrients that build neurotransmitters, reduce inflammation, and provide anxiolytic effects, your root cause of anxiety may be micronutrient deficiency. Individuals at high risk for this area are those recovering from an injury, excessive exercisers or marathon runners, individuals on specialty diets or limited from diversity for wide spectrum nutrient exposure, and mothers with demand from carrying and breastfeeding children. It is highly recommended to start with a quality bioavailable multivitamin with methylated Bs to support your foundational needs. Here are the panels I recommend:

Micronutrient Test

The SpectraCell panel uses white blood cell proliferation to assess the viability of the cells based on nutritional status. This test looks at 35 vitamins, minerals, and antioxidants in levels available on a cellular level in your body. The unique nutrition assessment of intracellular status provides information on micronutrient status for a more long-term assessment providing 3–6 month status as opposed to more of a snap shot focus.

Specimen: Blood test, white blood cell proliferation

Company: SpectraCell

Ideal range: No functional deficiency, <2 borderline deficiency

Vitamin D

The only vitamin that functions as a hormone, vitamin D plays a role in thousands of genes influencing the immune system, inflammatory processes, and metabolism via thyroid and sexual hormone balance. Beyond these mechanisms, seasonal affective disorder tends to trend with times of the year when vitamin D levels drop due to less sun access. One driver toward mood imbalances during winter is that both serotonin and dopamine rely on vitamin D for optimized function. Optimized vitamin D status can support your anti-anxiety program while boosting metabolism, balancing hormones, and reducing inflammation.

Specimen: Blood test, 25-hydroxy vitamin D

Company: Any, non-specific

Ideal range: 50–100 mg/mL

Red Blood Cell (RBC) Magnesium

Magnesium plays a role in over 300 enzyme pathways and influences neuromuscular relaxation. It directly hits the HPA-axis by suppressing cortisol and adrenal output, which reduces stress response that drives anxiety. Optimizing your magnesium can aid in sleep quality and reduced tension or muscle aches.

Specimen: Blood test, RBC magnesium

Company: Any, non-specific

Ideal range: 4.5–7 mg/dL

Zinc

Zinc promotes GABA expression and competes with copper, which can be expressed in times of panic and distress. See Chapter 5 for mention of condition, pyroluria, a genetic chemical imbalance where zinc and B6 are significantly depleted.

Specimen: Blood test, serum

Company: Any, non-specific

Ideal range: 0.66–1.10 mcg/mL

Genetic SNP Report

Single nucleotide polymorphisms (SNPs) influence the expression of a biochemical pathway. Understanding your body's SNPs can aid in understanding of the blueprint of your brain and anxiety tendencies based on how your body builds, converts, and excretes various compounds.

Specimen: Blood, saliva (ensure it includes: MTHFR, COMT, GST, SOD as minimum)

Company: Genomix Nutrition, Genova, 23 and Me

Ideal range: Least amount of SNPs or least reactive as heterozygous versus homozygous

HPA-Axis and Neurotransmitters

If you are dealing with adrenaline-like chemical surges that accompany your anxiety, experience chronic fatigue and interrupted sleep, or have chronic high stress demands, it is likely HPA-axis dysfunction is the root cause of your anxiety. Assessments of this axis should take into account the steroid hormones as well as neurotransmitters as they are so integrated in expression of anxiety and regulation of mood. Here are the panels I recommend:

Neurohormone Complete Panel

The Neurohormone Complete Panel for men and the Neurohormone Complete Plus panel for women by Labrix is the best place to start for a thorough assessment of HPA-axis function, including salivary assessment of cortisol at four points throughout the day, DHEA, estrogen, progesterone, and testosterone, as well as urinary assessment of eight+ neurotransmitters.

Specimen: Saliva and urine combo

Company: Labrix. Note: DUTCH and Genova provide reports for adrenals and sexual hormones but not neurotransmitters.

Ideal range: WNL of each marker

Thyroid Complete Panel

Often the thyroid function is broadly assessed with TSH only, which does not provide direct information on thyroid hormone production or conversion of inactive T4 to active form T3. It is important to look at free hormone when assessing function of the gland as this is the form available for use. Screening for Hashimoto's thyroiditis is important with family or personal history of hypothyroidism or symptoms of thyroid dysfunction, such as constipation, hair loss, brittle nails, fatigue, brain fog, insomnia, anxiety, and weight gain as over 80 percent of people with hypothyroid have Hashimoto's autoimmune disease.

Specimen: Blood test

Company: SpectraCell, any, non-specific

Ideal range: TSH 0.8-2.2 UIU/ML or lower (If on armor thyroid, glandular, or T3 compounded, may have medication suppressed levels of TSH)

FT4 >1.0 NG/DL

FT3 > 2.8 PG/ML

TPO negative or <15

TgAb negative or <8

Thyroglobulin <40

Thyroxine binding globulin 14-31

Selected References

For a full list of references, go to www.alimillerrd.com/
the-anti-anxiety-diet.

Anderson, S., J. Panka, R. Rakobitsch, et al. "Anxiety and Methylenetetra-
hydrofolate Reductase Mutation Treated With S-Adenosyl Methionine and
Methylated B Vitamins."*Integrative Medicine*15, no. 2 (April 2016): 48–52.

Bailey, M. T., S. E. Dowd, J. D. Galley, et al. "Exposure to a Social Stressor
Alters the Structure of the Intestinal Microbiota: Implications for Stressor-
Induced Immunomodulation."*Brain, Behavior, and Immunity* 25, no. 3
(March 2011): 397–407. doi:10.1016/j.bbi.2010.10.023.

Barrett, E., R. P. Ross, P. W. O'Toole, et al. "γ-Aminobutyric Acid
Production by Culturable Bacteria from the Human Intestine."
Journal of Applied Microbiology 113, no. 2 (August 2012): 411–417.
doi:10.1111/j.1365-2672.2012.05344.x.

Bercik, P., E. Denou, J. Collins, et al. "The Intestinal Microbiota Affect
Central Levels of Brain-Derived Neurotropic Factor and Behavior in
Mice."*Gastroenterology* 141, no. 2 (August 2011): 599–609. doi:10.1053/
j.gastro.2011.04.052.

Bjelland, I., G. S. Tell, S. E. Vollset, et al. "Choline in Anxiety and
Depression: The Hordaland Health Study." *The American Journal of
Clinical Nutrition* 90, no. 4 (October 2009): 1056–1060. doi:10.3945/
ajcn.2009.27493.

Blessing, E. M., M. M. Steenkamp, J. Manzanares, et al. "Cannabidiol as
a Potential Treatment for Anxiety Disorders."*Neurotherapeutics* 12, no. 4
(October 2015): 825–836. doi:10.1007/s13311-015-0387-1.

Boonstra, E., R. De Kleijn, L. S. Colzato, et al. "Neurotransmitters as Food
Supplements: The Effects of GABA on Brain and Behavior."*Frontiers in
Psychology* 6 (2015): 1520. doi:10.3389/fpsyg.2015.01520.

Bouayed, J., H. Rammal, and R. Soulimani. "Oxidative Stress and Anxiety:
Relationship and Cellular Pathways."*Oxidative Medicine and Cellular
Longevity* 2, no. 2 (April–June 2009): 63–67. doi:10.4161/oxim.2.2.7944.

Buydens-Branchey, L., M. Branchey, and J. R. Hibbeln. "Associations between Increases in Plasma N-3 Polyunsaturated Fatty Acids following Supplementation and Decreases in Anger and Anxiety in Substance Abusers."*Progress in Neuro-Psychopharmacology and Biological Psychiatry* 32, no. 2 (February 15, 2008): 568–575. doi:10.1016/j.pnpbp.2007.10.020.

Campos-Rodríguez, R., M. Godínez-Victoria, E. Abarca-Rojano, et al. "Stress Modulates Intestinal Secretory Immunoglobulin A." *Frontiers in Integrative Neuroscience* 7, (2013): 86. doi:10.3389/fnint.2013.00086.

Carhart-Harris, R. L., and D. J. Nutt. "Serotonin and Brain Function: A Tale of Two Receptors."*Journal of Psychopharmacology* 31, no. 9 (September 2017): 1091–1120. doi:10.1177/0269881117725915.

Chorney, D. B., M. F. Detweiler, T. L. Morris, et al. "The Interplay of Sleep Disturbance, Anxiety, and Depression in Children."*Journal of Pediatric Psychology* 33, no. 4 (May 2008): 339–348. doi:10.1093/jpepsy/jsm105.

Copeland, W. E., L. Shanahan, C. Worthman, A. Angold, and E. J. Costello. "Generalized Anxiety and C-reactive Protein Levels: Prospective, Longitudinal Analysis."*Psychological Medicine* 42, no. 12 (2012): 2641–650. doi:10.1017/s0033291712000554.

De La Mora, M. P., A. Gallegos-Cari, Y. Arizmendi-García, et al. "Role of Dopamine Receptor Mechanisms in the Amygdaloid Modulation of Fear and Anxiety: Structural and Functional Analysis."*Progress in Neurobiology* 90, no. 2 (February 9, 2010): 198–216. doi:10.1016/j.pneurobio.2009.10.010.

De Oliveira, I. J., V. V. De Souza, V. Motta, et al. "Effects of Oral Vitamin C Supplementation on Anxiety in Students: A Double-Blind, Randomized, Placebo-Controlled Trial."*Pakistan Journal of Biological Sciences* 18, no. 1 (January 2015): 11–18. doi:10.3923/pjbs.2015.11.18.

Dubey, V. K., F. Ansari, D. Vohora, et al. "Possible Involvement of Corticosterone and Serotonin in Antidepressant and Antianxety Effects of Chromium Picolinate in Chronic Unpredictable Mild Stress Induced Depression and Anxiety in Rats."*Journal of Trace Elements in Medicine and Biology* 29 (January 2015): 222–226. doi:10.1016/j.jtemb.2014.06.014.

Dum, R. P., D. J. Leinthal, and P. L. Strick. "Motor, Cognitive, and Affective Areas of the Cerebral Cortex Influence the Adrenal Medulla."*Proceedings of the National Academy of Sciences of the United States of America* 113, no. 35 (August 30, 2016): 9922–9927. doi:10.1073/pnas.1605044113.

Farach, F. J., L. D. Pruitt, J. J. Jun, et al. "Pharmacological Treatment of Anxiety Disorders: Current Treatments and Future Directions."*Journal of Anxiety Disorders* 26, no. 8 (December 2012): 833–843. doi:10.1016/j.janxdis.2012.07.009.

Forsythe, P., J. Bienenstock, and W. A. Kunze. "Vagal Pathways for Microbiome-Brain-Gut Axis Communication."*Advances in Experimental Medicine and Biology* 817 (2014): 115–133. doi:10.1007/978-1-4939-0897-4_5.

Freestone, P. P., M. Lyte, C. P. Neal, et al. "The Mammalian Neuroendocrine Hormone Norepinephrine Supplies Iron for Bacterial Growth in the Presence of Transferrin or Lactoferrin."*Journal of Bacteriology* 182, no. 21 (November 2000): 6091–6098. doi:10.1128/jb.182.21.6091-6098.2000.

Guo, S., R. Al-Sadi, H. M. Said, et al. "Lipopolysaccharide Causes an Increase in Intestinal Tight Junction Permeability *inVitro* and *inVivo* by Inducing Enterocyte Membrane Expression and Localization of TLR-4 and CD14."*The American Journal of Pathology* 182, no. 2 (February 2013): 375–387. doi:10.1016/j.ajpath.2012.10.014.

Herman, J. P., J. M. Mcklveen, S. Ghosal, et al. "Regulation of the Hypothalamic-Pituitary-Adrenocortical Stress Response."*Comprehensive Physiology* 6, no. 2 (March 15, 2016): 603–621. doi:10.1002/cphy.c150015.

Hollon, Justin, Elaine Puppa, Bruce Greenwald, Eric Goldberg, Anthony Guerrerio, and Alessio Fasano. "Effect of Gliadin on Permeability of Intestinal Biopsy Explants from Celiac Disease Patients and Patients with Non-Celiac Gluten Sensitivity."*Nutrients* 7, no. 3 (March 2015): 1565–576. doi:10.3390/nu7031565.

Jahnen-Dechent, W., and M. Ketteler. "Magnesium Basics."*Clinical Kidney Journal* 5, no. 1 (February 2012). doi:10.1093/ndtplus/sfr163.

Kennedy, D. O. "B Vitamins and the Brain: Mechanisms, Dose and Efficacy—A Review."*Nutrients* 8, no. 2 (January 27, 2016): 68. doi:10.3390/nu8020068.

Kimura, I., D. Inoue, T. Maeda, et al. "Short-chain Fatty Acids and Ketones Directly Regulate Sympathetic Nervous System via G Protein-coupled Receptor 41 (GPR41)."*Proceedings of the National Academy of Sciences* 108, no. 19 (May 10, 2011): 8030–8035. doi:10.1073/pnas.1016088108.

Kimura, K., M. Ozeki, L. R. Juneja, et al. "L-Theanine Reduces Psychological and Physiological Stress Responses."*Biological Psychology* 74, no. 1 (January 2007): 39–45. doi:10.1016/j.biopsycho.2006.06.006.

Kobayashi, K. "Role of Catecholamine Signaling in Brain and Nervous System Functions: New Insights from Mouse Molecular Genetic Study."*Journal of Investigative Dermatology Symposium Proceedings* 6, no. 1 (November 2001): 115–121. doi:10.1046/j.0022-202x.2001.00011.x.

Lakhan, S. E., and K. F. Vieira. "Nutritional Therapies for Mental Disorders."*Nutrition Journal* 7, no. 2 (January 21, 2008). doi:10.1186/1475-2891-7-2.

Lee, B., B. Sur, M. Yeom, et al. "Effect of Berberine on Depression- and Anxiety-Like Behaviors and Activation of the Noradrenergic System Induced by Development of Morphine Dependence in Rats."*The Korean Journal of Physiology & Pharmacology* 16, no. 6 (December 2012): 379–386. doi:10.4196/kjpp.2012.16.6.379.

Lenze, E. J., R. C. Mantella, P. Shi, et al. "Elevated Cortisol in Older Adults With Generalized Anxiety Disorder Is Reduced by Treatment: A Placebo-Controlled Evaluation of Escitalopram."*The American Journal of Geriatric Psychiatry* 19, no. 5 (May 2011): 482–490. doi:10.1097/jgp.0b013e3181ec806c.

Lionetti, E., S. Leonardi, C. Franzonello, et al. "Gluten Psychosis: Confirmation of a New Clinical Entity."*Nutrients* 7, no. 7 (July 2015): 5532–5539. doi:10.3390/nu7075235.

Maes, M., M. Kubera, J. C. Leunis. "The Gut-Brain Barrier in Major Depression: Intestinal Mucosal Dysfunction with an Increased Translocation of LPS from Gram Negative Enterobacteria (Leaky Gut) Plays a Role in the Inflammatory Pathophysiology of Depression."*Neuro Endocrinology Letters* 29, no. 1 (February 2008): 117–124.

McCarty, M. F. "High-dose Pyridoxine as an 'anti-stress' Strategy."*Medical Hypotheses* 54, no. 5 (May 2000): 803–807. doi:10.1054/mehy.1999.0955.

Meyers, S. "Use of Neurotransmitter Precursors for Treatment of Depression."*Alternative Medicine Review* 5, no. 1 (February 2000): 64–71.

Padayatty, S. J., J. L. Doppman, R. Chang, et al. "Human Adrenal Glands Secrete Vitamin C in Response to Adrenocorticotrophic Hormone."*The American Journal of Clinical Nutrition* 86, no. 1 (July 1, 2007): 145–149. doi:10.1093/ajcn/86.1.145.

Pizzorno, J. "Glutathione!"*Integrative Medicine* 13, no. 1 (February 2014): 8–12.

Reddy, D. S., B. W. O'Malley, and M. A. Rogawski. "Anxiolytic Activity of Progesterone in Progesterone Receptor Knockout Mice."*Neuropharmacology* 48, no. 1 (January 2005): 14–24. doi:10.1016/j. neuropharm.2004.09.002.

Risbrough, V. B., and M. B. Stein. "Role of Corticotropin Releasing Factor in Anxiety Disorders: A Translational Research Perspective."*Hormones and Behavior* 50, no. 4 (November 2006): 550–561. doi:10.1016/j.yhbeh .2006.06.019.

Russo, A. J. "Decreased Zinc and Increased Copper in Individuals with Anxiety."*Nutrition and Metabolic Insights* 4 (February 7, 2011): 1–5. doi:10.4137/nmi.s6349.

Sarris, J., G. I. Papakostas, O. Vitolo, et al. "S-adenosyl Methionine (SAMe) versus Escitalopram and Placebo in Major Depression RCT: Efficacy and Effects of Histamine and Carnitine as Moderators of Response."*Journal of Affective Disorders* 164 (August 1, 2014): 76–81. doi:10.1016/j.jad.2014 .03.041.

Sartori, S. B., N. Whittle, A. Hetzenauer, et al. "Magnesium Deficiency Induces Anxiety and HPA-Axis Dysregulation: Modulation by Therapeutic Drug Treatment."*Neuropharmacology* 62, no. 1 (January 2012): 304–312. doi:10.1016/j.neuropharm.2011.07.027.

Scimemi, A., and M. Beato. "Determining the Neurotransmitter Concentration Profile at Active Synapses."*Molecular Neurobiology* 40, no. 3 (December 2009): 289–306. doi:10.1007/s12035-009-8087-7.

Selhub, E. M., A. C. Logan, and A. C. Bested. "Fermented Foods, Microbiota, and Mental Health: Ancient Practice Meets Nutritional Psychiatry."*Journal of Physiological Anthropology* 33, no. 1 (2014): 2. doi:10.1186/1880-6805-33-2.

Straub, R. H., R. Wiest, U. G. Strauch, et al. "The Role of the Sympathetic Nervous System in Intestinal Inflammation."*Gut* 55, no. 11 (November 2006): 1640–1649. doi:10.1136/gut.2006.091322.

Taiwo, A., F. B. Leite, G. M. Lucena, et al. "Anxiolytic and Antidepressant-like Effects of *Melissa officinalis* (Lemon Balm) Extract in Rats: Influence of Administration and Gender."*Indian Journal of Pharmacology* 44, no. 2 (March 2012): 189–192. doi:10.4103/0253-7613.93846.

Tufan, A. E., R. Bilici, G. Usta, et al. "Mood Disorder with Mixed, Psychotic Features Due to Vitamin B12 Deficiency in an Adolescent: Case Report."*Child and Adolescent Psychiatry and Mental Health* 6, no. 1 (June 22, 2012): 25. doi:10.1186/1753-2000-6-25.

Wu, A., E. E. Noble, E. Tyagi, et al. "Curcumin Boosts DHA in the Brain: Implications for the Prevention of Anxiety Disorders."*Biochimica et Biophysica Acta (BBA) - Molecular Basis of Disease* 1852, no. 5 (May 2015): 951–961. doi:10.1016/j.bbadis.2014.12.005.

Index

Acknowledgments

Many thanks to:

- Brady, my amazing husband, who makes me laugh and keeps me grounded while providing support for our journey and my ability to share my passion with you all.

- Stella, my daughter, who brings light to my life and a daily connection to appreciating simplicity and nature's wonder.

- My mom, Nancy, and my dad, Jim, for encouraging me and teaching me to be kind and believe in myself.

I'd also like to acknowledge Becki Yoo, RD, LD, who manages my clients in the Houston, Texas, Naturally Nourished office and supports the brand with creative content and a rockstar hustle. She developed the following recipes for www.alimillerRD.com: Butternut and Brussels Breakfast Hash (page 190), Prosciutto Egg Cups (page 196), Smoked Wild Salmon Scramble (page 197), Whole Roasted Cauliflower (page 213), Sweet and Sour Pork Meatballs (page 235), Almond Flour Chicken Piccata (page 240), and Matcha Coconut Gummies (page 261). In addition, the following recipes were developed in collaboration with Becki and were originally featured on www.alimillerRD.com: Paleo Pumpkin Protein Pancakes (page 199), Coconut No-Oatmeal (page 202), Mediterranean Tuna Salad (page 237), Truffled Egg Salad (page 238), and Spaghetti Squash Bolognese (page 246).

About the Author

Ali Miller, RD, LD, CDE, is an integrative functional medicine practitioner with a background in naturopathic medicine. She is a registered and licensed dietitian, certified diabetes educator, and has contagious passion for food as medicine. She develops clinical protocols and virtual programs using nutrients and food as the foundation of treatment. Her Food-As-Medicine  philosophy is supported by up-to-date scientific research for a functional approach to healing the body addressing the root cause of imbalance. Ali's message has influenced millions through media with television segments, magazine features, her award winning podcast Naturally Nourished, and within the medical community as a keynote at many professional conferences. Ali's expertise can be accessed through her website: www.alimillerRD.com offering her blog, podcasts, virtual learning, and access to her virtual practice Naturally Nourished.